W9-BOF-677

THE

SPECTATOR

Also by Studs Terkel

American Dreams: Lost and Found

Chicago

Coming of Age: The Story of Our Century by Those Who've Lived It

Division Street: America

"The Good War": An Oral History of World War II

The Great Divide: Second Thoughts on the American Dream

Hard Times: An Oral History of the Great Depression

My American Century

*Race: How Blacks and Whites
Think and Feel About the American Obsession*

Talking to Myself: A Memoir of My Times

*Working: People Talk About What They Do All Day
and How They Feel About What They Do*

THE
SPECTATOR

Talk About Movies and Plays
With The People Who Make Them

STUDS TERKEL

THE NEW PRESS   NEW YORK

Published in the United States by The New Press, New York
Distributed by W. W. Norton & Company, Inc., New York

The New Press was established in 1990 as a not-for-profit alternative to the large, commercial publishing houses currently dominating the book publishing industry. The New Press operates in the public interest rather than for private gain, and is committed to publishing, in innovative ways, works of educational, cultural, and community value that are often deemed insufficiently profitable.

www.thenewpress.com

Printed in the United States of America

9 8 7 6 5 4 3 2 1

Remembering Alfred Lunt
and George Spelvin (The most favored pseudonym of actors who
assumed bit parts or walk-ons.)

—Contents

THE

SPECTATOR

—Introduction

Garry Wills

Most people know Studs Terkel from the prize-winning oral histories he has written about serious subjects—war, poverty, race, aging. But we in Chicago know him also for his radio interviews with writers, artists, and performers who come through our city. What I did not realize until I read this book is how far he has traveled to do similar interviews—to New York and California, France and Italy, where he talked with movie actors and directors, stage actors, musicians, authors. (I do not understand how he gets around so well, since he has never learned how to drive.)

The most important part of an interview, so far as the questioner is concerned, takes place before the interview. Studs is the best prepared interviewer I have ever met. Over the last eighteen years, whenever I had a book come out I was privileged to discuss it on the air with Studs. My bran-new book was always dog-eared, its margins filled with his notes. More than that, he had prepared radio clips or recordings of related material to use in the interview (or not, as the flow of things determined). Those who have done book tours know how rare this is. Some interviewers do their homework on selected books. But Studs would not have anyone on his show unless he had read carefully the book in question and related it to the author's whole body of work. I heard him once turn down a producer who was eager to have a visiting playwright on the show before he left Chicago. Studs said he could not do it, since he did not have time to read the man's work before the time for his leaving.

Over and over in the interviews presented here, Studs surprises the people he is interviewing with how much he knows of their work, their colleagues' careers, their predecessors. As a stage-struck young man, Studs made it a point to see everything he could in the theater or opera house, at the concert hall or the movie palace. When he meets performers, he is usually able to call up some high point of their career, when he saw them decades ago, or to compare notes on actors the performer worked with in the past. Since Studs himself has acted on stage and on the radio, he has great empathy with the pride, the vulnerabilities, and the craft of those he admires. They respond, as you will see, with appreciation for his knowledge and sympathy, which makes them answer questions with more than the normal self-revelation.

Studs sees through the dumb blonde act of Carol Channing. After he says he admires her for her intelligence, he learns about her past as a student at Bennington studying classic drama. Channing, a shrewd analyst of her own art, tells him she must play the accommodating type because she is too tall to push people around: "The most potent women in the theater are, say, Tallulah Bankhead, not five feet tall, Lynn Fontanne, five feet, Judith Anderson, tiny, dynamic. They're smaller, so they're not afraid of mopping up the floor with you." Even the rhythms of her speech radiate intelligence.

When he is talking with Edward Albee about his play *Three Tall Women*, Studs not only knows the play but saw a performer on whom one of the characters in based. He surprises Satyajit Ray with a memory of *Kanchanjungha*: "Where did you see that? Very few people have seen it." Vittorio De Sica tells him: "I am so enthusiastic over you because you remember the names of my characters." Because Studs knows so much about these people, they tell us more about themselves—how Ian McKellen used John McEnroe's brattiness to help him sharpen his own performance as Coriolanus, or how Jonathan Miller focused King Lear's tragedy in terms of Lyndon Johnson's character. Though Studs admires all his subjects' talents, he is also good at getting out of the way when a man wants to reveal his smugness (Arnold Schwarzenegger) or pretentiousness (Marlon Brando). Above all, Studs can play the straight man for an improvising genius like Zero Mostel, who breaks out of this book like his own rhinoceros in the Ionesco play, smashing the stage set.

Much as I admire Terkel's other books, I think this one is his best. He has show business in his bones. There is no better description of the way movies shape our own identities than the opening riff Studs does on the memories of cinema that twitch in his imagination as he goes through a single day. He also interweaves the interviews as their subjects remember one another, calling up complementary responses from Studs's vast repertoire of tapes. It may seem odd to put a book about performance above his work on more serious themes, on war, or poverty, or race. But those concerns are never absent. He knows that they are reflected to us in our culture because they are the abiding problems of the nation. The political implications of popular culture are not analyzed here; they are just embodied. His ear for the false political note shows in his savaging of *The Deer Hunter*. Most people did not catch on to Michael Cimino's emptiness until he did *Heaven's Gate*. Studs was on to him from the start.

I could go on, but I must break off and head for the video rental store. I just found out from the interview with Ruth Gordon that I missed a brilliant bit of acting (by Albert Basserman) in *Doctor Erlich's Magic Bullet*. I had never heard of Basserman, but Studs had. It was only because he brought him up that Gordon recalled a precious moment on the set with him. It is that kind of book.

—Acknowledgments

M y thanks to the Chicago Historical Society, my place of
work; especially to Douglas Greenberg, its president, and
to my colleagues, Bernard Reilly, Sharon Lancaster,
Maria Latière, Sylvia Landsman, and Usama Alshaibi, the gifted
sound engineer.

My gratitude to radio station WFMT, where for forty-five years I
had experienced the delight of encountering the subjects of this
book, along with thousands of other guests in different spheres. I
am especially grateful to my colleagues there, who through the years
have been so generous with their time and efforts, beyond the call of
duty: Lois Baum, Linda Lewis, Jim Unrath, Norm Pellegrini, Ray
Nordstrand, Tony Judge, and Steve Jones.

A salute to my voluntary scouts, whose tips and leads have been
of inestimable value: Carlo Baldi, Cindy Bandle, Zev Braun,
Eleanor Bron, Ann Barzell, Ben Bentley, Roger Ebert, Bob Ed-
monds, Lee Eisenberg, Bob Howe, Carol Iwata, Frances Loving,
David Shepard, Milos Stehlik of Facets Multimedia, Dan Terkell,
and Michelle Vian.

To my publisher and editor, André Schiffrin, who has been my
guide through this work as well as ten others; along with Jessica
Blatt and Ted Byfield.

Finally, to Sydney Lewis, who, with an assist by Tammey Kikta,
has been a valued commentator as well as transcriber.

And, of course, a low bow to Al Hirschfeld for his caricatures
that grace the cover of this book.

OVERTURE

In 1927—or was it '28?—I saw a play, *Burlesque*. I remember the curtain line. As the drunken hoofer (Hal Skelly) and his loyal young wife (Barbara Stanwyck) go into a soft shoe, he wonders why she has stuck with a bum like him. She says, "I married you for better or for worse." With a touch of resignation as much as guilt, he rasps, "Yeah. Better for me and worse for you." As the curtain falls, they're still dancing.*

For better and for worse, I've set a track record of sorts: a forty-five year run as host of a one-hour radio program, five days a week, come rain, come shine. It was on WFMT, Chicago.

James Cameron, the nonpareil of British journalists, referred to his work as neither vocation nor calling; he simply said, "It's my trade." I figure what's good enough for Cameron is good enough for me. Among my guests have been jacks of all manner of trades and, in a number of instances, masters of some.

In the pages that follow, you'll hear the reflections of fifty or so of these masters. Theirs was the world of theater and films: playwrights, actors, directors, and critics. Most are long gone, but their visions still haunt me.

In contrast to my earlier book, *Working*, the subjects of this one are celebrated, more or less, by "the public." Yet, my approach toward them was perceptively no different than it was toward those more anonymous. There is, above all else, a common thread: the pursuit of their craft, their trade.

Many of the conversations here took place at earlier times in my subjects' careers. Much has happened to them in their work since: a fact with which many of the readers may be familiar. In the case of Marlon Brando, for instance, his jobs in *Last Tango in Paris* and in *The Godfather* were yet to happen. My conversations with him and the others reflect their state of mind at that time.

---

*Some years later, Clifford Odets wrote a variant on the theme: *The Country Girl*, with Paul Kelly and Uta Hagen.

If there is a pointed difference between this book and my others, it is in me. The journeyman carpenter or the dedicated school-teacher, in recounting his or her life and work, affected me, of course—but not in the same way, nor to the same degree, as those in the world of the lively arts.

I know that my life—certainly my dream life—has been touched in more ways than would have been the case had I lived in some other epoch, before the magic lantern had been invented.

Ever since Year One, the play has been the thing that caught the conscience of commoner as well as king; but it was the moving picture that has fueled our fantasies. For better and for worse. Consider the case of my city's reputation, worldwide. It is not simply Chicago; it is Chicago Boom-Boom.

Chicagogangster. It may not appear in Webster's as one word, but it is so regarded in many quarters of the world. A proper noun, though our city's chamber of commerce may consider its usage somewhat improper. To some extent, our local hornblowers have a point. Though other cities have been found equally corrupt, equally Mob-influenced, it is Chicago that is universally honored as the Big Daddy of them all. Ever since the '30s. I attribute this in no small part to the rub-off power of the magic lantern, the movies.

Foremost are Warner Brothers and their two archetypal gang-sters, Jimmy Cagney and Edward G. Robinson. Their job in per-verse public relations has been astonishing.

Case in point: In 1962, I found myself in the Italian city of Bres-cia. I had gotten off the train too soon; my destination was Verona. I was somewhat discombobulated. I'd be late for a celebratory ban-quet in the city of Romeo and Juliet. (As it turned out, I subse-quently arrived two days early, to the discomfiture of my gracious hosts.)

It is four o'clock in the afternoon. The next train to Verona is not due till 8 P.M. *Madonn'! Madonn'!* I'll miss the ceremonies. The friendly stationmaster advises me to take it easy. "*Piano. Piano.*" He indicates a little trattoria across the tracks. "*Mangia,*" he sug-gests. Not a bad idea. A sweet-faced, white-haired old lady, a dead ringer for the venerable actress Emma Grammatica,* appears to be the proprietor. The young man who waits on me asks if everything is OK. What with the north Italian wine and a meal washed down with grappa, I assure him it was a Lucullan feast. "*Grazie, mille grazie,*" I say. "*Prego,*" he says. He and Emma Grammatica are delighted.

I notice something about their eyes. Are they grandmother and grandson? *Si, si.* They seem even more delighted now. They study me—a curiosity. Where do you come from, Cotton-Eyed Joe? I tell them Chicago. The young man's eyes widen. He is definitely impressed. *Aahh, Chicago.* He aims his two index fingers at me, two forty-fours. Boom! Boom! He thinks I'm Scarface. I shrug helplessly, I smile forlornly. I am Marcello Mastroianni in *La Dolce Vita.* If Fellini could see me now, I'd be his next existential hero. Why not Chicago? Rome ain't the only decaying apple in the barrel.

He tells me he has seen oh-so-many American movies. His favorites are gangster movies, even more than westerns. He calls them "Chicago movies." Of course he idolizes Jimmy Cagney and Eduardo Robinson.

Another case in point: It is 1965. Axsel Schiøtz and I are seated at a table in the L&L Lounge, a gathering place for some of Chicago's more picaresque citizens. I point out to my awed Danish guest a few of the regulars.

There is Chuckie E., all 300 pounds of him, freshly talced, a diamond ring flashing on his pinkie. He is a collector, I tell Mr. Schiøtz. A collector? Yes, he pays occasional visits to tavern owners who are remiss in their payments, who may have fiddled with juke-box receipts.

What if they don't pay? I explain to Mr. Schiøtz that Chuckie E. persuades the man to be honest, to pay his bills like a responsible American citizen. If the man persists in his recalcitrance, there may be a broken ring finger, or one leg shorter than another, or further action, if need be.

---

*An honored character actress in Italian films. She is especially remembered as the old lady who cared for the little orphan boy in De Sica's *Miracle in Milan.*

The Dane's eyes light up. "James Cagney!" Yes, he had seen *Public Enemy* years ago in a Copenhagen movie house. And *Little Caesar*, too, of course.

I indicate the handsome, gray-haired, nattily dressed man in the favored booth; an ex-judge who's had a contretemps of sorts with the Chicago Bar Association. He is a dead ringer for Otto Kruger, the movie actor who on occasion played crooked judges. This man is a dear friend of the boys who employ Chuckie E.

"Is this a Mafia place?" Mr. Schiøtz wants to know. I explain that enterprises of this sort are beyond ethnicity — they are multicultural in nature. The cadaverous one at the bar is a nephew of Doc Graham, who in the glory days was a soldier in the army of Bugs Moran, Al Capone's bête noir. I remind my companion that Murray (The Camel) Humphries, a grand vizier in the high court of the Mob, was a Welshman. Perhaps the one whose presence here, at this moment, is the most dramatic, is Maishe Bear, Jewish. The guy at the center table. See? The one with no neck, who looks like a sumo wrestler. I confess that I am astonished by his presence. Several months ago, he was sent up to Joliet, five to ten, for hijacking a truckload of silver. How did he get *here*?

Stupidly, I ask Dorothy the waitress about it. Dorothy, usually the most voluble of women, is speechless. She stares at me in the manner of a weary teacher facing an incurably backward student. At length, she says, "Want dessert?"

I should have known. The authorities may have granted him a leave to attend his grandmother's funeral. (A year later, Maishe Bear is found in the trunk of a Lincoln Continental. He never did get to finish his sentence.)

I try to explain that this is just an ordinary restaurant, not much different from any other. Here is where small-time entrepreneurs, who have seen better days, gather, not simply for auld lang syne but to reflect on futures, the vicissitudes of venture capitalism, and, hopefully, to pick up a buck or two.

Schiøtz, with an air of wonder, says this is the most memorable lunch he has ever had. And one of his most exciting experiences. He can't get over it.

A word about my guest. Axsel Schiøtz was Denmark's most admired and beloved singer. Though his fellow Dane, the Wagnerian heldentenor Lauritz Melchior, may have been better known in the United States, Schiøtz was, in Europe, the artist most associated with Denmark's high musical tradition. To hear him sing a Scandinavian art song was an exquisite experience.

Another word about my guest. He was a hero in the Danish Resistance, during the German Occupation of 1940–45. It was he who sang at the funeral of the martyred patriot, Kaj Munk, aware that a platoon of S.S. men were scattered among the mourners.

Recently, I received a letter from his ninety-year-old widow, Gerd.

As you know, during our five-year German Occupation, Axsel sang at hundreds of protest recitals: open-air gatherings, church concerts. Whenever it came to serious clashes, the Danes called on him and he always 'popped up.' Funerals, so many. When he was asked, he went. Where there were bombings, sabotage, victims buried. Twelve victims in small churches. Fourteen in Copenhagen's Cathedral. Axsel would sing *Comfort Ye, My People* in English.

Wöldike, the conductor and Axsel's mentor, called it 'Axsel's private resistance war.' The leader of the underground resistance army, the rector of Copenhagen University, broke down from laughter when Axsel volunteered to join. He answered, 'You! You of all people want to join the underground! We can't use *you!* Every kid in Denmark knows you. You are tall and conspicuous. We need little gray people, who can pass unnoticed. Oh no! Continue your private war. We can send you to Sweden only when it will be absolutely necessary for your safety. We are aware of all the great risks you are taking.'

We received many warnings, in notes, small pieces of paper. Especially during 1943–45 when the Germans were very desperate and murderous. Some good-music lovers among the Germans followed Axsel and were present at many of his concerts. They always asked him to sing in Germany, but he said, 'Never!' And he never did, from 1933 to 1945.

I might add a small story. In 1943, when Axsel and I were extremely active, many Jews came to our Copenhagen apartment to be secretly shipped to Sweden. At Easter time, the teacher in our small boy's class told the kids about Jesus' crucifixion. Little Mike, six years old, asked, 'But, ma'am, why didn't he escape to Sweden?' The little jars had big ears at that time.

Come to think of it, the lunch at the L&L Lounge was as memorable to me as it was to my guest. Consider this: Axsel Schiøtz, highly gifted artist, honest-to-God hero, a rare and noble bird, was enchanted and held in thrall by a wretched assemblage of featherless vultures. There is but one explanation—the movies. In this instance, blame Warner Brothers. Blame Edward G. Robinson. Blame Jimmy Cagney. (see Jimmy Cagney on p. 105)

Nineteen thirty was an especially rewarding year for me, the moviegoer. It marked not only Cagney's debut on the screen; it was Spencer Tracy's, too. I had seen Tracy on the stage, a year or so before, as Killer Mears in the death-row play, *The Last Mile*. He was a rough customer, frighteningly good.

It was in his first movie, *Up the River*, that he casually exploded: at least for me, an eighteen-year-old. I had never before seen a movie actor with so light a touch, aside from Charlie Chaplin and Raymond Griffith, in wholly different circumstances. (On the stage, there was Alfred Lunt, but then he was, as the Welsh would say, something spess-ial.) I have been unable to find a print of *Up the River*, but that's OK. It has stuck with me.

It was a parody of prison-life movies. Tracy is St. Louie, an insouciant gangster, whose air of bonhomie is so expansive that he enchants his dim-witted cellmate, Dannemora Dan, even as he double-crosses him. Warren Hymer, in a class by himself, is the befuddled buddy.

In the sequence that follows, Hymer, "saved," in a Salvation Army uniform, offering street-corner testimony, spots the genial Tracy in a fancy roadster with two blondes. He busts the Army bass drum on St. Louie's head. A riot. Fade-out. The two are once more cellmates. All that ensues is quite wonderful.

It was Tracy's performance—or seeming nonperformance— that set the movie's tone. Though he may never have heard of Mies van der Rohe, his credo, too, was less is more.

I had always assumed that the movie was written by Joel Sayre, whose satire on prison life had appeared in H. L. Mencken's monthly, *The American Mercury*. When I ran into Sayre, some forty years later, I acted out *Up the River*, playing all the roles, inspired by a dram or two of his excellent Scotch. Sayre appeared to enjoy it, laughing all the way. I thanked him for a work that had offered me such long-lasting delight. He was bewildered. "I don't know what you're talking about. I had nothing to do with it." His short story was wholly unrelated to this movie.

Thanks to a young friend's computer (I avoid such apparati), I have since found out that *Up the River* was written by Maureen Watkins,* with noncredited assists by John Ford and William Collier, Sr., who played an old con in the movie. This may be a telling anecdote concerning my approach to this book. Assiduous movie buffs—and playgoers, for that matter—may detect a number of boners and will undoubtedly point them out. Remember Franklin Pangborn, the sharp-nosed accountant, sniffing out something askew with the bookkeeping of W. C. Fields in *The Bank Dick*?

It is a matter of memory against statistic. I'm trying to be as close to fact as possible, but there may be occasions when I might add a grace note or two to highlight the fact and thus lift it closer to the truth: *my* truth. This is, I'm afraid, a habit of mine. Like Marlene Dietrich's Lola falling in love again, I can't help it.

Nineteen thirty was the year of another treasure: *Laughter.* I had no luck finding a print of this one, either. Harry d'Abbadie d'Arrast was the director of that one. How come he disappeared?

It was sixty-eight years ago, yet two sequences are indelible. They told me all I needed to know about power, in one instance, and rue, in the other.

Nancy Carroll, a beautiful ex-Follies girl, is married to the powerful tycoon played by Frank Morgan. She runs off with the impoverished young composer, Fredric March, abandoning her furs, jewels, everything. Morgan, on discovering her disappearance, picks up the phone and simply says, "C. Morton Gibson speaking." Cut. Sirens are heard as police motorcycles, paddy wagons, and fire engines are tearing all around town. Talk about power.

The second sequence: Carroll and March are seated at a sidewalk café. Paris. They are drinking and laughing. A limousine pulls up. We see a woman's hand protruding from the rear window. It is

---

*Her play, *Chicago*, was a hit in the late '20s.

heavily bejeweled, rings on her fingers and probably bells on her toes. Nancy Carroll sees it, too. She simply stares. Fredric March glances at her. She, embarrassedly, turns toward him. They break out laughing once more, though, you suspect, not quite as light-heartedly as before. Talk about rue.

For that matter, talk about freedom. Wynne Gibson experienced it in a stunning moment. The film was *If I Had a Million*, a series of six episodes, each with a different director. The common thread was the sudden good fortune of the protagonist of each: a million-dollar check from an eccentric rich man.

Charles Laughton, a lowly clerk, much abused by his boss, gives the razzberry to Mr. Big. W. C. Fields and Alison Skipworth, long pushed around in their flivver by road hogs, buy a vehicle of steel and demolish their tormentors. It is Wynne Gibson, as a weary hooker, in a sequence directed by Ernst Lubitsch, who experiences the most glorious of moments. She rents a hotel room. Undresses, climbs into bed, pulls up the sheets, and remembers her good luck. She sits up, ungarters her stockings, and ever so slowly, so luxuri-antly, rolls down her stockings, takes them off, and flings away the second pillow. Talk about liberation.

I discovered the silent movies of Raymond Griffith not too long after experiencing the delights of Charlie Chaplin, Buster Keaton, and Harry Langdon. I was about ten; the walk from our rooming house was a short one. The doctor had prescribed exercise of this sort for my rheumatic fever.

Griffith, with his well-trimmed mustache, silk scarf, opera cape, and top hat, was really Charlie, dressed to the nines. He was the most congenial companion you could possibly hope for; the most thoughtful and gracious of beings.

Walter Kerr writes, in *The Silent Clowns*, "In hearing that a friend is not really married after all, the first thing Griffith does is to retrieve the wedding presents he had given him. The act is not an unsocial one; it merely—and quite genially—takes cognizance of the facts. He looks as though he is courteously saving his friend the terrible trouble of returning the gifts." Who wouldn't be blessed to have him as a friend?

In another movie, he's in love with two women and they with

him. Each, generous-heartedly, will give him up to the other. He doesn't want either to feel bad, so the three of them blithely ride off to Salt Lake City.

Come the talking pictures. Bang! I remember my first look at the Vitaphone shorts, put out by Warner Brothers. A compote of celebrated actors and singers could be *heard* as well as seen in their most celebrated routines. Boy, oh, boy! John Barrymore offered his Hamlet soliloquy: "To be or not to be, that is the question . . ." I had never seen him in the flesh, so this was dynamite.

Many wretched years later, I did see John Barrymore, a tragicomic shell, a burlesque of himself. He was in something called *My Dear Children*. At the Selwyn Theatre in Chicago (or was it the Harris?). Doris Dudley, the ingenue, recalled the horror and sorrow of other cast members as the audience—oafs and boors—howled and "cheered" the lost artist humiliating himself.

Anthony Quinn (or was it John Carradine?) remembered one glory moment. It was a floor show at a posh nightclub. The patrons were delighted by Barrymore's mortifying act. They enjoyed a further bonus as an unfortunate girl in the chorus, plain looking, awkward, and scared, missed every step. Out of the wings appeared Barrymore. Bowing graciously to the girl, he invited her to dance with him; a slow waltz. Apparently, it was quite moving and beautiful. The audience responded with genuine cheers. Barrymore stepped toward the footlights, stared out front, and with the fervor of young Hamlet, said, "Fuck you."

Also during that Vitaphone afternoon, I heard and saw the Italian tenor, Giovanni Martinelli. It was Canio's aria from *Pagliacci*, after he does in the faithless Nedda and tells us that the comedy has ended.

When I visited Edith Piaf in her dressing room at the Mayfair Room of the Palmer House, I asked her about her Pagliacci song, *Bravo pour le Clown*. In her simple black dress, surrounded by a squad of slick young hangers-on, she patiently explained. "I feel good when I sing a sad song and sad when I sing a happy song. When you're happy and up, where can you go, but down? When you're sad and down, where can you go but up? *Comprenez-vous?*" Yeah, sort of.

It was the first full-length talkie, *Interference*, that convinced me the *heard* word was here to stay. Doris Kenyon was the long-suffering good woman; Clive Brook, an English actor, was the steady-as-she-goes good man; and Evelyn Brent was the no-good girlie. All believable to the ears as well as to the eyes. But it was the born-again William Powell, until now a silent-movie rotten egg, who most impressed me. Hearing his plum-rich voice, you knew instantly that he was a good man; a self-sacrificing one, who did in Evelyn Brent to ensure the happiness of the other two.

At that historic moment I understood that, though seeing may be believing, hearing as well made you a true believer. How else could you explain Billy Sunday and Aimee Semple McPherson?

As 1930 was my vintage movie year, 1935–36 were rich ones for me as a playgoer. It was during a year's absence from Chicago that I saw a dozen or so Saturday matinees in Manhattan. No matter how big a hit the show was, you could always pick up a single at the last minute.

Winterset was Maxwell Anderson's verse play, inspired by the Sacco-Vanzetti case. Burgess Meredith was the feverish young Mio, on a quest to clear his father's name. Margo was Miriamne. Richard Bennett was the guilt-possessed, out-of-his-mind judge. (Unfortunately, I missed him at the matinee; he was ill. The understudy was okay, but I wanted Bennett. He was the star of the first stage play I had ever seen, *They Knew What They Wanted*, by Sidney Howard. It was 1925 and my eldest brother took me.) There was Eduardo Ciannelli as Brock, the gangster.

FLASHBACK. *For some unaccountable reason, there is one line from* Winterset *I best remember. Mio's buddy says to the young hero, "Restrain your chivalry." Why does that three-word throwaway by a supporting actor stick with me more than any of the major speeches? I was quite moved by the passion of Mio, as played by Burgess Meredith. Obviously, I disagreed with his pal's advice. It was the actor himself—Myron McCormick—who had that indelible effect on me. I had seen this guy so many times in plays and in occasional films; and, always, no matter how minor the role, he was indubitably there. If ever there were a flesh-and-blood embodiment of the noncelebrated, taken-for-granted journeyman craftsman, it was he.*

Imagine my astonishment, a few months later, in seeing Ciannelli as the Bishop of Beauvais in *St. Joan.* I was not bowled over by Katherine Cornell as the Maid (see Sybil Thorndike, page 211). But the ensemble of men in the cast — wow! Brian Aherne was Warwick; Maurice Evans was the dauphin, Arthur Byron was the inquisitor; and there was Ciannelli as the bishop. Thumbs up for all four.

Pauline Lord as Zenobia Frome and Ruth Gordon (see Ruth Gordon, page 186) as Mattie Silver in *Ethan Frome* killed me. Raymond Massey as Ethan didn't lay a glove on me. As usual, he was Abraham Lincoln with the solemnity of a cigar-store Indian. I left the theater wondering what these two impassioned women saw in this guy.

Some sixty years later, I knew. During that matinee, *I* saw Raymond Massey. During that matinee and all the matinees and nights that followed, Pauline Lord and Ruth Gordon saw Ethan Frome. That was the difference between a callow spectator and two masters of their trade.

I saw Avon Long a week or so after he had replaced John W. Bubbles as Sporting Life in *Porgy and Bess.* I was prepared to be disappointed because I had, years before, when I was about ten or eleven, seen Buck and Bubbles in vaudeville at the Palace Theatre in Chicago. More than disappointed. I, a twenty-three-year-old spoiled playgoing brat, was actually sore at Avon Long for not being John W. Bubbles. I imagine myself, seated in that theater, arms folded, being Sergei Diaghilev, the ballet impresario celebrated for his imperious demand: *Étonnez-moi.* Astonish me, buddy. And that's precisely what Avon Long did. I don't see how anyone, even John W. Bubbles, could match his sinuous, snakelike *There's a Boat That's Leaving Soon for New York.* It persuaded me as well as Bess.

Helen Dowdy, the original Strawberry Woman, toured in revivals of *Porgy and Bess* well into the 1950s. During her appearance as a guest on my radio program, she recalled the excitement and the anxieties of those early rehearsals.

She spoke of George Gershwin's deep respect for the cast. He was open to any suggestions or memories they had of the songs and street cries of the South. She told him of her mother's remembrance of a woman who sold strawberries "right off the vine." Her mother's voice was with her, she told me, every time she cried out—"Straw-w-berrie-ie-s. . . ."

(On hearing Mahalia Jackson segue from *Sometimes I Feel Like a Motherless Child* into *Summertime,* you suffer a revelation. George Gershwin's celebrated ballad is a mimetic tribute to the old spiritual, almost note for note.)

I hit the jackpot that season in seeing the Russian actress Nazimova as Mrs. Alving in Ibsen's *Ghosts.* What was memorable to me, aside from her riveting performance, was my encounter, some years later, with McKay Morris, who played Pastor Manders.

I had since become a gangster in radio soap operas airing out of Chicago. Reading the scripts had become, mercifully, a matter of rote. It was in and out of the studio as quickly as possible. During my run on *Ma Perkins*, McKay Morris joined the cast! I was bowled over and yet felt a certain sadness I couldn't put the finger on. During a break, I reminded this weary old actor, still handsome, that I had seen him with Nazimova in *Ghosts.* He thought I was putting him on. He could not believe he was remembered.

I had a similar experience with Glenn Anders during my run at WFMT. He had a bit part in a Chicago production of a forgettable comedy. By this time, he had the appearance of a tired, old bantam ballet dancer. During the course of my interview, I told him that I had seen him in 1925 as Joe, the ranch hand, in *They Knew What They Wanted.* He stared at me for what seemed an interminable span of time. Then he grabbed my hand and squeezed it tightly.

I had neglected to tell him that I had seen him in 1929 from a second balcony seat at the Blackstone Theatre. He was Dr. Ned Darrell, Judith Anderson's lover, in *Strange Interlude.* Eugene O'Neill's nine-act play.

During the two-hour intermission at the end of the fifth act, I strolled toward my dinner at Pixley & Ehlers, a short block away. I'll never forget the taste of that hamburger, smothered with fried onions, followed by cherry pie á la mode. Much of that time I spent leisurely watching the short-order cook, whose name had to be Slim, flipping those burgers with the éclat of a Chinese juggler. A master of his trade.

My affection for the theater and for its masters had a lot to do with the casualness of advance men. They were theatrical press agents who came to town a couple of weeks before the company itself. It was their job to herald the play: visiting newspaper drama critics, feature writers, and hotels where tourists and visiting dignitaries gathered.

The hotel my mother owned, the Wells-Grand—"Rooms For Men"—was a walking distance from the Loop, Chicago's theater center. The advance men, an easygoing lot, decided it was close enough. In return for my putting up theater posters on the lobby wall, I was given two free ducats.

It was of small matter that our guests, a rough and ready crew, had as much interest in attending theater as they had in getting into the ring with Jack Dempsey. Their taste ran more toward the offerings at the Rialto, our city's blue-ribbon burlesque house, where Margie Hart did a slow striptease, as Buster Lorenzo, "The Little Man with the Big Voice," sang *Songs My Mother Taught Me*.

In any event, hanging an occasional theater poster on the lobby wall, between a portrait of Abraham Lincoln and *September Morn**—an American triptych of sorts—was a small price to pay for my education as a playgoer.

---

*A calendar picture of a pretty girl wading in the water and daringly lifting her skirt just above the knee. It was the most popular calendar artwork of the '20s and early '30s.

PROLOGUE: MORNING, NOON, AND NIGHT

As I awaken in the morning, after a hard day's night, I open one squinty eye and turn toward the window. I see, or imagine I see, a sliver of sun racing like crazy through the trembling leaves. It is not the warming, rising sun that worshippers kneel toward on salubrious mornings. There is something moonily cool and sickly pale about this one. And ominous. It is Kurosawa's sun.

Both eyes open now, I stare at the greenery. It is that early morning in *Rashomon* as the woodcutter trudges through the forest. The man stops abruptly. Stares. A woman's hat on a bush. A man's hat on another. Entangled on a third, a rope. Boy, you know something horrible has happened.

Something *has* happened. I've overslept. Damn that Benadryl. "Rise and Shine." Oh, no. It is Laurette Taylor in Amanda Wingfield's "blue dress, sort of beaten up with an eggbeater."* I feel as rotten as her son Tom, who has heard that cheery reveille on too many mornings. I stumble toward the bathroom. A finger of water dabbed at one eye, a finger at the other; and I'm on my way. I'm Henry Hull as Jeeter Lester in *Tobacco Road*. When he did that turn, the audience laughed. When I do it, nobody is laughing; certainly not me.

———

JACK KIRKLAND

He adapted produced, and directed the play *Tobacco Road*, based on Erskine Caldwell's novel. It ran for eight years. I interviewed him for my book *Hard Times*.

———

*Claudia Cassidy, Chicago's preeminent drama critic, covering the world premiere of *The Glass Menagerie*, a play by a young man from St. Louis. It was during the blizzard of 1944. There were very few patrons in the house. Thanks to the extraordinary reports of Miss Cassidy and her colleague Ashton Stevens, I saw it the second night.

In the spring of '32, I woke up with a violent hangover. An agent gave me this book to read that afternoon. "You're a Southerner. You'll dig this." I went home with my hangover and read it and said: This is a play. So I took the book under my arm and went to live in Majorca for three or four months. I was quite broke at the time.

As a screenwriter, I did make a few bucks on a Shirley Temple movie. You might say Shirley was really responsible for *Tobacco Road*. [Laughs]. It opened December 4, 1933. The reviews in the dailies were not too good for the play. Until Captain Patterson fell for it and wrote an editorial for the *Daily News*. The next day we were in. Later on, the monthlies came out—George Jean Nathan, Bob Benchley, Dorothy Parker, all came out for it. The play was dealing with poverty. The audience understood and was concerned. It was the Depression of the South, before the Wall Street Crash. Mrs. Roosevelt loved the play and helped a lot.

Recently, I suffered a small accident. On my way to the bathroom, I slipped on a wayward dumbbell lying in my path. It is a bad neck sprain, causing the need for a cervical collar. As I stare into the bathroom mirror, I am Erich von Stroheim, as Colonel von Rauffenstein, the German commandant of the prison camp in *Grand Illusion*. I call out to one of the French officer-inmates, Captain de Boldieu, a fellow aristocrat, who is on the roof helping two other prisoners escape: "Captain Boldieu, have you gone insane? I do not want to shoot you. Please come down, I beg of you."

"*You* come down, the breakfast is getting cold." It is my wife.

As I walk toward the bus, on my way to work, I have a habit of humming, whistling or ta-da-ing a piece of music; a song or a passage from something. It makes the time go faster. It may be that poignant German folk song, *Der treue Hussar*, about the soldier who will be forever faithful to his dead sweetheart. Instantly, the image appears of that young girl in the final scene from *Paths of Glory*. It is the Stanley Kubrick movie adaptation of Humphrey Cobb's World War I novel. It is the tavern in a town near the front; it has passed from German hands to the French. The soldiers are having one last fling before being sent to the slaughter. A frightened German girl is pushed toward the stage. There is the expected whooping and hollering. She softly begins to sing, hardly audible because of the noise. As the tone of longing and loss comes through, we see the faces of the soldiers. They are listening. They may not know the words, but a sense of longing and loss overcomes them.

On another morning jaunt, I'm rasping an old Japanese tune, "Uta No Gondola" (Song of the Gondola). It is the recurring theme of Kurosawa's *Ikiru* (To Live). The elderly civil servant, dying, needs one meaningful deed to justify his life. The actor, Takashi Shimura, sings of the passing nature of existence, youth to old age. It is a hurtful sound, from deep in his throat. Though I can't get this wistful melody out of my head (I'm humming it now, as I type), it is the movie I remember.

Some sixty years ago, I heard Lucienne Boyer, the celebrated French chanteuse, sing "Plaisir d'amour." It was at the old auditorium in Chicago. I was seated way, way up in the second balcony. She was the star of Balieff's *Chauve Souris.** I was knocked out. But when I hum what is now a popular café song, it is the movie, *The Heiress*, that immediately comes to mind. In this adaptation of a Henry James novel, the music track is based on this tune. Fran Warren sings it as "My Love Loves Me." As I'm crooning it on my way to the bus, it is not Lucienne Boyer I see. It is Montgomery Clift, the predatory suitor, having the door slammed on him by Olivia De Havilland.

There's a certain passage from Franck's D Minor Symphony which never fails to spring forth the image of Renée (Maria) Falconetti, the French actress, as Joan on her dying bed in the silent-film classic, *The Passion of Joan of Arc*. It was the masterwork of Carl Theodore Dreyer, the durable old Dane. As I remember, the soundtrack, added, was all Franck. Joan, feverish, is implored by the Bishop of Beauvais to recant. (I still see the wart on the old actor's cheek.) As I'm listening to the music on the phonograph, on

---

*Nikita Balieff, the ebullient Russian conferencier, had gathered international artists in a sort of vaudeville potpourri. Among them were Escudero, the elderly flamenco dancer, whose one accompaniment was his snapping fingernails; and Raphael, the Italian concertina virtuoso. Boyer was the headliner.

the radio, or in a concert hall, it is not Bruno Walter at the podium I'm envisioning, but Falconetti as Joan.*

I leave the bus and approach my workplace. A monstrous piece of modern kitsch architecture. The subterranean caverns are labyrinths that disorient me daily. I am a shuffling old Theseus in need of Ariadne and her ball of thread. It is a funhouse of hair stylists, videogame parlors, fast-food emporiums, adult-food shops (X-rated?), and places with charming French names. To hasten my dark journey, I whistle the blind flower girl's song from Charlie's *City Lights*: "Who Will Buy My Pretty Violets?"

I am often lost in this frozen tundra, as the catatonic young pass me by. I seek the attention of one who may help me find the way. Taking a cue from the blind flower girl, I become Conrad Veidt, as Cesare, the somnambulist, in *The Cabinet of Doctor Caligari*. I hold forth my hand, brushing it softly against the wall, and slowly, slowly stalking *misterioso*. Once in a while, a young woman pauses and gently shows me the way. It is a rare moment.

On a cold wintry morning, very few birds are about, other than

---

*There appears to be no print extant that has such a soundtrack. "A few months after release in 1928, a fire destroyed the negative and all existing prints. Dreyer reconstructed the film from what still existed. The second version was also destroyed in a fire. Around 1950, a French film historian, Lo Duca, pieced together his own version and added a score that was a montage of Albinoni, Vivaldi, and other Baroque composers. Dreyer was horrified and disowned Duca's version. Then, in the early 1980s, a print was discovered in a closet of a mental institution in Oslo, Norway. The film was sent to the Norwegian Film Institute where it was found to be a copy of the original 1928 version, with Danish intertitles" (The Internet Movie Database, Ltd.).

In the 1990s, Richard Einhorn composed an oratorio, *Voices of Light*, specifically for the film. There were special showings across the country, with a live orchestra, chorus and the Anonymous Four, singing Ambrosian and Gregorian chants. It was wonderful. In any event, I saw *The Passion of Joan of Arc* and I heard passages from Franck's D Minor Symphony as its music track. It was in 1929 or the very early 30s. It was at an old art film house on East Chicago Avenue that some thirty years later was named the Cinema Theatre. Obviously, I can't prove it. If you choose not to believe me, that's your prerogative. Why else do you think the memory of Joan's feverish moment fused to Franck's larghetto passage still haunts me?

the tough little sparrow. Naturally, I'm burbling, ". . . His eye is on the sparrow and I know he watches me . . ." It was the theme song of Mahalia Jackson's CBS radio program, of which I was the host. We had agreed that of all the spirituals, gospel songs, and hymns of her repertoire, this was to be her hallmark. Yet, it is not Mahalia that so frequently comes to mind. It is Ethel Waters singing it, during the second-act curtain of *Member of the Wedding.*

It was an adaptation of Carson McCullers's short novel. She is Bernice, the maid, comforting Julie Harris, glowing as Frankie, and eight-year-old Brandon De Wilde, as John Henry.

For years, I have been addicted to cigars. Lately, I've been advised to abandon this foul habit. The task has been made somewhat easier by the yuppies, who have adopted the stogie as the hallmark of success; as a result, these smokes have become obscenely expensive.

How I came to this habit, I attribute to a Soviet movie, *Chapaev.* It was in the late '30s. This people's hero was a self-educated peasant general who rallied his bewildered, raggle-taggle army of *muzhiks* by charging forward on his trusty stallion in the manner of George Armstrong Custer and Crazy Horse.

I was impressed by this scene, but not nearly as much as I was by the enemy, the trained Cossacks. As they marched forward in formation, their rifles and bayonets at the ready, *they were smoking cigars!* The subtitle read: "The Psychological Attack." I was bowled over. The next day, I bought my first cigar, a fifteen-cent Bock panatela. From that first hitherto-forbidden puff, I was delightedly hooked. Whether it was a nickel Red Dot cigar, smoked in the john of the PX at Fort Logan, Colorado (while the younger recruits were engaged in calisthenics in the blustery mountain air), or blowing smoke rings on an H. Upmann given to me by a generous member of the Chicago mob, I felt like I belonged. The movie Cossacks did it.

Though the word best remembered by moviegoers from *Citizen Kane* is the tycoon's dying gasp, "Rosebud," I was most impressed by Joseph Cotten's wistful request of the investigative journalist: "You wouldn't happen to have a good cigar on you, would you?"

Immediately after seeing that classic, I bought a twenty-five-cent Anthony & Cleopatra.

A friendly doctor has told me there's nothing wrong with my having a cigar now and then. That's when I remembered Charlie Chaplin in *City Lights*. The little tramp is embraced by a drunken millionaire and then booted out when the rich man sobers up. In one scene, Charlie is reclining in the back seat of the chauffeured Rolls Royce as he spots an old bum on the sidewalk reaching down for an abandoned cigar butt. Charlie jumps out, shoves the old boy aside, picks up the butt, and hops back into the Rolls. Inspired by Charlie, I slice my cigar into three butts and thus am able to puff away daily — my now-and-then cigar.

On occasion, I have a late-night rendezvous at the refrigerator with yesterday's cold chicken. As I gnaw at the drumstick, I am Charles Laughton's Henry VIII, having a go at it with a capon. It is the film's last shot. I am squinting at my mind's-eye camera as guiltless as the wayward monarch. And so to bed.

ACT ONE

1—Beginnings

1949. It was a summer stock production of *Three Men on a Horse*. The successful Broadway farce had become a perennial favorite at summer theaters. Buster Keaton is disentangling himself from the contrary bedsheet. He is not fighting it as much as trying to understand it. The linen is not an adversary; it is a puzzle to be solved.

W. C. Fields would have dealt with this circumstance in a somewhat different fashion. Consider his hard times with the hat rack and the picket fence. And Baby Leroy. They were there as antagonists, by nature ordained. Or by some dark conspiracy. He, besieged human, elbowed, poked, shouldered, juggled his way through these ordeals, abetted, now and then, by a surreptitious kick. His bumptious dignity was somewhat diminished (if only for a moment) by these malign forces of nature.

For Charlie Chaplin, there'd be no challenge at all, nor a puzzle. The sheet was simply there; not to be ignored, of course; to be embraced, perhaps; to be worn as a robe by a Martha Graham dancer. Yet, ballet was his forte, not the modern dance. There would be a pirouette, segueing into a pas de deux with his compliant partner, the sheet: a touch of Nijinsky's dalliance with that scandalous scarf in *The Afternoon of a Faun*.

FLASH FORWARD. *During some troubled times, in the early 1950s, I had difficulty holding on to jobs. A thoughtful acquaintance, who owned an art movie house, engaged me as its manager. I hadn't a clue about bookings and matters of that sort. I made a mess of it; a total disaster. During that month, I had one idea—a letter to Charlie Chaplin.*

Charlie had experienced some troubles, too. He had left the United States and settled in Switzerland. Until some years later, he forbade the showing of his feature films in this country, classics such as The Gold Rush, City Lights, *and* Modern Times.

My letter suggested renaming the movie house I was managing as the Chaplin Theatre. After all, I reasoned, there were established houses, Warner's, Loew's, Fox, Goldwyn — named after commercial producers. If they were so honored, why not the artist who above all others helped create our most popular entertainment? It was his face, his walk, his first name, Charlie, that had become the most renowned in the world. Whether it be among the Inuits of the frozen north or the pygmies of Africa's Ituri Forest, as well as among the sophisticates, the Little Tramp's appearance from the magic lantern said it all. "Charlie" had become the eponym for the moving picture. James Agee had said it better, but I figured this would do. Further, I added, it would be an irreparable loss, indeed a shame, if the younger generation that had never seen his classics be denied this delight. If he granted me permission to show these films at the Chaplin Theatre, it would enrich their lives as well as ours.

I addressed the letter: Charles Chaplin, Vevey, Switzerland. About three weeks or a month later, I received a reply. Unfortunately, in my slovenly way, I have misplaced the letter that had lain in my desk for a couple of years and have had no luck in recovering it. However, I do remember certain passages. I have no doubt that he typed it himself because there were typographical errors that no seasoned typist would commit. He was deeply appreciative, he wrote. However, for my sake, because he took me to be a decent man, he would not allow me to be hurt. Anyone living in the United States at this time would become something of a pariah if associated with Charles Chaplin. There is one sentence that I will never forget: "My name is an anathema in the United States." The article "an" was inserted.

It was the loveliest rejection I had ever received. Duke Ellington could not have been more elegant. Duke, in firing Charlie Mingus from his band, sang his praise, suggesting that he was too creative to be just a sideman, that he was a natural-born leader and should have a group of his own. Mingus felt great until it occurred to him that he had just been sacked. I simply felt great. And moved.

For Buster Keaton, the bedsheet was a wholly different matter. With the silent perseverance of a microbe hunter, searching out a cure for a plague, he transforms the sheet into something else. His was the spirit of the alchemist transmuting dross into gold. If only to get out of the jam he was in.

In the bed, he twists, turns one way, then another. No soap. The sheet ravels itself around him even more tightly. He stands up. It is a toga. He is a solemn Roman senator, surveying with fixed gaze something out there. Once more, stone-faced though perplexed, he tries to free himself. The sheet is maddeningly enveloping him. Another move—nothing desperate, simply a move. It becomes a flowing robe, the caftan of an Arabian sheik.

Again, he is at it. A winding sheet! We catch our breath. It has become the white shroud of the three dead little sons returning to haunt *The Wife of Usher's Well.**

It is not a moment of fright we are experiencing, as much as antic anxiety. Our unsettlement is not unlike that of the little children in Truffaut's *400 Blows*, caught by the violence of Punch and Judy, yet delighting in their terror.

FRANÇOIS TRUFFAUT

1960

He is the French film director, on an American tour, promoting *400 Blows*. He is twenty-eight.

How did I capture that moment? The faces of those children watching Punch and Judy, the terror? Very simple. The camera was hidden under the puppets. The operator had loaded his camera. I was standing in front of him with a newspaper. When the show began, I would lower the paper and we simply shot the scene. It was filmed during a festival.

The idea was to show that, contrary to what people ordinarily believed, a puppet show does not relax children or amuse them. On the contrary, it makes them tense and fills them with all sorts of anxi-

---

*"Green grass is over our heads, mother / Cold clay is over our feet, / And every tear you shed for us, / It wets our winding sheet." (Child Ballad #79)

eties. That's what we intended to show. Yes, I had something of a documentary in mind.

During this puppet show, the two characters who had taken the little girl to see the puppets were coolly discussing their plans to steal a typewriter, while the other children were sitting there watching Punch and Judy.

I meant it as a sort of farewell to childhood, a loss of innocence, the passing from petty misdemeanors to real theft. In the puppet show, everything revolved around the concept of good and evil; the blows that are inflicted and the ones received. This particular scene is the turning point, the focal point of the film; the point at which everything is going to change and take shape.

It's a difficult world. The phrase, 400 blows, does not refer to Punch and Judy. In France, doing the 400 blows means leading the unruly life, in which you commit misdemeanors that lead into major delinquency. The young woman, the mother of the boy, did her 400 blows before she got married.

To begin with, the boy has no admiration for his parents. When she's being kind to him, she's playing a role. The boy knows this. At no time is she natural. It's about separation of parents from child. This is the age that the child discovers that the world is not absolutely just. It's the time for hunger for independence, without parents, without teachers, without being told what to do by adults.

This life creates that solitude. That's it. It would have sounded a false note to have a cheerful or a pessimistic ending. At the edge of the water, I had this child come forward, look straight into the eyes of the public and, in effect, say, "Well, here I am. The story's over." There's a refusal to judge.

————

Buster is a prisoner with no apparent means of escape. Does this call for Houdini? Pause. He makes another, somewhat acrobatic turn, and he is free. He gets out of bed, puts on his clothes, and that's it. End of scene.

Three Men on a Horse concerned a timorous writer of greeting cards, who was kidnapped by three racetrack touts because he had a clairvoyant's knack of picking winners. I was one of the touts. Buster Keaton was, of course, the gate attraction as the kidnapee. That it was not his ideal vehicle was beside the point.

Standing in the wings, awaiting my cue, I was enthralled, watching a master. During each of those moments, there was an ever-so-slight improvisatory riff, as though he were doing it for the first time. He was Casals playing Bach, as though discovering him that moment. Even more remarkable, I missed my entrance cue only twice.

The production was mercifully reviewed as "adequate," a gentle critic's most damning report. I remember nothing of those forgettable two weeks, other than Buster's ten-minute scene. It had nothing to do with the play, but did that matter? Fifty years later, I remember Buster and the bedsheet.

When recalling the Brutus of Tyrone Power, Sr.,* it is Buster I see in the Roman toga. As Rudolph Valentino carries Agnes Ayres into the tent, it is Buster, rather, in the caftan. As I hear Alfred Deller sing of the haunted mother and the dead little sons, it is Buster in the winding sheet.

BUSTER KEATON

1960

He was once more on tour; this time, promoting a movie, *When Comedy Was King.* It was an assemblage of two-reelers, featuring the clowns of the silent past, the great ones: a piece of Chaplin, a piece of Langdon, a piece of Keaton. . . . It was eleven years since I had seen him perform magic in that less-than-magical summer stock production.

No words were spoken. Subtitles said it all?

Your lips moved. You spoke. In the cutting room, you'd simply run the film through your fingers down to where you got your mouth

---

*Power was a featured actor in Fritz Lieber's Shakespearean repertory company that appeared in the Civic Theatre, Chicago, during the 1930s.

open. On the second syllable, you'd cut, slap in your subtitles.
Then you'd come back to pick it up just as your mouth is about to
close.

We eliminated subtitles just as fast as we could if we could possibly tell it in action. Charlie Chaplin and I would have a friendly
contest: who could do the feature film with the least subtitles? Charlie won that. He had this picture down to something like twenty-one
titles. I had twenty-three. The average picture had 240 titles. The
most I ever used was fifty-six.

*In the movie I saw the other night, you gummed up a big police pa-
rade. You didn't mean to, but somehow you did. They were chasing
you, thousands of cops. It became something out of a bad dream.*

I tried to cut through the parade, but couldn't do it, so I joined it
before they could stop me. I was in a wagon, a moving man. Some
anarchist on top of the building threw a bomb down and it lit in my
wagon. So when it went off, the whole police force was after me.

*Thousands chasing this one man, never quite catching him. The way
you moved, your acrobatics, knocked me out. How much was planned,
how much improvised?*

Oh, no, it was just a hit-or-miss routine, just ducking cops in all
directions. Just a common, ordinary chase sequence. We never did
repeat gags. About fifty percent you have in your mind before you
start the picture and the rest you develop as you're making it.

*James Agee wrote: "Keaton's face ranked with Lincoln's as an early
American archetype. It was hauntingly handsome, almost beautiful.
Yet it was irreducibly funny. He improved matters by topping it off
with a deadly horizontal hat, as flat and thin as a phonograph record.
One can never forget Keaton wearing it, standing erect at the prow,
as the little boat is being launched. The boat goes grandly down the
skids and just as grandly straight onto the bottom. Keaton never
budges. The last you see of him, the water lifts the hat off the stoic head
and it floats away. The hat."*

That's called *The Boat*. I had a similar hat on the stage before I went
into pictures. I was twenty-one. That's in the spring of 1917. My

family was all on the stage. I was born with the Keaton/Houdini Medicine Show Company on a one-night stand in Kansas. They tell me that Harry Houdini gave me the name of Buster.

My old man was an eccentric comic. As soon as I was able to get on my feet, he had slap shoes on me and big baggy pants. And just started doing gags with me, especially kicking me clean across the stage or taking me by the back of the neck and throwing me. By the time I got to about seven or eight, we were called the roughest act in the history of the stage. I always played it deadpan as if it was the most natural thing in the world. If I laughed at what I did, the audience didn't. The more seriously I took my work, the better laughs I got. It was just automatic, mechanical.

You've been called the master of the mechanical gag. Iris Berry said: "Buster Keaton gazes with frozen bewilderment at the nightmare reality: inventions and contrivances with deck chairs and rail engines seem animate. They seem alive to him in the same measure that human beings become impersonal. He's like the inhabitant of another planet."

I get my best material working with something like that. I guess I was one of those original do-it-yourself fellas. I may not know how to do a carpenter's job, but I set up to build a house. Everybody knows you're going to get into trouble when you start that.

FLASHBACK. *The late '20s. Willie West & McGinty was a headline act in the top-flight vaudeville houses. They were Irish brick masons, blithely working on a house, fortified with a touch of the water of life. They were having some difficulty; the more the shambles, the more we howled. It was pure Keaton.*

I liked dream sequences. Some of those two-reelers were full of dreams. That cop chase was one. We went wild and crazy in them. We lost all that when we started making feature pictures. We had to stop doing the impossible gags, what we called cartoon gags. They had to be believable or your story wouldn't hold up.

For instance, I'm the fellow who got up on a high-diving platform at a country club and did a swan dive off of it and missed the pool and went through the ground. And the scene faded out. And the title comes on and says, "Years Later." And it faded back into the country club. And the pool was empty and the grass growing onto it and the whole place neglected and nobody around. And I came up out of the hole with a Chinese wife and two kids. That was the fade-out of a two-reeler. We wouldn't have dared use that in a feature picture.

You'd just sit around, talk for quite a while before starting the picture. And then take advantage of anything that happens. Neither Chaplin, Harold Lloyd, nor myself ever had a script. That sounds impossible to anybody in the picture business today. We never thought of writing a script. Somebody would always come up with a start. We'd say, "That's funny. That's a good start." All right, we want to know the finish, right then and there. There's nothing to work toward but the finish. If we can't round out something we like, we throw it away and start on a new one.

When we get the start and the right finish, we've got it, because the middle we can always take care of. That's easy. We're all set. My prop man knows what props to get, the wardrobe man, the same. The guy who builds the sets knows what it's all about. I help him design them. There's no need for a script. We all know what we're going to do. Gags that don't work, we throw out, and the accidental ones come.

Another thing we didn't do in those days that they do today: we didn't rehearse a scene to perfection. In our big roughhouse scenes, there's a lot of falls and people hit each other. We never rehearsed those. We just sat down and said, "He drops that chair, then you come through the door and come through fast. This person here throws up their hands, you come through and just about hit him. If you miss, get her, the girl." That's how we laid those scenes out. If you did those roughhouse scenes, invariably somebody skinned an elbow or bumped a knee, so now they'll shy away from it on the next take or they'll favor it. So you seldom get a scene that good the second time. You generally got 'em on the first one. Anybody in the scene is free to do as he pleases, as long as he keeps the action going. Even your extras can use their imagination.

Hank Mann was a newcomer. Mack Sennett never heard of him. He got in as an extra during one of those cop chase scenes. A building had caught fire. The police and fire department are there. Mann came out of the burning building, put a cigarette in his mouth, lit it off the burning building and walked off. He hadn't the slightest idea he'd do it till the last minute. In the projection room, Sennett saw it and said, "Who's that so-and-so?" I says, "One of the extra guys." He says, "He's all right. We'll keep him here for a while."*

In the Mack Sennett two-reelers, I always remember authority being comically challenged: the befuddled cop, the confused boss. . . . The snowball thrown at the top hat. . . .

Oh, sure, like throwing pies. But you got to be careful. There are certain characters you don't hit with a pie. Hit the wrong person, the audience gets mad at you.

You hit girls with pies, lots of them.

Oh, that they didn't mind. I remember a lot of people wanting to hit Lillian Gish because she was always so sweet and innocent.

FLASHBACK. *The '30s. Clayton, Jackson, and Durante at the Palace Theatre, Chicago. Jimmy, in an indignant peroration, sees "an ol' man hittin' a little boy wit' his umbrella. I walks up to 'im an' says, 'Why ya hittin' dat cute little boy wit' yer umbrella?' He says, 'Dat's why I'm hittin' 'im, 'cause he's so cute.'"*

Now, in television, about eight years ago, Milton Berle got Ed Sullivan with a pie. The audience froze up. And Milton didn't get another laugh while he was on that stage. There's just some people you don't hit with a pie and that's all there's to it. Ed Sullivan was one of them.

If I had a grand dame who was dogging it and putting it on, she was gray-haired but she was overbearing, the audience would like to hit her. Then you could hit her with a pie and they would laugh their heads off. But if she was a legitimate old lady, a sincere character, you wouldn't dare hit her. If she's a phony, that's different. The same thing goes with a man.

---

*Hank Mann is best remembered as the mean-looking prize fighter in *City Lights*, who is befuddled by Charlie Chaplin's fancy footwork in the ring.

There are certain set rules when it comes to getting a laugh?

You bet. I did a silent called *The Camera Man.* I was a newsreel photographer. I got into a tong war in Chinatown. They didn't want me to take the picture, so they started chasing me. This was going to be a big laugh picture. I'm down to the last reel. At the finish, they're chasing me down fire escapes and over rooftops and I was doing everything to get away. We thought it was great.

We previewed it and in that last reel, it took a nose dive. We finally figured that one out. I had deserted the camera and the audience didn't like it. I had left the camera when the Chinamen started chasing me. So we went back and retook the sequence. The camera followed me all the way and it was all right. They took our stories seriously and we had to always remember that. (A touch wistful.) Some of those routines we did forty years ago, we can't do today.

Yet Chaplin's Limelight *was not that long ago: his bouquet to his English music-hall days. You and Chester Conklin and Charlie did a routine in which you bounced around like rubber balls. . . .*

Oh, I can still turn over as far as that goes. I guess some of us are lucky we can still move fast.

When we first met that summer, some eleven years ago, you spoke of Charlie Chaplin as a director and you specifically mentioned A Woman of Paris.

Charlie was one of the best ever in the picture business. Edna Purviance was the girl. She had been his leading lady and he made this a high-society drama. It was suggestion all through. It was the first time ever this approach was used—something that had to be explained and not something head-on. Every director in the business went to see this picture.

Chaplin wanted the audience to know that Adolphe Menjou paid for the apartment she was living in, that he was keeping her. Nobody had to explain it. Menjou calls on her one evening to take her out. He looks in the mirror, sees a little spot on his collar. He takes the collar off, went over to the bureau and got a clean one. That told the whole situation, no diagram needed. He respected the audience. He left it up to them to figure it out.

Roscoe Arbuckle didn't feel that way.* His pictures were the first ones I appeared in. I was with him a short time when he said, "The average mind of the motion picture fan is twelve years old." I'll never forget that. I was with him for only a few months when I said to him, "Roscoe, something tells me that those who make pictures for twelve-year-old minds ain't gonna be with us very long." It was only a couple of years later that the scene in Chaplin's movie proved it. The minds jumped faster than we were making pictures.

I always tried to challenge the imagination of my audience. I always challenged them to outguess me and then I'd double-cross them.

As far as laughter goes, we'd go into a movie house where our picture was playing and we'd hear those people laugh out loud at what they saw on the screen. No prompting. The canned laughter we hear on television today is absolutely no good at all. There is a false note all the way. It saddens me to hear it.

I'll never forget your encounter with that bedsheet in Three Men on a Horse. *Eleven years ago* . . .

Ah, well. It was there, you use it. Don't fight it—and that's it.

LILLIAN GISH

1963

> The quintessential heroine of D. W. Griffith films: frail, vulnerable and fair-skinned. She starred in, among others, *Birth of a Nation*, *Intolerance*, and *Broken Blossoms*.
>
> At the time of this conversation, she was appearing in *Passage to India*, a dramatic adaptation of E. M. Forster's novel. She had, at one time, played Ophelia to John Gielgud's Hamlet.

I was in the theater when I was five years of age, playing children. That was about 1902, 1903. When I was eleven, twelve, I got to be

---

*Roscoe "Fatty" Arbuckle was one of the most celebrated and successful movie comedians in the '20s. A headline-making scandal involving a wild party and the death of a girl, Virginia Rapp, ruined his reputation and career.

awfully long-legged and long-armed. A tall child found it difficult getting roles. There were few demands for lanky children. Leading ladies in those days were short.

In the films at that time, they needed young faces. So they dressed up the young ones in long skirts and they played heroines until they were eighteen. Then they were too old and went into character roles. An old hag of eighteen was passé as a heroine. The photography was so cruel and so prying. Their liability was an asset to me.

Before I could read, I was taught my lines on the stage. I never knew anything else. I never had the choice of saying, "I want to be *that*." Acting was all I knew. I would love to have been a librarian, because I like to read.

I was very envious of all my cousins, who went through universities, and I used to have a great inferiority complex. But I soon learned they couldn't hold their own on many subjects that I knew about. I had been educated in films and in theater, on the spot, and my knowledge was quite different from theirs. I didn't know arithmetic and geometry, but I knew lots of other things they didn't know.

Think of the education of *Intolerance*. That was the greatest film ever made. All the different centuries of struggle. Mr. Griffith was sympathetic to the sufferings of the poor and all the injustices throughout history. So we had to know all about Babylon and all about the Crucifixion. When I visited the Holy Land, I thought, "Griffith built this." Everything about it was so familiar that I expected him to call "camera!" any minute.

When we came up to the French period, the Eve of St. Bartholomew, we had to know that. And then the modern period, the battle between capital and labor. So each film was an education. When we did the fifteenth-century Florentine time, we had to know not only the history of Florence and Italy, but the world around it. So this *used* to be a great education.

We were immersed in all those periods. You went around with those little books and if you had a minute, you were reading. You worked seven days a week. You never stayed at home because after all, it wasn't as interesting. There was no social life whatsoever.

There were no scriptwriters. Griffith did everything. Very often he changed his name. He would use a nom de plume because, he said, people wouldn't like it if they thought you did everything. He had the courage of his ideas and was very strong on the side of the working man against the boss.

We worked for a medium we believed in. A lot of us took personal responsibility for what we said in the films. We were told we were much more influential than the press, the printed word. It weighed heavily on our conscience.

What Griffith had was the way of telling a story. He invented the form. He knew it had to be different from the stage. On the stage, we see people walk on stage and off. Everything was literal. He saw that the film can move as your mind moves. The camera has no proscenium arch. The sun, the moon, and the stars are the proscenium arch. There is no *limit* to the camera. So we had to learn a new form of acting.

When Charles Laughton took on the job of directing *The Night of the Hunter*—James Agee was doing the screenplay from Davis Grubb's novel—he spent a great deal of his time at the Museum of Modern Art in New York. Do you know why? He was running all the old Griffith films.

He called me one day and asked me over for tea. He said pictures today have lost the excitement they used to have. A certain spirit. That's why he was studying these old Griffith films. He had them sent to the coast so he could study them again, while making his movie.

Charles was so *frightened* of directing. You would try to help. If you had a suggestion, he would say, "Oh, you don't like what I'm doing." "Oh, that isn't good." He was like a scared kid.

We ended up by putting props under him, just saying, "Everything is wonderful, Charles." He was so unsure. It was that he had such enormous respect for Griffith, the man he was trying to imitate. The Russians did quite well imitating him. Look at Eisenstein.

Perhaps the most celebrated shot in Birth of a Nation *is that of a sad sentry, a droopy-faced Union soldier leaning against his gun.*

He was a sailor out of work. He came to work as an extra in films. His name was Freeman. He helped carry our costumes, they were heavy. They were doing a scene at hospital, and this man, Freeman, was just tired, leaning against his gun. Griffith said to Billy Bitzer, his cameraman, "Look at that face, Billy. Get a picture of that." That's how pictures were made in those days. We improvised on the set. If we as actors had an idea, we were allowed to put it in. We were a creative people.

Author's note: At one moment, I casually mentioned the overt racism of Birth of a Nation. *She was clearly unsettled. "He was from the South, you know."*

KING VIDOR

1975

A film director, notably in the 1920s and 1930s. His World War I movie *The Big Parade* was his most celebrated work. His films have been, in my life, benchmarks. When I've seen a King Vidor film I remember the time and place because my memory of it has been so indelible. He was visiting Chicago during a midwest film festival sponsored by a local college.

You're celebrated for a number of films but I'm thinking at this moment of Our Daily Bread, *a movie of the Great Depression.*

I think it was '34. Milk trucks were being overturned and people were selling apples on street corners and they had the Hoovertowns. Farms were being sold, mortgages were being sold for a small amount of money. And I read a thing in *Reader's Digest*, where some fellow at Duke University said that the only solution to this was to exchange services and know-how. That was the way to overcome the economic depression. That's all I needed to put the whole thing together. It was a commune. A man who knew how to lay bricks, he exchanged with a plumber, or a tailor who knew how to press pants. They exchanged their abilities and goods. In a time of depression, life becomes too complicated, the middleman, the wholesaler, and all the people that get a cut out of everything. So you think of people living together, sharing their work, and all pitching in. It was sort of a natural sequence to solve depressing times. It just came about naturally. People always ask me was I trying to do socialist or communist propaganda. I was called pinko quite a few times. When *Our Daily Bread* opened in Los Angeles, we had a full-page ad in the *Examiner*. Just before the picture opened, they threw the whole page out. It was the Hearst press, and the reason they gave was that it was pinko propaganda. A month or so later, a Russian delegation came over to Hollywood to present awards from the Moscow Film Festival. I got second prize for *Our Daily Bread*. They said, "We would have given you the first prize except we considered it capitalistic propaganda." [Laughs]

You got it both ways! You can't win. You did not use celebrated stars. You deliberately sought people not known, anonymous ones.

Exactly. Somebody would cast John Gilbert, or James Cagney, or Gable. I thought they were identified with some set image. And I was looking for a fellow that didn't have an established image. It's a feeling I had very much in those days. I believed the character, and I believed the story. You can't take a Gable or a Tracy and make him an average man.

They call it neorealism, I guess. The Italian director Vittorio De Sica always gave my *The Crowd* credit for starting his career. He always said it inspired him more than anything. The result was his *The Bicycle Thief*, *Shoeshine*, *The Roof*, and *Umberto D*. De Sica always told me it inspired him. He said it up until he died.

The Bicycle Thief is one of my favorite films of all time. The fact that De Sica said your film, The Crowd, *played a role in his becoming a director does not surprise me at all. You made* The Crowd *in 1928, just before the Crash. The actor you used was James Murray, an unknown.*

Do you know how that happened? You're familiar with *The Big Parade*. At the time of *The Big Parade*, I wanted to take an ordinary G.I., an ordinary guy, and let him walk through and observe and react to what he saw. He didn't cause the war and he wasn't parading against it. That was my feeling, and that was the way I directed John Gilbert. He said, "Oh, now we're in a French village. Oh, there's a pretty girl." And then one day, they said "Now you're going up to the Front." This is the way most American G.I.'s, ordinary men, go through a war.

I imagine it can go over today because it deals with the real horrors of war. I wanted to make a war picture from the G.I.'s viewpoint. The war pictures always had been from the officers' viewpoint. They caused the war—the generals, the colonels. And I wanted to make one from the G.I.'s viewpoint—where he got dirty in a sloppy uniform and bloodied and killed. And you know, we weren't just satisfied to make a little thing, just a little psychological thing. It had form. It builds up to an exciting climax just before intermission. You come back, there's a big orchestra playing, you got your money's worth.

Afterwards, Irving Thalberg, who was running MGM, said to me, "This is such a success, what are you going to do next?" And I said, "There must be other things that a fellow can walk through and observe." And he said, "What, for example?" And I said, "Life." And he said, "That sounds like a good idea. Why didn't you mention that before?" I said, "I never thought of it before." And he says, "You got a title for it?" And I said, "One of The Mob." He says, "That's good." He says, "Might sound like a gangster mob." So we changed it to *The Crowd*.

It was the guy walking through life and observing life. You know, he was born, his father died, and he had to go to work and he's just one of the mob. And then he meets a girl and he gets married and he has a baby. The baby gets into an accident and dies. So he's just observing life . . . the ordinary man observing life. He's not causing situations; he's not bringing them about. It's the carrying out of the idea of *The Big Parade*. *Our Daily Bread* is still carrying out that theme, a subjective theme of a man observing his world.

The character Pierre of *War and Peace* appealed to me because he was trying to find out what his world was, going to the battlefront. My feeling is that when I look at me, I have one thought about it; when I look at you, I have the same kind of thought. You're just as important to me as when I look down and see me. A psychiatrist friend of mine refers to it as "my you." There's an old saying, "You can't love anybody else until you love yourself." There's a certain divinity about each individual. I look upon everybody just the same as I look upon myself.

I don't like the word director. Filmmaker is more general. If he can discover himself, something is going to rub off in whatever he does. Examples are Hitchcock and Frank Capra, DeMille and Griffith. Their individuality dominated everything, or rubbed off. That's what's lacking in pictures today. A fellow will make one kind of picture and the next time make another kind of picture. Certainly, with Fellini, the individuality is right there every time. And with Bergman. It's right there. And I'm waiting for the young American directors to establish some individual quality that will rub off on everything they do.

I was influenced by Griffith a lot, in the form of the film, but it still has to come from the insides. When I see a Fellini film, I think, instead of going to a psychoanalyst, he's doing films. The same thing with Bergman. You see the religious life of his early training, Bergman coming out. Give the man enough rein for him to discover himself.

I'm also a film fan. When I hear a new Fellini film is coming out, I don't have to know the story or anything. I just look forward to seeing a new Fellini film. I look forward to any Fellini film because I know it's going to interest me. It doesn't have to be sensational. I was standing in line once and I turned around and said, "Why are you here?" And he said, "It's a Fellini film." A film. That's what I wait for. I think of many of the films of today, the technique is great, but something's missing: feeling.

I was at Dartmouth in October, showing *The Champ*, one of my films. Remember when the door opens and Jackie Cooper's mother is standing there, and he looks at her and says, "Mother"? From the students, yak, yak, yak, big laughter. Afterwards, I said, "That's a funny reaction." One of the professors said, "When the freshman comes in here he wants to be accepted and he thinks he's supposed to laugh at everything that has any sort of mother or feeling about it, and he's supposed to brush it off; he wants to let the seniors know that he's laughing at the feeling."

This fear is interesting. Recently, there was a showing of the New Deal documentaries, The Plough that Broke the Plains *and* The River. *A young friend of mine says some of the students who saw it started laughing. They thought it was corny. The people fighting to save the land, cooperating, together. It's this looking inward, this sinister fear of feeling.*

It's an interesting change. Interesting to see what we can find in it.

I remember a Vidor movie with an entirely black cast. It was called Hallelujah, *I saw it at the Castle Theatre, across the street from the Boston Store, corner of Madison and State. It was known as the busiest corner in the world. [Laughs]*

We could not get a booking in the big theaters. Balaban and Katz controlled the theaters. They would not book it, although it was an MGM film. . . .

The MGM sales department said, "You go to Chicago, get the critics to see the film, get the reviews written, and maybe some theater owner will read it and say it must be important." Which we did. Ran the film. Got the reviews. No theater yet. And this place that you saw it, I'm glad to hear the name.

The banker who really ran the company, Nick Schenck, was saying no. I said, "I'll put my money in with yours." My salary. Those were some of the obstacles we had with making an all-black film at that time. He booked the film, had a black-tie opening, and we packed the theater for Schenck for a while. And then the big theaters — Balaban and Katz Theaters — they took it over and it had a pretty good run. It took me three or four years, but I finally persuaded MGM to make it. Recently, a friend of mine went to MGM with a story and they said, "Haven't you got a story that features black people? That's what we're looking for right now. It'll make money." [Laughs]

By some of today's standards, Hallelujah *is full of stereotypes. But at the time, it was quite explosive.*

Yes, yes. At the time, you must remember there were no black players in major league football, major league baseball. I realize it was not a story about what the blacks have accomplished. Of course, I wouldn't make that picture today, but it was a true record of scenes that I had seen in my boyhood, rural southern America. I was born and raised in Texas. And I'd seen all these people milling around in a church, revival, ecstasy, inside a church, as a boy, a young man in Arkansas. I reproduced exactly what I saw. There was no opposition on the part of the black actors. They were there, they lived there, they ad-libbed a lot of the dialogue. Some are out of the stage in New York, and some are off the streets of Chicago, and we went to churches, black churches here, and walked the streets and picked up people, took them to Memphis. Some were right out of Memphis—boys dancing, right out of the Peabody Hotel in Memphis, Tennessee.

I was thinking of what happened to Jimmy Murray. You said he's the actor, an unknown actor, who was the star of The Crowd. *What happened to his moment of celebrityhood, his moment of recognition?*

I got a letter of how he died in New York, as a bum. I started putting the whole story together. He becomes an alcoholic. I won't talk too much about it. But it's a good basic theme, isn't it?

VITTORIO DE SICA

1962

Rome. He is seated in his office. His classic face betrays weariness. I observe we're within hailing distance of the balcony from which Mussolini addressed multitudes. He smiles. He quotes Baudelaire on Napoleon. "'A dictator is not as dangerous alive as when he lives on after death.' You had your sorry period, McCarthyism. We had a bad one after the war." Closet fascists had given him a hard time. They were high in the circles of government.

Once a matinee idol, De Sica still acts in films, too many of them bad ones. Reason: He must raise much of his own money to finance the ones he directs. It is better now, but in the beginning the government was intransigent. They abhorred his chosen themes.

> Following the fall of Mussolini and the end of World War Two, a group of Italian film makers brought forth a style known as neorealism. It portrayed the lives of working people in cities and villages, and their day-to-day survival in postwar Italy.

After the ruins of the war, everybody, every artist in the cinema in Italy needed to tell the story, to say the story with sincerity, with truth.

To be courageous. To tell the truth. Because to tell the truth is very difficult. Finally, after twenty years of fascism, we have perceived this possibility to be free. Every artist is fighting for this freedom. My first picture, *Shoeshine*, is a small stone in the rebuilding of Italy. It's about two small shoeshine boys. A small story, of ruined lives maimed by the war. For everybody, the war was horrible. I felt the necessity to say something about these boys. Absolutely no actors, boys in the streets. One now is a great, a good actor. He was one of the boys. I find him in a street. All the others are real shoeshine, real shoeshine.

The father of the boy in *The Bicycle Thief*, Lamberto Maggioranni, was a workman who sent me his boy, to show me his boy to be in the film. I find this man who had the face, the face that I need in this moment for the father.

This story of the father and son was so emotional for me, so sincere, so true. I give them, these characters, my love, my conviction, and I have already half of the role with the face. The other half for me is very easy because of the feeling I have for their daily problems.

The idea of making *The Roof* came to Zavattini* and me together. Passing by these villages of huts, these hundreds of huts that were springing up around the big cities, around Rome, in this particular case. The fact that they had to be covered with a roof within one night hit particularly Zavattini's and my imagination. You know that if the hut was built and roofed within a night they could keep it on the ground, otherwise it would have been taken down.

If the roof can be set up before nightfall, the house belongs to them, even though they're squatting. Which made for suspense of the film.

---

*Cesare Zavattini, the writer of most of De Sica's films.

The fact that these villages were a product of the war, were part of the social situation of Italy after the war, was very interesting for us. Therefore, we made this little story.

We hear talk these days about the day of neorealism being over, you know. There's a poetic style coming into the Italian film industry. To me what you did is poetic.

Neorealism is not absolutely realism, it's realism figuratively. *Miracle in Milan,* for instance, is a fable. Reality as a fable.

It was a different style than your other works. Miracle in Milan *dealt with this boy who was almost saintly, this boy where the poor people lived in their jungle. I'll never forget the humor when the freezing men are trying to get into that sun. And they're pushing each other around. This is not a realistic thing, yet it could be.*

A fable, a wonderful period of my career, this of *Miracle in Milan.* The idea was from a book by Zavattini for children. I told him I would like to translate this book in the picture, *Miracle in Milan.* We come back again with the story of the truth with *Umberto D* and *The Roof.*

The way you make children behave like children and not like midgets. Bruno Ricci, the little kid in The Bicycle Thief *or the boys in* Shoe-shine. *How do you make them be children?*

I am so enthusiastic over you because you remember the name of my characters.

I saw it twelve times.

I am so grateful to you because it's very emotional for me that an American would remember the name of a little boy like Bruno Ricci. Bruno Ricci, I find him after four months. I heard many boys, many boys. Always they give me nice sweet boys. I don't like. I would like a boy with eyes very human eyes and a strange face—I begin the picture without the boy, without Bruno Ricci. Because I could not find the one exactly how I prefer. I begin the picture, and at a certain moment, I see a boy near me just standing around in the street watching as we shoot the movie. A miracle. Because there was

Bruno Ricci near me. I said, "*Como,* how, you are here?" He says, "I am here; I am enthusiastic to see a picture." "What is your name?" Enzo Staiola is his name. "How old are you?" "Five years." "Would you like to make a picture with me?" "Yes." "All right. Go." He begins his role, and this is the miracle of Bruno Ricci. It is fortune, a miracle for me.

In Italy, nobody wish to make this picture. In France, in London, nobody. . . . Only an American producer, Selznick, offered me, because he was interested in this picture, *but* he would like to put an American actor for the father. I didn't like to make an actor for the role of the father. Simple people, poor people, I can't make this role a bourgeois. Impossible. Our actors are all bourgeois. In this role it is impossible to put a bourgeois actor.

We had many problems at the beginning in our career. Now very easy to find producer because now a producer trusts the new ideas. But after the war, after a period of old-fashioned comedy, it was very difficult to suggest new ideas. For me, for everybody it was very difficult to find money. At certain moments I spend my own money to make this picture. I was an actor, and took the money I made as an actor and put it in the film I was directing. *The Roof,* for example. My money. What a pity. It was not commercial. I lost all my money. But I am glad to lose my money, to have my story, my life, the souvenir of a picture like *Bicycle Thief* and *Umberto D* and *The Roof.* There is always a marriage between humor and tragedy because life is always so tragic and so funny.

My films always had a social impact. How can artists be insensitive to these problems, to social injustice? Through the small stories of small people, they expressed these big problems. So it is *Miracle in Milan,* the dreams of the poor people. *The Bicycle Thief,* the problem of unemployment. *Umberto D,* the problem of the old, retired civil servant, old age. *The Roof,* the problem of housing. These small stories about small people, with their poetry, they always, always have a social meaning.

Now it's different, because the audience prefers this kind of picture. It is a necessity to resolve certain conditions of human beings. Everybody feels this. Now everybody is interested in this problem of poetry, misery, and social unjustice.

This is very revealing of you, Mr. De Sica. Even though you knew at that time that some of those films would lose, you wanted to make those films for yourself. You had to make them.

When I made *Umberto D*, I was sure to lose my money. I made this picture because I needed absolutely to make this picture in favor of an old man. In this period we read in the newspapers about many, many, many suicides of old people. It's a horrible, horrible story. Because if a young man makes a suicide, it's desperate, crazy. But the suicide of an old man is even more tragic. Because it's a maximum desperation. I made this picture, I was sure to lose completely my money.

The plight of old age must be recognized. The character was irritating, this civil servant who might turn down a begger himself, if he had money. Yet we felt the plight of old age. The story was also about me. A producer wanted to make this picture with a great actor, an aristocratic actor, and I refused. I needed an absolutely real old man, because the *real* old men are not sympathetic. No sentimentality. No self-pity. Real old men are always so angry with people, with society. And I find this professor of the University of Florence. A professor of languages. I find him in the street. He was my real Umberto D. I take this man who, for me, was perfect in his role because he was not sympathetic, but a real, old, un-acting man.

Not many people saw *Umberto D* because there was a strong, resentment by the government, the official authorities, against this film. It emphasized, put in clear light, the problem of the old civil servant, of the people who were living on a pension. It was not said, not open, but there was a strong ostracism against this picture. So not all Italians had the chance to see *Umberto D*.

Certain moments, after the war, the Italian audience wished to see American pictures, because after twenty years without American pictures, you understand, it's true, it's sincere. Myself, I want to see American pictures because I admire very much Hollywood pictures. Many actors, many directors like King Vidor, I admire very much. So the Italian people don't want to see the daily misery. This is the reason I lost my money, because the audience refused to go to see these pictures. I had a very unhappy life with the government; it was against my pictures. I fight. I continue to make my pictures. And now the government accepts my pictures but it was a sorry, very unhappy period. This period, fortunately, is finished, and now our lives are a little more free. We can make our pictures without too much trouble. Before, no. Before, for me it's been a very unhappy career, because every, every picture I made was considered antigovernment. A heritage of fascism. Baudelaire was right then and he's right now.

A certain resistance to freedom was still alive in Italy after the war, among certain groups of people. They did not want to discuss certain problems, especially with the cinema. They said we shouldn't put on the screen these problems. They still had the fascist mentality, that everything was all right. During the fascist times, there were no suicides in Italy, they said. Everything was all right. There were no poor people, they said. Everything was beautiful, it was new, it was great. This mentality is still in many, many people.

After the man is gone, Mussolini is gone, hanged by his feet, there are still the remnants of his rule. When I first read Children of Sanchez, *about this Mexican family, the actual words of these people, this father and four children, and I heard that you were going to be the director, it seemed the most natural thing in the world.* *

I am unemployed now, because the government, the Mexican government was against this. Here it is again. The artist as a rebel, as a questioner. It is always so, no?

---

*Children of Sanchez, by Oscar Lewis, was the oral history of a Mexican family. De Sica was close to directing the film adaptation when we spoke.

2—Say It with Music

EUBIE BLAKE

1973

He and his colleague, Noble Sissle, wrote Shuffle Along *in 1921. It was the first all-black musical.*

"After Shuffle Along, *nobody dared produce a musical that didn't have syncopation in it or have some jazz dancing. It really revolutionized the whole Broadway musical": William Bolcom.*

He, ninety, smoking cigarettes like crazy, is in the radio studio. His companions are Robert Kimball, musical biographer, and Bill Bolcom. Bolcom's interests range from ragtime to opera.

You want to hear how *Shuffle Along* was launched? It was launched on nothing or something pretty close to nothing. The producers had had a couple of flops and all of a sudden they wanted to put on this show. Nobody had any money. It was all done on a shoestring. Everything was really done completely on the tick.

All of a sudden we found ourselves with all these bandanna-type, handkerchief kind of costumes. So we had to write a number for it. And that's how "Bandanna Days" got written.* Over the phone. Sissle was in Boston and I was in New York. One of the chorus girls was Josephine Baker. Paul Robeson was in the quartet. The Harmony Kings. A regular member of the quartet had to go back to Kansas City, someone in the family had died. Paul said, "I've never been on a stage." I said, "Listen, you don't have to do anything but sing."

Bolcom interjects: "He had just come out of Rutgers. All-American football, Phi Beta Kappa." Kimball interjects: "That pit orchestra had William Grant Still at the oboe and Hall Johnson

---

*A hit song from *Shuffle Along*.

at the viola."* Bolcom: "Those guys supposedly couldn't read." [Laughs].

Adelaide Hall was in the chorus. And Florence Mills, boy, she was the most dynamic woman I've ever seen on the stage. Gertrude Saunders was great, but she made a big mistake. She left *Shuffle Along* to go with a burlesque show for five dollars a week more.

I guess the most popular song in Shuffle Along *was "I'm Just Wild About Harry." That served as Harry Truman's campaign song. About twenty-seven years later.*

I wrote that as a waltz. I played it as a waltz for Lottie Gee one of the stars of the show. She just passed while I was in Los Angeles. She says, "I like the song but I can't sing it." I knew her range. She had a D above the staff and I took it no further than a B flat. I was taught never to take people to the last note. I said, "Why can't you sing it?" She said, "Because it's a waltz. Who ever heard of a waltz song in a colored show?" She says, "If you put it in one-step, I'll sing it."

I played it in one-step and that's what made the song a hit. We almost threw it out of the show.

Talk about hits, you heard about James Reese Europe? He traveled all over the continent playing our songs. Sissle was the singer. I played the piano.

Bolcom: "Europe was responsible for the fox-trot. He worked with Vernon and Irene Castle. They changed the tempo and the rhythm on 'Memphis Blues' and that became the fox-trot."

This was before World War I. Then he had the military band that went abroad. I didn't go to war. I'm not fighter, you see. Know how they'd introduce me to the girls? "Meet slacker Eubie Blake." [Laughs]

Bolcom: "Europe came back after the war in triumph. He was all set to just absolutely clean up the country. Then one day he got stabbed

---

*Still was to become a distinguished American composer. The Hall Johnson Choir was one of the most highly regarded choral groups in the country.

to death by one of the orchestra members. It was actually Sissle and Blake who were doing most of the work by then."

In 1919, we formed the vaudeville act, Sissle and Blake. I'm at the piano, he's singing. I'd be talking to him and playing piano fast. All the tricks I'd put in that piano. Then came *Shuffle Along*.

[We are listening to a recent Columbia recording of Eubie Blake playing "Dreamland." John Hammond had brought him out of years of retirement. Bolcom says he's playing as well as ever.]

When people ask me about my longevity, I just don't know. I practice more now. My father lived to be eighty-three, and that was a miracle. He and my mother were slaves, you know. My mother never owned up to it. It's the only willful story she ever told. "No, no, I was never a slave." My father was nineteen years older than my mother and he'd say to her, "Did you pick cotton?" She says, "Yes." He'd say, "Did the man pay you?" She says, "No." Then he'd wink at me and says, "Slave right along with me." He wouldn't say it out loud, because she'd jump at him and kill him, you know.

My father used to tell me about slavery. While he was cracking walnuts for me, he'd show me all those stripes on his back where they whipped him. They didn't allow them to talk or have meetings.

You know cotton doesn't grow high. It would make them bend over like this from sun up to sun down. The old man told me he'd never had on a pair of leather shoes until he went in the Civil War. Carpet shoes. That guy lived to be eighty-three years that way.

My mother and father used to go to market late Saturday night so they could get things cheaper. It was a street in Baltimore called Broadway. The market was near the wharf and I was toddling behind. I don't remember it, but my mother told it to me. I was about five.

She looked back and didn't see me. She gave one scream. "I lost my boy." This white man behind her says, "He went over in that music store across the street."

I had never touched a piano in my life. It was an organ. This guy was demonstrating. You pump it with your feet. When he finished demonstrating I tried to play it. It wouldn't play. My mother walked in and you know what the man says? "He's a genius." He wants to sell this organ. You can get it for a dollar down and twenty-five cents a week. So that makes you pay for it for the rest of your life. That's how I got the organ and that's how I started to play.

Some years later — I was 'bout thirteen — Jesse Pickett heard me playing at some lawn party. He was a gentleman of leisure. He had diamonds on, a big shot. I was playing in the house. He rapped on the door. He says, "Who's that playing the organ?" She says, "Eubie." He says, "Tell him to come out." The woman wouldn't invite him in her house, because he was a gentleman of leisure, you know. High up on the echelon, those people were. Jesse says to me, "Come to the corner and I'll show you how to play something." He taught me how to play "The Dream Rag." People think I wrote that. I didn't. But I did write a lot of songs I had forgotten I wrote. I once heard a fellow named Willie Gant playing something familiar. I said, "What are you playing? I don't know it but it sounds like I heard it somewhere." He laughs and says, "You wrote it. You taught it to me."

Sometimes you forget something you wrote until somebody reminds you and then you realize you wrote an awful lot of songs and they're not half bad.

[The hour ends as we listen to a recording of "Memories of You." He murmurs,] "That's from *Blackbirds of 1930*. I wrote it for Ethel Waters."

AGNES DEMILLE

1960

She is best known as the choreographer who introduced ballet into musical comedy. *Oklahoma* was her first such venture.

I grew up in Hollywood, and I loved Hollywood. It is the custom now for people to say what a dreadful place it is and how miserable everyone is. They weren't when I was there. The studios were building, and it was full of excitement. There was a sense of pioneering, and a new art form. I can't tell you how excited and full of zest the men were. And it was a country town, there were dirt streets and Hollywood Boulevard was shaded with pepper trees, avocados, and palms. It was a city in a state of most delightful growth and flux. Isadora Duncan was a Californian; Martha Graham, our greatest, was born in Pittsburgh, but she grew up in California; Doris Humphries spent her whole youth and learning period in California. My love for dancing is not exclusive of my other interests. My father was a writer. My grandfather was Henry George, the political scientist.* So I'm aware of other fields that impinge on dancing, because I think all art is interrelated with life.

Martha Graham is the nonesuch: there is nothing like her in the world. She is probably the greatest choreographer living. She's one of the greatest American artists in any field. She's no longer young, but she's done two new works, brand new in point of view and in content. She's like Picasso. Each couple of years she comes out with a brand-new set of ideas, and with all the excitement and energy of a very young, creative talent.

It's magnificent, it's like Verdi. It's a great inspiration to everybody in the art world. When the curtain goes up, you know something extremely important and wonderful is going to happen. And it does.

As a small girl, you saw Pavlova.

This was not a unique experience. I met so many girls and women whose lives were quite changed by her. We hadn't seen much great dancing and almost no ballet dancing, so our eyes were innocent. But she had that sense of electrifying excitement that Callas has. I don't know anybody else that has quite that. There were technicians in the day that could out-dance her technically, and now I think she could be out-danced in many ways. But she could not be out-performed. And what she did in the way of reaching an audience, and making them sit up straight and feel that they had a regen-

---

*The American economist who advocated the single tax based on the right of all to the use of land. *Progress and Property* was his most celebrated work.

erating experience, is just extraordinary. I used to go out and just cry with sheer excitement.

Like most little girls, I wanted to put on a fluffy skirt and twinkle around. When I was a little girl, young women didn't go into dancing schools, and my father had a horror of it. He was just dead against it. So I wasn't permitted to study until I reached my teens, which is a little bit late.

I had a stiff body anyhow, lumpish. I can't think for one moment what I look like when I'm on stage. When I look in the mirror I'm generally affronted. But if I *feel* it through—I think this is the essence of performing—if I really feel what I'm doing and keep my mind on that, then you will see what I want you to see. And you'll forget. Well, I hope you'll forget. [Laughs]

My father wanted me to go to college, so I had to give up dancing for that. After college I said, "I've done it. Now please may I go back to the barre?" So I did go back to the barre, but it was late. Then I met Martha Graham. She had a tremendous influence on me, but she wouldn't let me study with her. She said I had to find my own way. "You stay by yourself and sweat it out by yourself. If you come to me, you'll imitate me, and it'll harm you." So I did stay by myself. It was long and dreadful. I felt that my field would be folk dancing. It was difficult to see a lot of very good dancing when I was a student, because there weren't many traveling companies here. Since there are no libraries of dance to study, the way young musicians can study music, or young playwrights can study the literature of the theater, the only thing that was available were the folk forms. There's not a bad folk dance in the world, because if it didn't work, it wasn't danced.

I thought I might be able to be a very great folk dancer if I worked *very* hard. I couldn't be a great ballet dancer, that was obvious, because I'd started late. And I didn't have the imagination or the vision to become a great innovator, the way Graham is. But I thought with taste and love and patience, I could remind people of what had gone before, through the folk forms. And that's what I made a specialty of. I went to England and studied folk dancing there. I studied all the preclassic forms. I also studied ballet in London.

I went to England because I couldn't get on in Hollywood or the

New York stage. I found myself smack in the middle of the big British renaissance in dancing. And my barre mates—I don't mean the drinking type now, but the pliéing type barre—were Frederick Ashton and Anthony Tudor and Alicia Markova. I was slow at catching on, but I suddenly realized that this was history, where I was.

My uncle thought that I was not photographable, not pretty enough. He said so all the time.* And that hurt my feelings. It also kept me out of the studios. But if I'd been taken in, I might not have searched and found something as individual. If I'd had a quick success in the Broadway . . . If I hadn't had to go to England and study . . . I might not be doing what I so love today. Look at the people I worked with. My colleagues now are leading the theater. I gave Jerry Robbins his first solo bit. In the long run it's more fun.

You could have had an easy way, really.

I couldn't have, really, because the passport was a pretty face, and I didn't have that.

Your uncle, Cecil B. DeMille, was a flamboyant figure, one of the most colorful in all Hollywood. He said to you he'd put you on the road early, if you got something set in two months. You said it would take two years. He said he couldn't wait for you.

I don't think he realized the need for slow growth. The real unfolding of the individuality. He himself had been slow to reap success. As a young man he was a failure. He was a failure in New York, and he was a failure at almost everything he did, but he smashed his way through with the most tremendous courage and stamina and verve. Only we were poles apart in all our tastes. Strangely enough, though, he did appreciate me, and when finally I did *Rodeo*, and performed out there, he liked it. And he said to me, "Well, you could get into pictures," and I said, "But you said I was ugly," and he said, "Well, you *are*, but it doesn't seem to matter. Nobody minds." [Laughs]

When I came back from England, Lucia Chase was forming the

---

*Cecil B. DeMille, the famous movie director, especially celebrated for his biblical spectacles.

Ballet Theater. There was a young man named Richard Pleasant, who'd seen me rehearsing in a studio in Hollywood, and he had said, "Some day I'm going to have a big company, and I'll give you a chance to choreograph." I thought that was just talk. But here he called me up and he said, "We're forming this company. Will you come to lunch?" So I met Miss Chase. She had a pencil and a paper and just said, "Think of twenty good choreographers." So I thought of twenty good ones, she wrote them all down, and the wires were going out that afternoon, all over the world. And they were going to bring over Frederick Ashton, who's now the head choreographer of the Royal Ballet. But I said, "There is one that is not recognized in London, that I think is equally great and in some ways more original, and it's Anthony Tudor." He came over then at their request, and he did a series of ballets that have made history: *Lilac Garden*, *Pillar of Fire*, *Gala Performance*, *Undertow*. One masterpiece after another.

I did *Rodeo* for the Ballet Russe. I did several ballets for Ballet Theatre, but they were small ones, and I was left out. Then I met someone who said—the war came, you see—they said, "Ballet Russe is looking for a novelty, and the novelty would be an American ballet done by an American for a change." They said, "Have you got a story?" I didn't have a story, but I made it up on the subway.

I got down there quick and shoved it under Serge Denham's nose—he was the administrative director of the Ballet Russe. He was very startled, because he didn't seem to think it was a spectacular type of thing. And he kept saying he wanted a red barn, and I wanted to do cowboy things. I said, "They don't have barns out in the West, Mr. Denham, because the herds are roughly eight thousand to twelve thousand head, and that would be some barn." "Well," he said, "A red barn would be so pretty." We had fights like that right along, but in the long run we got it done, and it's *Rodeo*.

They said, "Who do you want for a composer?" I said, "Let's start at the top, let's get Aaron Copland." Well, they phoned Aaron Copland and he said, "OK, send me a scenario." So he came down to tea and I told him the story and he said, "That's all right, that's fine." Then he went home, and he said, "I've got a nice lyric piece," and I said, "I can't do lyric dancing," and he said, "Well, that's too bad, because I've written it." I think he was lying, I think he had something in an old drawer. But he did play it for me and it was perfectly lovely. So I said, "Well, I'll try." And then he said, "Break it down into minute lengths. How many minutes for each scene," which I did. And then he went away to Tanglewood, where he taught, and he composed the piece.

I went away and started working out the dance steps. Then I went up to Jacob's Pillow—Ted Shawn's dance theater—and I was on the program which opened the new theater there, doing square dances and one thing and another. Copland came over from Tanglewood with a young pianist and played me the score that night, start to finish, and it was marvelous. He had it on that thin paper they use, multigraphs music, and it kept falling off the keyboard, and this boy kept picking it up and putting it back on, and playing at sight *superbly*. And then he'd say to Copland, "That's pretty dull. You'd better fix that up." And I thought, Well, of all the insolence. It was Lenny Bernstein. That figured.

So that's the way we worked. I made them dance in a way that they had never danced before, and I introduced tap dancing. And the *régisseur* (that's the man who rehearses them) put his eye to the keyhole—because I worked behind locked doors—and he phoned Mr. Denham and said, "She's reducing us to the level of a nightclub." But you see, it was all in Russian, so I couldn't understand. It didn't hurt my feelings any. And the audience loved it. I think they loved it especially because it was war time, and we were reminding ourselves . . .

When I got on the road with the Ballet Russe, I realized that I was going to change the end of the story a little bit, and the girl was going to get the man I hadn't thought she was going to get. She only had eight bars to change her mind, and that didn't seem very decent somehow. So I said, "Could we have sixteen bars for her to change her mind in? It's more ladylike." And Copland said, "No, you could not." So she changes her mind in eight bars. [Laughs] And that's the way it stands.

I don't think one single episode ever changes your life, but there are moments when the culmination of years slip over into the next era, and the direction alters. And it just happened at that time on the clock that night. We got eighteen or twenty curtain calls, and the whole of the Theater Guild and Rodgers and Hammerstein were sitting in a box. This did not go unnoticed. The eighteen calls were not lost on them. So then came *Oklahoma*.

I had to fight for it. Oscar Hammerstein wanted me. He's always liked my work. He'd seen it way back when I was doing concerts with Sybil Shearer.* But he never knew how to use it. And Dick Rodgers had never seen me. He said, "Well, this is great fun and it's dandy and all, but we're not sure she can handle the rough-and-tumble of Broadway rehearsals around the clock, with a mixture of dancers." It's a much rougher kind of work. I was taken in, probably on sufferance. I didn't realize this, but Rodgers sat in the rehearsal fixing me with beady eyes in a way that was just absolutely unnerving. And I remember two or three of the girls came up to me in a sweat and said, "They're watching us and we're going to be fired." I said, "Toots, they're not watching you, they're watching *me*." The third day he slapped me on the back and said, "OK, kid," and then he relaxed.

This is the first time ballet and modern dance were ever integrated in a musical comedy, isn't it?

Balanchine had done some very fine things, and then in *Slaughter on Tenth Avenue*, in the revue *The Little Show*, with Fred Allen, Clifton Webb, Libby Holman, Zorina.†

But in *Oklahoma*, we used dance as a part of the story, and the dancers as characters in the environment, so that they maintained their character through the whole play. It was something new.

After some years, Rodgers and Hammerstein had me do a play called *Allegro*, which was to be largely dance/action. That was not a success, but it had certain scenes that were very, very imaginative.

---

*Sybil Shearer, one of the most respected and least recognized of American choreographers. The Chicago area has been her locale.

†I saw this revue in Chicago and was bowled over when the delicate Clifton Webb, a dancer, knocked Zorina around and about in *Slaughter on Tenth Avenue*.

That same idea came to fruition in *West Side Story*. I think that through this sort of musical theater, through lyric action, we may get a kind of opera which is indigenous to us. It will be largely in movement, with some voices, and it will be as successful and as meaningful and beautiful as the Italian singing opera in the nineteenth century.

I think we're movers. I think the sixteenth- and seventeenth-century people were speakers. I think language was their medium. And I think the eighteenth- and nineteenth-century theater people were singers and musicians, and music was their medium. But this is an age of visual movement, and I think TV and movies are augmenting this thing. I think our theater is going to develop extraordinary action dramas, lyric action dramas. I hope so.

There's a thread throughout here. There would be no Oklahoma *without* Rodeo, *there could have been no* West Side Story *without* Oklahoma, *and whatever else will follow could not have been without a* West Side Story.

This is history.

You as choreographer say that the line is very narrow now in what you do between dancing and acting. The dancers are really characters. They're not just beautiful dolls, as in many of the classical ballets, but individuals.

The classical ballet is an old form, and it was long in developing. It developed out of the folk dance forms and out of the court dances, which in turn developed out of the folk dance form. This is highly abstract movement, as always. But the closer we get to theater, you get more and more realistic acting. Now I feel that I am a better director than I am a choreographer, and I am a better actress than I am a dancer. Since I had to work out of my own body, I put my own stamp on things.

The idiom has been enriched somewhat and has gotten away from the highly stereotyped pantomime of the nineteenth century, which was in tone with the very stylized ballet dancing. Now you find dancers doing things that aren't exactly realistic, but they are easily recognizable and understandable by an ordinary audience. I think you shouldn't have to go through an initiation before you can understand what people are doing on the stage.

I think art, to be communicating, should be this way. Now, I'm not saying all art must communicate immediately. The newer music is not readily understandable at first hearing, and the new painting is not readily understandable at first seeing. But in the theater there's not much time. You have to get something before you leave that evening, because there's no retrospect in the theater, you see. And I think this particular form has to get through emotionally, and if it doesn't, it has failed.

I try to do as much work beforehand as I can, because dancing is difficult. Choreography is hard because you're working on living bodies, and they get tired and they get bored. The equivalent would be if a conductor actually composed for his musicians while they sat before him. The job of a choreographer is to be immersed in the idea, and to be creative, and to work out all the technical problems, and still hold the attention and energies of his group. He has to work on many levels at once.

Dancers are very patient. They're the most disciplined people in the theater. But if you're fumbling, past a point, their legs hurt and they just plain sit down, and everybody gets depressed. And I despair myself. So I work out as much as I can beforehand. I do it on my own body, and I do it on paper, and I do it everywhere I can.

I can work out acting very well because, as I told you, I am an actress. But I can't work out all the technical lifts and things, because I'm one person, and a woman. So when I'm transferring my ideas onto a man's body, enormous changes have to take place. Well, sometimes this is disappointing, and things I thought would work don't work. But sometimes it's very revealing, and they will catch on to an idea, and expand it and explode it way beyond what you thought. These are the rewards of the trade.

I work a great deal beforehand, preparing. In New York we have to work on union hours, and they're very expensive and circumscribed because of the expense, so you have to deliver right on the clock. This is nerve-wracking.

I had a long talk with Freddie Ashton, who is the chief choreographer of the Royal Ballet, and he said he prepares very, very hard

and long, and that he has vomited his way to rehearsals. I understand that perfectly. Sheer nervous funk. And this man has done
more ballets than anybody else, including Balanchine. And with
greater success, I would say, than anyone in the field. But he said he
always made allowance for what he called the accident of the theater.
Something might happen which would clarify or change, and he
would use this. You see, the thing is that there's nothing on paper. I
have to say, "Do you remember what you did Tuesday, but not
Thursday?" And they do, if they're experienced. It's a most incredible act of memory. They say, "Well, you got this far. You got eight
bars of this on Tuesday, and Wednesday and Thursday we did
this." And I say, "Well, we won't do that now, we'll do what we did
Monday." [Laughs]

*Didn't you have a problem convincing commercial producers that
these dances would be acceptable?*

I certainly did. I remember I went to Walt Disney, whom I had
known when we both were not successful, and I said, "I'd like very
much to do a short on the ballet." And he said, "Well, I'd like to do
it with you, but nobody would be interested at all." I went away, of
course, disconsolate.

Later on, I was doing *One Touch of Venus*, and I was rehearsing
in the place and the woman who ran the studio said, "There's someone on the phone. Says he's Walt Disney, and I cannot make him say
who he really is. And he won't get off it." So I went there, and he
said, "Agnes, this is Walt, and I've seen *Oklahoma* and my doors are
wide. You come out and do anything you want."

I was told by everybody that people don't like dancing. They
don't like *bad* dancing, and quite right, too. They hadn't seen good
dancing. When you see good dancing, and easy-to-understand
dancing. . . . I think my service has been that I'm the sugar on the
pill, you see? Lots and lots of ordinary American men saw *Oklahoma* and *Carousel* and *Brigadoon* and things like that, and they'd
seen a hunk of dancing, and they didn't mind it! That was the great
surprise. That's easy-stages-taught *Swan Lake*, you see.

I did a long ballet, in *Bloomer Girl*, on the Civil War. Everybody
was very dubious about that. We had a terrific fight keeping it in.

The people are always uneasy when you do anything that's sad in dancing; they want dancing to be very gay and, you know, a quick beat. But in *Bloomer Girl* I had a very sad ballet, and the whole company split up fighting over it. But the audience just sat there weeping. So they left it in, and it gave the play some weight it might otherwise not have had.

And then in *Brigadoon* there was a funeral dance. The authors were so infuriated over that, they almost went to the union to get it removed. They have that right in the Playwright's Guild. They have absolute say.

Here's the case where Loewe and Lerner* were not sure.

They were sure: they loathed it. They were perfectly sure. It was the director who said, "Give it two public performances." And Loewe, who's a good friend of mine, said, "Agnes, I'm sorry." He said, "Of course, it gets the press everywhere as the distinguished thing in the show, but it's where I have my second whiskey, and I just always have it at that point." [Laughs]

I stuck to my guns. You have to! What other guns do you have? They're *your* guns. And I remember when I was doing *Paint Your Wagon*, again they came to me. "This is," Loewe said — he's Viennese, you see — he said, "So boring. It's so boring, I can't stand it." And I said, "Well, Fritz, I'll have to resign. You fire me, or I'll get out. I think it's marvelous. And I think it's one of the best things I ever did. And if I'm *that* wrong, I'm wrong for your play." [Laughs] Well, they went out and had a drink. Had a lot of whiskeys. Then they did *My Fair Lady*, and there isn't very much dancing there, and it's been the success of the century. So leave me not brag at all.

Today in America I feel that all the different techniques are coming together. They're not exclusive. Ballet, I think, is the best technique the world has evolved for the feet and legs, and for elevation. Elevation is rising off the ground easily. And it gives the body the most beautiful stance. It was built on the king's posture, and it was

---

*Lerner and Loewe were the librettist and composer of *Brigadoon*.

built on the nobles of the court of France, and they were very superb people. But the modern technique uses the ground, and uses the whole torso in an emotional way.

Graham uses arms with a dynamism that the ballet dancers don't have. Then we have our own indigenous techniques of tap dancing, and don't let anyone ever underestimate that, because that's beautiful. That came out of the clog — the clog dancing of England and Ireland, meeting up with and marrying, so to speak, the Negro dancer. The Negroes were forbidden to use drums after an uprising in the South, and they beat out the rhythms on the ground. But they did it on the African upbeat, and the clog was always on the Northern European downbeat. So they started doing the clogs on the upbeat, and that's where you get syncopation and jazz. And that's ours. And that's wonderful. All of these techniques are practiced, sometimes by the same person. In Broadway now, we demand a ballet technique and enough modern work so that they can get to the floor and get off the floor and all that knee business. Add tap to it, and you've got something close to total dancing. [Laughs]

CAROL CHANNING

1959

Her most celebrated role, at this time, was as Lorelei Lee, in *Gentlemen Prefer Blondes*. The musical was based on a collection of short stories by Anita Loos — of the '20s, the jazz age, sugar daddies, and their girlfriends.

She is appearing in Chicago at the Empire Room of the Palmer House. Her act is a gallimaufry of song, monologue, and seemingly unrelated matters. There is an improvisational air, though I assume it is carefully worked out. Her throaty laugh is a frequent obbligato to her conversation.

You have a sparkle and an intelligence. . . .

An intelligence? That's the first time anyone ever accused me of that. The day you get perspective on yourself is the day your act is lousy. As soon as I think I've got it—ah, there's the answer—I'm self-conscious for the next show. Your joke is no longer funny.

Here's this character singing, saying things—the moment you get off that—this little jumping across each pebble, and stand back and say, "Look how I'm doing it," the joke is gone. There's no laugh all of a sudden.

It's all so frightening, because the audience tells you immediately—you're off the track. They don't laugh. Where did the laugh go? What are you doing that's wrong? It has to be wrong, because it was boffo last night.

My very first professional job was in Marc Blitzstein's *No for an Answer.** For heaven's sake, you have the record!

[We listen to "I'm Simply Fraught About You," a comic song from Blitzstein's musical play *No for an Answer*.]

I was eighteen years old at the time, would you believe it? I was this Bennington College girl. They teach you the arts and everything. I glued scenery together and was doing small theaters and wrote a thesis on stage design. Every weekend I went down to New York to see the shows. Ethel Waters in *Mamba's Daughters*, Ethel Merman in *Stars in Your Eyes*, Gertrude Lawrence in *Susan and God*.

I decided to crack Broadway. I had little bits of characterizations ready to audition. I was seventeen, my second year at Bennington. I walked into William Morris, the biggest agency in the country, and said, "I want to see the president." That was Abe Lastfogel. Somehow, the secretary got confused, she thought I was somebody else. I'm also a pretty big girl. So she waved me in.

I walked in and started doing things. I did the "Haitian Corn Grinding Song," which they loved at Bennington. They stomp out the kernels with their feet and then they sing. It was written in some kind of French verse and some Gaelic. [She goes into a wild, strange

---

*His most celebrated folk opera was "The Cradle Will Rock." (See Hiram Sherman, p. 91). He also adapted Lillian Hellman's play, *The Little Foxes*, into the opera *Regina*. His adaptation of *Threepenny Opera* had a longer run than any other production of the work.

series of sounds.] Lastfogel is chewing on his cigar, sitting there, trying to figure out what is happening to him.

Then I did a thing called "Orestes' Funeral Chant." It was done to a drum beat. [She bangs on the table.] I had one of those terrible drums they use in Greek tragedies about the ravages of war. And these three women are down in the footlights, with this one big piece of jersey over their heads and all you could see is a kind of a triangle of elbows and heads. It's bloodcurdling. About the massacre of children, my gosh. [She goes into something quite bloodcurdling.]

Lastfogel is still sitting there, his hand to his head, "What is this? How did you get in?" He's hollering. I said, "Wait. Wait—I got another one." In my Middle European studies on culture, I found one that goes—[She sings something that sounds wild—Russian or Turkish or Urdu or something]. And here's this big shiksa, ten feet tall, towering over him and singing some Yiddish song.

All of a sudden, he perks up and says, "Say, that's very interesting. I'll tell you what to do. Instead of doing Orestes and those others nobody knows, why don't you do somebody everybody knows, like Sophie Tucker."

That was his ultimatum. Sophie Tucker. So I did research on Sophie Tucker and people like Carmen Miranda. And he sent me to Marc Blitzstein to audition. He said, "You're just the girl I want." And he wrote this song for me.

I'm this girl in a café who thinks she's better than Bea Lillie, Ethel Merman, Ethel Waters, and all the queens of the day put together. I was the silly girl, who didn't realize that by being all these people at once, she was nobody.

An act is a personal thing. You have to find *you*. With this blonde, Lorelei Lee, going around threatening homes, well, I can't help it. Anita Loos wrote this character, and I'm just trying to be faithful to her. But an act, it's *you* and that's the hardest thing in the world to find.

I remember Tallulah Bankhead saying [imitating her], "I know, darling, but is it Amanda?" It was opening night in *Private Lives*. We kept saying, "Who cares whether it's Amanda, Talullah. Everybody paid their money to see and hear you laugh like that and romp around."

TALLULAH BANKHEAD

1960

| She was in Chicago in a summer stock revival of *Craig's Wife*. |

I have to be part of whatever I play, darling. I don't think any actor or anybody in the public eye can completely lose their own personality. You have to bring out the part: say, "I happen to be Tallulah Bankhead." Whether they like it or not. I think very often a strong personality antagonizes as much as it attracts, do you know what I mean, darling? If sometimes you have overenthusiastic admirers, it rather annoys people that don't admire you so much. They don't see what's so unique about her. That applies, of course, to any politician, statesman, preacher or lawyer. Anyone in the public eye.

It's difficult for someone like me sometimes to stay in character. So I try to stay in character and keep talking through the applause — that is, when I make my first entrance. At the same time, you don't want to be discourteous, darling. When they go on and on, just to slightly bow my head and smile, but out front, to the curtain, never to that fourth wall, the audience. You might make this slight gesture in a summer stock play, where you know they came to see you as Tallulah. But I'd never dream of doing any such thing in, say, *The Little Foxes*. Lillian Hellman would have torn me apart, darling.

I remember the designer Oliver Smith saying to me, "I love that ad-lib character at the end. I've never seen that before." We've known each other for years. I was doing *me*! He was the scene designer who coproduced *Gentlemen Prefer Blondes*. He decided [imitating], "You've got to get Carol to play Lorelei. Don't cast your five feet two, eyes of blue. The way to do Lorelei is to get a girl exactly off it and have her comment on it. That'll make it funny. It's a satire on an era of musical comedy."

The jazz age was before your time.

No, it wasn't. I had memories. Yvonne Adair, who played Dorothy with me—we were the same age—kept saying, "Teach me the Charleston." Of course I knew it. My grandmother and I were movie happy and we went from one Marian Davies movie over to Colleen Moore, Jack Mulhall, Richard Barthelmess. We'd start out at ten o'clock in the morning on Saturdays and get milk shakes between movies. Then to a Wheeler and Woolsey comedy, and to a Rear Admiral Byrd movie across the street. Then we'd go home and do the Charleston. I was three-and-a-half, four, five. This was in San Francisco.

When we'd get home, I'd make her up like Anita Paige, with a worried look. Remember, her eyebrows went up in the center? When Jean Harlow came in, my poor grandmother had to go to church with her eyebrows shaved in the center and those two hooks and a big black pencil going in a circle from the center of the eye out.

People asked, "What happened to your grandmother?" She wouldn't let on, that dear woman. I finally evolved a makeup that looked surprised, bewildered, like that Dorothy Lee baby-doll look of the '20s. So I knew all about makeup by the time I was six, seven.

I kept fooling around on my grandmother. She must have been awfully old because when I put the pencil on her, her skin would stick to the pencil and it would kind of sag a little.

You always went against type. Here in Chicago, you played a sophisticated and literate Ruth Sherwood in Wonderful Town.*

George Abbot directed *Wonderful Town*. His pace, a fast one, is probably the most infallible in show business. When it came to Chicago, I took over for Rosalind Russell. I have a slow pace, naturally slow. I remember Mr. Abbott saying, "I never thought I had to slow

---

*A musical adapted from the play *My Sister Eileen*, which was inspired by Ruth McKenney's short stories of her girlhood in Columbus, Ohio.

down my pace, but if it isn't true to you, let's see if yours works better." Because of my slow pace, we needed a fast patter number to make it dramatic, otherwise it's dull.

For this show, we brought in Fred Ebb, a songwriter, for a fast patter number. He asked me, "Where are you the most a fish out of water?" I said, "Off stage. I can't put my right foot in front of my left." "Where are you the worst?" I said, "Trying to be hostess at a party." It isn't my nature to say, "You go here and you go there and you sit down here." If I'm a guest, fine. I'm malleable, I sit wherever they tell me. But it's just mayhem, chaos, if I try to give a party. Maybe it's because I'm tall and I hate to push people around. I think little people are cute when they push people around, but being tall . . . Have you noticed that? The most potent women in the theater are, say, Tallulah Bankhead, not five feet tall, Lynn Fontanne, five feet, Judith Anderson, tiny, dynamic. They're smaller, so they're not afraid of mopping up the floor with you. I can't tell anybody where to go or what to do, 'cause I'm too strong. It's just native for me to go wherever I'm put. Even horseback riding: if the horse wants to go there, let's go with the horse, let's not argue with him.

I'm just an unorganized person all day. But when it gets around six, seven o'clock, I start getting organized. Fred Ebb said, "You're getting ready for the show, you know exactly what you're doing. Boom, the eyelashes go here, the glue goes there, where's the sheet music? Where's the orchestra? Where's my conductor? But until six o'clock at night, you're a mess."

So it works out beautifully with the orchestrator, the drummer, the pace—I'm all set when they double up the tempo of the music of the party and I have to keep up with it. [She rattles it off, speedily.] "Mr. Schnurr, this is Mr. McSchleen; Mr. McSchleen, this is Mr. Shaw; Mr. Shaw, this is Mr. Schnurr; Mr. Schnurr, this is Mr. McSchleen." The second time, we go into . . . [She does the orchestra.] They go umpa, umpa, umpa, and it sounds like I'm going faster. They're pushing me more and more, the party gets more frantic, musically, and it's really hard for me, Carol, to keep up with it. But somehow I do.

I enjoyed doing *Wonderful Town*, but actually my favorite field is the revue. They're out of style now because we haven't had a good one for a long time. A musical comedy has a book and it follows a plot. A revue is more like vaudeville. It has no plot connection. It may be a comedy sketch, a beautiful ballet number or a monologue. Sometimes it's a topical revue about present-day happenings.* Sometimes it's nontopical, such as Charlie Gaynor wrote. He writes some of my best stuff now. Brooks Atkinson said of Charlie, "Just luckily enough, Mr. Gaynor seems to tear down only what needs to be town down and has no caustic tongue about things that ought to be preserved."

Charlie cast me as the Gladiola Girl, the flapper, in his revue *Lend an Ear*. That was really the first time I made anybody laugh. Charlie said, "I think you're funny," and he hired me. I thought I was funny but everybody was telling me for ten, twelve years that I wasn't. Finally you come to believe it.

You ask where my energy comes from? Thank goodness, I've worked out my life so I can just go ahead and do what I'm free to do. And enjoy doing. That's the source of my energy.

1961

It is Channing's second appearance at the Empire Room, where she has become something of a familiar as well as favorite.

When I do Sophie Tucker or Marlene Dietrich or, for that matter, Mrs. Alving in *Ghosts*—I did that at Bennington—there's a moment of *complete*, severe focus before I go on. People pass through my dressing room and say, "How are ya?" I don't hear them. Isn't that awful? I hate to be one of those Stanislavsky method artistes who crawl into their own little emotional shells, but I do *concentrate* like crazy. So it doesn't disturb me if people come through. I don't hear

----

*The most trenchant topical revue during the Great Depression of the '30s was *Americana*. Its most celebrated song became the epoch's anthem: "Brother Can You Spare A Dime?" The lyrics were by E. Y. (Yip) Harburg, the music by Jay Gorney. (See Harburg, p. 94)

them. It's exactly the same science doing Dietrich or Tucker as doing Joan of Arc, which—would you believe it?—I also did at Bennington.

It's first of all, how does she feel? What's her emotional track? Is she a biting person or soft? What's her goal? You feel the chemistry. You have to be in love with the person, not nasty.

I remember falling in love with Lorelei Lee. I remember the whole world was different, walking down the street, my feet off the ground. Such a *doll!* Such a little baby powder puff. [Inhales] Oh, this is the way she walks, there's a girl went by, she walks like Lorelei. Unless you feel that way about a character, don't ever do the part.

I remember Dietrich, after I saw her in Las Vegas. She lingered with me for weeks. I'd feel that funny mood she creates, that strange blau angel spell, a funny European, something Viennese, that cellarlike mood, that old rathskeller, a good stein of beer. She's a man's woman, that sort of thing, let the boys all put their feet up on the table.

Your eyelids automatically get heavy, like Dietrich's, your cheeks automatically sink in, and you automatically feel thin and lean and you're not a human being, only a presence. [She slips into Dietrich's accent.] She's only a mere presence, a blithe spirit or something, you know, mein Herr. If you touch her, she's gossamer, she'll blow away. Pull your cheeks in. No, that doesn't cut it. You have to feel like her and automatically you get thin all over.

I can't get rid of that spell. It's all around me, the blue angel feeling. My son would ask, "Who's mother today?" I'd say, "I still feel Dietrich." So Charlie Gaynor said, "All right, I'll write you a Dietrich number."

To do that twice a night, promptly at 8:30 and at twelve midnight, is really rough, unless you feel the mood she casts over the audience. People say she's not talented. Coming through as herself, that's the highest form of talent.

No, my portraits are not etched in acid. It depends how the audience feels about her. If they like her, they say, "Oh, what a loving thing it is." If they hate her, they say, "Oh, what a sarcastic, biting, caustic bit." I always thought Sophie Tucker was great. Did you ever see her?

At the old Palace in Chicago, two-a-day vaudeville.

I once played the Palace in *Show Girl.* I *smelled* those old entertainers on that stage. Sophie claimed she played the old Palace in New York when it burned down. She was standing on stage in this sequin dress — the talkies were coming in at the time — she said, "I thought to myself, this is the way to go if you gotta go. I'm going down with vaudeville." And she stood there and said, "All right, you people, go slowly up the aisle." Later, she found out that she was the only one in danger. The fire was backstage and if her sequin dress caught on fire, she'd have gone up just like that. Everybody says it, whether you're a big-name entertainer or a small-name, this is the way to go.

We're doing Gian Carlo Menotti's *The Medium* now. I'm Marie Powers, that big-voiced, heavy contralto. I sing "Love Is a Sickness." [Sings in a deep, way-down voice.] She's a heavy woman in a basement where the rental is low. It's the most utterly miserable song you ever heard. I notice the laughs go the minute I try to be funny, if I'm not dead-on sincere. You have to respect the audience, let them see what makes her run, get them on her side. Otherwise, forget it. Of course I admire Marie Powers.

1972

We are listening to a recording of *Archy and Mehitabel.* It is a musical adaptation of Don Marquis's classic tales of Archy, the little cockroach and his undying, self-sacrificing love for Mehitabel, the large cat with the roving eye and the wayward heart. Channing is, of course, Mehitabel. "It didn't work as an off-Broadway production. It's an idea, something of imagination."

Mehitabel is a dirty, rotten alley cat. You and I wouldn't have anything to do with her. She's totally amoral. She is enormous, with the tribal quality of Mae West and Ethel Waters. Mehitabel is a terrible, grabbing cannibal. Imagine drowning your kittens in the lake. She says, "A mother's love is so unreasonable." Archy is crazy about her because he can't imagine anybody being as awful as Mehitabel. The more she pushes him around, the more he worries about her because he knows she's walking over a cliff and he wants to make her happy.

She just *stands* there and doesn't have to do much about getting that little cockroach. The eternal quality of the great big thing for the little. To me, Anita Loos was the perfect little package, too tiny for words. Her friends told her she chose me as Lorelei " 'cause you wanted to be as tall as Carol." She's the cutest little button, not five feet tall. Black-eyed, with those '20s bangs. She has to get children's furniture to be comfortable in.

During rehearsals of *Gentlemen Prefer Blondes*, Anita and I used to follow girls down the street and say, "Oh, she walks like Lorelei," and we'd follow her for blocks. She wanted me to meet all sorts of people of that jazz age, when Lorelei was living it up. She knew many Loreleis. She introduced me to Peggy Hopkins Joyce.* Anita said she was Lorelei. Now, the younger generation says, "Peggy who?"

Lorelei gets along very well without doing any work.

I disagree. She works very hard. Her scheming is really work. She's like the president of General Motors, don't you think?

So she and Mehitabel have something in common?

Oh, no. She's smarter than Mehitabel. Mehitabel just flops into whatever comes, whatever she wants to do. That's no work. Lorelei is not just a little girl from Little Rock, naive and wide-eyed. She's shrewd. It's the duplicity of the old, reactionary regime. It's the cheating on one side but standing upright in front of people. She stands for it all the way—kings, queens, nobility, everybody. She just keeps quiet about it and gets her own. She never comes right out. Nobody ever knows, did she or didn't she? That's what keeps her innocent. Naturally, I love her.

In a 1950 review of Gentlemen Prefer Blondes, *Brooks Atkinson, drama critic of the* New York Times, *wrote: "Carol Channing's*

---

*The most celebrated multi-divorcée of the '20s. Her name became the eponym of any woman whose marriages were brief and divorces many.

Lorelei Lee is the most fabulous comic creature of this dreary period of history, and dreary it was. Her rapacious innocence is uproariously amusing. There never has been anything like this in human history."

Ruth Sherwood, in *Wonderful Town*, was truly innocent. She could only express herself on the printed page, but she was a total introvert, who can't come down in one and [sings out] "Diamonds are a girl's best friend." She's got to hide her heart's soul. It was so difficult to do a musical about someone like her. Her sister, Eileen, wide-eyed, oh sure, was the knowing one, had a snappy mind. She was like Lorelei.

[Suddenly] Here, I'm just *about* to enter the prime of my life, and suddenly, talking to you, I feel like a relic. I realize I'm hitting that horrible veteran bracket.

Cut it out. It's full speed ahead for you. Consider the roles you've played. What one attribute do they have in common?

Shoot.

Lorelei Lee?

She survived.

Mehitabel?

She survived.

Ruth Sherwood?

She survived.

Dolly Levi?

She survived.

And who is the character you most delighted in playing?

Carol Channing. I guess she'll survive. I hope.

3—Hard Times

1980

Charleston, South Carolina. His latest play, *The American Clock*, is having a week's run at the Spoleto Festival in this city. Its theme: the effect of the Great Depression of the '30s on the American middle-class family. It was, the playwright says, inspired by my book, *Hard Times: An Oral History of the Great Depression*.

Some time ago, you said the two most traumatic epochs in American history were the Civil War and the Great Depression. You, as a young man during the hard '30s, were obviously affected.

I probably had a distorted view because I was right at the bottom. I had the usual American upbringing: everything was going to be better every year. An endless boom. I thought the system was foolproof because it was advertised as such. The bursting of the bubble was devastating because it had been blown up so big.

What disintegrated with the Depression was any kind of faith in government. I'm speaking of '29, '30, and '31. There was a scoffing at authority. It had in it the seeds of the '60s. There was one basic difference—the question of guilt.

In the '30s, people, in order to believe they were real Americans, believed they were responsible for their own fate. If a man found himself making $15,000 a year (a lot of money then), he credited himself. When he lost it, he blamed himself. We've all heard about the psychic crippling, the suicides. I remember where I was living, in Brooklyn, a stunned air all over the neighborhood. You'd see a lot of perfectly able-bodied men in the middle of the day. They had aged enormously. You'd sit in a room with these guys, many of them fathers of my friends, and you'd sense a premature senility. Thinking back on it, they were young men, in their forties. They blamed themselves.

A Southern woman of my acquaintance remembered some of this. People saying: "If we hadn't bought that radio . . ." "If we hadn't bought that second-hand car . . ." She was horrified by the preachers who'd tell the people they suffered because of their sins. The people believed it, God was punishing them. Their children were starving because of their sins.

It was part of our theology: as ye sow, so shall ye reap. Remember, Americans had hardly participated in contemporary society. We had no social security at that time, no unemployment compensation, hardly any income tax. The average American could live and die without getting next to a government form, aside from a visit to the post office to sign a receipt for a letter. He had no personal connection with the government, so how would he deduce that "society" had the slightest effect on him? Today, since the New Deal, the relationship of the individual to society is altogether different. He expects certain things from society. He lives side by side with government measures from the time he's born. We've got a whole class of people that have never been off relief, have never had a job. Businessmen, really, have never been off relief, especially the big ones. There are many government measures that support industry. You can't conceive of business being really free of that any more. Look at the interest rates, maneuvered and manipulated. They're no longer acts of God. It is decided how much people are going to pay for their money. They didn't do that in the old days, at least not in public. Now when something goes wrong, you'd have to be an idiot to really blame yourself altogether. When you lose your job now . . .

I wanted to be a professional crooner. It was a quick way up. I sang on a radio station. If I may so, I had a terrific tenor voice. [Laughs] I did that until I got tired of working without pay. It was a crap game.

You and Russ Columbo. *

I would have settled for that any time. [Laughs]

---

*A crooner, celebrated in the '30s.

The warehouse you once worked in was, I assume, the locale as well as the metaphor in A Memory of Two Mondays.

Working anywhere was perfectly normal though in those days. You got all the jobs you could get. People got fired at three o'clock in the afternoon. A guy would come through and say, "Well, it's all over, go home." There were few unions, no severance.

I have since come to believe that we have a lot more to do with our fate than that play implies. But at the time, say, between 1932 and 1937, there seemed no conceivable way of escaping it. Nor did there seem the slightest hope any more by 1937. We were thinking every three months that something was gonna work. The New Deal came up with one experiment after another, but nothing really happened. It would gasp for a few months and settle back to where it was. It was a despair that was matched only by the post–Civil War South. It lay there and seemed to have been mortally wounded.

There are images that spring to mind in this play. When I was sixteen, I decided to go to sea. I walked into one shipping office after another, till I found the U. S. Lines. They had these tremendous liners all tied up in the dock. I'll never forget the image: gigantic floating cities that were empty, stuck. In *The American Clock* I have a guy who was the captain's steward on the S.S. *Manhattan*. He ended up in Brooklyn trying to stay out of the rain.

You're not calling the new play The American Clock *for capricious reasons, I'm sure. Time is obviously on your mind, now as well as then.*

Time is what it's about. It is in the past. The hands of the clock are being turned back. There's also the racing against the clock. How much time do we have to fool around before the whole thing collapses again? It is a menacing image as well as a benign one. My interest in this play is formal as well as reflective. I was fascinated by the idea of having an objective view of society and, running through it as a counter-motif, the story of a family. The members of the family may be more coherently drawn because they are continuous, but they are as objectively seen as the Iowa farmer and the black hobo who also appear.

If the Depression does come again, wow. During my travels while working on Hard Times, *I asked scores of Depression survivors, "Would the public's reaction be the same?" Invariably, the response was: Hell, no! There is no longer the feeling of personal guilt. Sally Rand, the fan dancer, was astonishingly powerful. She spoke the thoughts of the great many. "I don't think there will be any more people queuing up in bread lines waiting to be fed by charity, god-damn it. I think they will just go out and take what they need. The middle class look upon the deprived smugly: the poor we'll always have with us. Oh, yeah?"*

There is unquestionably a potential in the American people of ex-treme measures, if they are provoked enough. When a man loses his job, he loses his identity. This is not simply an economic question. He's sore. It's like he's gotten beat with a stick. Especially if he's in his middle age and he's put his inventiveness, his time, his hopes, everything into his job and suddenly he's nowhere.

Status, feelings about his manhood, it's all there on the hook. I was told about some miners in Pennsylvania during the Depression. While they idled on the benches, whittling away, they were considered such failures — they looked upon themselves as such, too — that their wives refused to go to bed with them. A guy in Kansas City told me about his father, a good carpenter. One day he came home with the tool chest on his shoulder, laid off. With his loss of job, his authority, his sense of self, was gone. Now began the tension, especially between fa-ther and son. This theme has always attracted you, hasn't it? The conflict with Biff and Willy Loman in Death of a Salesman. *Joe Keller and his surviving son in* All My Sons.

The American Clock is a culmination of that concentration I've al-ways had on what society does to the inner life of a man. The reason is obvious. I saw it happen in a cataclysmic fashion. About ten years ago, *Esquire* magazine sent out a questionnaire to fifteen writers. What had they in common psychologically? You know what it was? A failed father. Either a suicide or a drunk, an economic disaster, a father who fled — the disillusion of the boy at about the time of pu-berty. Hemingway, Faulkner, Steinbeck, go down the list . . .

And myself. It's practically foolproof.

In one of your theater essays, you spoke of your father. You implied there was hardly any communication between the two of you. You hardly spoke to the man in years.

I had no animosity toward him. I simply had no great relationship with him. It was like two searchlights on different islands. As I grew older, we became much closer. I began to understand what it was all about, too.

Combine a father's failure with the society in which he lives — after all, he brings into the house the social system in which he wholeheartedly believes — you'll see what's gonna happen.

The guy brings the society into his living room, pretty sure of himself. Suddenly, that which he believes in fails, collapses. So the guy himself collapses. I'm thinking of a kid who recently drove me through Kentucky. He talked of his father, a fantastic salesman, a great con artist, a self-styled big shot. For one reason or another, he goes down. Suddenly he's an old man, a dead failure. He sits at home, plays solitaire, works crossword puzzles, watches TV, hardly walks more than ten feet out of his room. Know what the kid said to me? "My father is Willy Loman. Death of a Salesman *is about him." The two older brothers and their wives don't want the old man around. Shame and fear. His failure terrifies them.*

They might catch it. [Laughs] The question is whether anybody can avoid identifying himself with his failure or his prosperity. In *The American Clock*, the father *is* his business. Even when he's not around his business, he's busy working at it. It's probably one of the reasons that, as a class, businessmen have created more than anybody else. In a way, they're like artists. They really pour themselves into their work. There's no way of divorcing themselves personally from what they're doing. And if he fails by virtue of nothing he may have done, it's like a lightning stroke. It's the closest thing to fate. I wrote an essay once about the equivalents we have for gods. The closest thing we've got is an economic system. In the old times, God spoke and you didn't know why or what. He just knocked your brains in. Look at the story of Job. Good man, did everything right. Suddenly, for no acceptable reason, his faith and existence are being challenged. He asks questions, but there's no answer. The Greeks had the Sphinx.

There's another element in this play which is in my other work, too. The son moves in to assert the life force. It does not end in total surrender, which is remarkable, given the insanity and the surrealism of the social situation. The play ends on a very positive note. The teller of the tale is still alive to tell it, and hopeful.

And growing. As the old man is slipping, the son takes over. You're also talking about an individual's growth during a moment of trauma in society.

To me, that's most important.

It's reminiscent of Biff realizing the truth about himself at the time of his father's death. He knows who he is. Willy never did. For that matter, it's Joe Keller's boy, too, in All My Sons.

The father in *The American Clock* is absolutely the opposite of Willy Loman. He does not have illusions. He is a realistic man and does not surrender to his own defeat.

I found this fascinating. He accepts relief, without self-flagellation. He goes to the welfare station. He is not encumbered by false pride. I talked to quite a few businessmen who lost everything during the Depression. A remarkable number went on relief. Though they recalled the moments of humiliation, they realized in retrospect it was not their fault. Others erased the memory and the shame of it.

This man, under duress, is able to separate himself from his condition. He is not a guilty man, by any means. He's quite different from the incoherent hero. Not that he's voluble nor an intellectual. The son in this play is more the intellectual.

It's a pretty large canvas you're painting. Calling it a mural is, I imagine, not accidental.

I have experimented with formal problems since the time I started writing. There's an attempt here to do two things at the same time, which is the nature of a mural. Rivera's and Siqueiros's in Mexico are prime examples. Large Renaissance paintings are of that order.

When you look close at any face, it may turn out to be a real person's. When you step away, you see a whole pattern, the grand movement. It's fundamentally a picture of many people interacting with each other and with the heavens. In the case of a Mexican mural, with the Revolution. That's the form I'm trying to create: a picture of people interacting with each other and with a significant historical event, the Depression.

I don't care for a theater that is absolutely personal and has no resonance beyond that. We've become so accustomed to that we've forgotten that for most of mankind's history the theater was quite the other way. Theater was involved with the fate of the kingdom, and the importance of power, of rank, of public policy. It's in Shakespeare. It's absolutely essential in Greek drama. Ours is almost excessively bourgeois in that it presumes the world really has no effect upon us.

Challenging solipsism in the theater has always been your impulse. You've been racked up on more than one occasion for this.

They call this political in a condemnatory sort of a way. In Greece's best times, they regarded people who were nonpolitical as idiots. It was the idiot who didn't understand that man was social, that our fate in the deepest sense of the word was bound up with all of mankind.

The air we breathe is political, you might say.

Let's be more literal about it. The fact that the air is poisoned now is a political fact. Had there been a different attitude on the part of the society toward the abuse of the earth and the air, you would not have people now in Love Canal dying of unnatural causes, of poisons. Of course it's political. Does that take away their character? At this moment in our country is this imminent sense of some deep dislocation about to take place. For many, it has already happened.

What is positive about it is the impatience of the people with the empty reassurances that politicians give them. That's terrific. They took it for far longer in the '30s. Now they feel the mess is man-made. They have secularized the economic system. They think: What the hell, we made it, we can unmake it. We can readjust, tinker with it. Don't tell us we can sit around, waiting for three years before we eat again.

A lot of people who lived through the Depression would just as soon not hear about it any more. It's bad-luck time. It's the younger people who are really thirsty for the news that this play brings. I suppose it's because they never got a straight story about what really went on at that time. The schools have covered it up pretty well. Yet it may have been the ten most important years in American history. You'd hardly know it from our text books.

We are told that Roosevelt was elected four times, that some poor guys sold apples on street corners, a passing reference to the CIO, a war came along, and that was it. Paradoxically, it was also a time of great excitement, of neighborhood rallies and demonstrations, of wildly creative federal arts projects. And there was a camaraderie: the passing of a cigarette butt to another, a streetcar transfer changing hands, a morning newspaper handed over to the next guy.

There was also a cheerfulness I've tried to capture in the play. Some of the great songs in our popular repertoire came out of the Depression. I've called upon quite a few. And the humor, which was fundamentally positive. It had a bitter edge to it naturally, but it was not black humor. It was healthy.

I've attempted a play of about more than just a family, of forces bigger than simply overheard voices in the dark. It's a story of the United States talking to itself.

EVA LE GALLIENNE

1964

> She is the founder and artistic director of the National Repertory Theater. During its three weeks in Chicago, we saw Chekhov's *The Seagull*, Miller's *The Crucible*, Anouilh's *Ring Around the Moon*, and Ibsen's *Hedda Gabler*.

I was only twenty-five when I started organizing this theater. Two years later, in 1926, we opened. During our seven years in New

York, we were an endowed theater. It was intended to be. In those days, there were no foundations, so I had to raise money from individuals. I managed to do this until the Depression and then people I knew who had the money didn't have it.

I had lived my childhood in Europe and my early youth was enriched by this type of theater, endowed by the government. It was a matter of course, taken for granted—the highest type of productions at very popular prices. Money was important to us, because so many of us had so little of it. In Paris, I was able to go up in the *poulailler*—the peanut gallery—and for twenty-five cents see the greatest acting you can imagine at the Comédie Française and the Odéon. Even in little Denmark, they have one of the best repertory theaters in Europe. And in Russia, of course, and all over continental Europe. The people in all these countries would be enormously outraged if these theaters were abolished. They wouldn't stand for it.

I do believe there is a people's theater. It really boils down to prices more than anything else. If people can afford to go to the theater, they get the habit of it. I know this is the case with the people who attend these government-endowed theaters. They have a very catholic range: classics, modern plays, avant-garde. Tennessee Williams and Arthur Miller along with Chekhov and Ibsen. Molière, Shakespeare, of course. Schiller, especially in Germany.

I came to the United States when I was sixteen years old and the first thing I noticed was that there were no such theaters here. I was astonished. I thought this was strange. There were a lot of theaters on Broadway, but it was all commercial and expensive. The type of plays were not the sort that would live or be of any importance. It was simply show business, not art.

Show business means simply that: it is a *business*. There is no such thing as a medium run. It's either a flop or it's an enormous hit that runs for years.

Even at sixteen, I thought, if I ever get to a position of power, I'll start a repertory theater here. I was out to win the Battle of Broadway and when I was something of a hit in Molnar's *The Swan* and in a few other plays, I decided to take the step: establish this kind of theater.

I had never directed before. Here I was twenty-five, just swept away by my fanatic conviction. I just never had any other thought. Here's a job that ought to be done and I'm going to see if I can do it.

Aside from classics, we did a lot of modern plays. We did the first Girardoux plays in this country. We did several modern French and German plays. We did Susan Glaspell's *Alison's House* that won the Pulitzer Prize.

The critics didn't like *Alison's House*. They disdainfully dismissed it. Had this play been produced in the regular commercial way, it would have closed in a week or two. Being in repertory, we played it three times a week over that whole season. So the Pulitzer judges had a real chance to see it. They did and gave it the prize. They wouldn't have had time to see it if it had been run out of town.

Our company had apprentices as well as professionals. Burgess Meredith was an apprentice, I saw his talent and gradually fed him into the company, so that he began playing small parts with the company. We had Madame Nazimova, Joseph Schildkraut, Jacob Ben Ami.* My whole point was that our standards must be high and our prices must be low. Our prices were $1.50 top. How did we subsist? How did we make it? People who believed in our work, individuals. Mrs. Edward Bach gave us $50,000 a year. Others gave what they could. When the Depression hit, we were knocked out. An eight-year run, 1926 to 1934.

We had many, many young people in the audience. Long after we closed, I received letters from people who now had children of their own. "If only the Civic Repertory still existed, our sons and daughters could learn about the great theater of the world as we did."

President Roosevelt at that time asked me to head the Federal Theater thing. I didn't do it because I didn't agree with it.† I felt it

---

*A star of the Yiddish theater, who appeared in English-language classics.
†One of the federal arts projects under the auspices of the New Deal (WPA), the Federal Theater Project was an idealistic concept to encompass the whole country—to make the unemployed theater actor an entertainment worker. To do his share. It employed not only legitimate theater actors and dancers, but vaudeville and circus performers as well. Hallie Flanagan of Vassar College sub-

was encouraging mediocre theater at best. I felt it was true in all the fields of the Federal Arts Projects: music and painting—all those horrible murals. I saw some of those murals in Westport, Connecticut, and they're so awful.

Just because it was federally funded, did that make it bad? You spoke of European theaters that were federally funded and great, you said.

That was altogether different. Here, it was a social thing, helping people who couldn't earn their livings and had to be subsidized by the government.

Many good actors were out of work, too. Orson Welles did some remarkable stuff with the Federal Theater. A black Macbeth, Cradle Will Rock. If there was an artistic standard applied, you'd see no objection to that, would you?

Oh, no, of course not. But the purpose of this program, as a whole, was to provide work for the unemployed. I, as a perfectionist in the theater, could not go along with it.

Aside from being the manager/director and actress of a repertory company, your new translations of Ibsen plays made us aware that he was far from dated.

Ibsen, as a genius, will never be dated. William Archer deserves a lot of credit for introducing Ibsen to the English-speaking world. You must remember, this was in the 1890s. Archer was a Victorian *literateur*, and his translations, by today's standards, are much too literal and stuffy. He was not really an affinity of Ibsen's. Being a Victorian, there was a thought barrier, as well as a linguistic one. He was so slavishly faithful to Ibsen that he often translated Norwegian idioms quite literally into English so they made no sense whatsoever. I don't think Archer really translated the spirit, the subtle thought of Ibsen's intention. My asset as a translator is in being an actor. I know what sort of rhythm of speech will make a point on the stage. Archer's translations are almost impossible to act in. I could

---

sequently became the director of the Federal Theater Project. Her memoir, *Arena*, is a recounting of its trials and triumphs.

never have done *Hedda Gabler*, Archer's version. I think I've done Hedda more than anything I've ever played. [Laughs] She is someone who will never be dated.

It's really the study of a woman, rather than a play. There's very little story in it. She's a woman who outwardly appears quite ordinary, but inside is ridden by this demon, which one gradually discovers as the play goes on. I think Hedda would have been an extremely fascinating, brilliant, successful woman if she hadn't been trapped into this very petite bourgeoise, dull atmosphere which she got herself into. If she'd been married to a brilliant diplomat, and traveled all over the world, and had an interesting salon, she would have been a very successful woman in the sense of fulfilling herself. She would have been a great hostess. She was undoubtedly a clever woman. She was a coward, of course. I remember Elsie Janis* saying to me, "I've met so many Hedda Gablers in this country and everywhere I've been in the world. The trouble is they don't all shoot themselves." I think the only brave thing she did was to shoot herself.

Scandinavians have always been a little bit avant-garde, really. They've always done, outwardly, things like smoking, before any other women. For instance, in *Hedda Gabler*, which was written in, say '86, Tesman says to her at one point, "Would you like a cigarette?" I used to smoke in the play occasionally, and people always said, "Smoking?" And I said, "Well, it's in the text." My mother smoked from the time she was fifteen years old, in the early '80s, in Scandinavia. So there's nothing peculiar about that. I think that women there were much freer and much more advanced than they were, say, in England.

Aside from Hedda, you've translated A Doll's House, Ghosts, The Master Builder — *you call those his social plays, rather than his poetic plays.*

I wouldn't have had the temerity to translate *Peer Gynt*, because in the Norwegian, it's wonderful. The music of the Norwegian is so

---

*A celebrated wit and comedienne in the '20s and '30s.

strong and so exciting that in order to give it the same effect in English, you'd have to be a very great poet. The only languages I do speak well are French and Danish, which is the same as Norwegian, and English. I used to speak Russian not too badly, but I haven't for so many years that I wouldn't dare *speak* now.

That leads us to the other giant: Chekhov. He's very different, isn't he? I always think that Ibsen appeals more to the mind, and Chekhov to the heart. It seems to me one *loves* Chekhov, and one is fascinated by Ibsen. Chekhov has such *compassion*, you know. He knows humanity so well, but he's never hard on it, he's never bitter, the way Ibsen is. Ibsen has enormous comedy in his plays, but it's a very harsh comedy—he tears people to shreds. In *Ghosts*, Pastor Manders has one of the most powerful invectives against the state religion of Norway, the hypocrisy of that type of clergyman at that period, and it's very funny. But it's a very bitter, ironic, sarcastic humor. Whereas Chekhov has a very tender humor.

Oh, Ibsen was ferociously attacked by all sorts of people. I don't believe Chekhov ever was, except of course in the beginning. They did say he couldn't write plays. [Laughs] *The Seagull*, for instance, that we're playing now, was first done in St. Petersburg, by the Imperial Theater, by the sort of actors that had never encountered that kind of material at all. It was much too simple, too human. And they had been used to playing very theatrical pieces that were not true. They didn't know what to do with Chekhov. It was a complete flop because people said it wasn't a play at all. Then, when the Moscow Art Theater, a group of young people, who had no clichés as far as their acting went, who were there to try and evolve a method of acting of their own . . . when they did *The Seagull*, it sprang to life. They were wonderful in the Chekhov plays. I saw them do three of them when they were in New York in '24. The material that Chekhov gave them and their way of playing suited each other perfectly.

In *The Seagull* Chekhov meant for Irina Arkadina to be a great actress of the old school. She's what I would call a theater ape. She never stops acting, she acts all the time. In life, as well as off stage. [Laughs] And she has that sense of slightly overcharged vitality, in the voice and the action; everything is a little bigger than life. It's a comedy part, undoubtedly, and he meant it to be.

She has a scene with her lover, Trigorin, and she's of course an older woman. She's desperately trying to keep him from leaving her, and this scene is in a way very moving. But at the same time she is giving a performance in it. It's one of her better performances, because much is at stake for her. I'm not really that kind of an actress myself, but I know a lot of them, and I think that there's no question that they really believe they're being true. I'm sure of that. It isn't that they don't mean what they say, but somehow it's a performance all the same. He meant that scene, for instance, to lead up to a comedy point, because she pleads with this man and she, as I say, gives a very good performance and *means* it, because she doesn't want to lose him. After she has won him back, there's quite a long pause in which she powders her nose and recovers. Then she quite casually says, "But of course, you must stay if you like." Which naturally gets a laugh, and Chekhov meant it to get a laugh. Thereby proving that he knows the woman very, very well indeed.

We think of all the nonprofessional actresses who are actresses in life.

I suppose there are a lot of nonprofessional theater apes. [Laughs] I dare say. I hadn't thought of that.

She's a terribly selfish woman, frightfully selfish. I don't think she really ever thinks much of anything but herself. And the boy, her son, has a very interesting scene in the play, where he speaks of his mother and really analyzes her very brilliantly. He says that she really is a complete egoist.

This leads to another point, since you said the boy analyzes his mother. Chekhov and Ibsen and Freud, in a way.

Of course Ibsen was way ahead of Freud, and I don't think that Chekhov knew anything about Freud. I think that genius has a kind of a sixth sense. I don't think they'd have to know about Freud in order for those men to know these things. Ibsen knew everything. Look at Shakespeare, Shakespeare knew everything too.

Not too long ago, in Chicago, I saw you in the adaptation of Schiller's Mary Stuart, you were Elizabeth.

Yes, indeed, that was a great challenge. Heaven knows, nobody could be less like Queen Elizabeth than me. [Laughs] But it was a wonderful thing to attempt to play that great, extraordinary, fascinating woman.

I remember this memorable moment when you weren't sure who your allies were. You were on the throne, studying Mortimer. Could he be trusted? He was treacherous, but you weren't sure. That's that one moment, the concentration. It seemed like about five minutes. You were just on the throne, just staring at him, trying to figure him out.

Hmm-hmm. To weigh him and see whether I could trust him or not. But she made a mistake, the Queen, even though she did stare at him that long. Because she figured she could trust him, and then it turned out that she couldn't.

That silence, that moment of concentration and silence, it's a long moment, and yet it's very gripping.

The moment is just happening, that's all. You see, a silence is no good if it's empty. It's got to be inevitable. And so therefore during that moment, Elizabeth, all sorts of things were going through her mind as she looked at that man. She examined his whole body, from top to toe; she looked at his hands; she looked at his eyes; she looked at his mouth. She thought, can I? . . . All these things are going through her mind. It's got to be an inevitable thing, otherwise a silence is not good—it can be very dangerous. If you impose deliberately a pause that doesn't mean anything, then it wouldn't have been gripping if it hadn't been inevitable. It wasn't an empty, but a full silence.

I was seated way up in the second balcony, but it's still with me. I'm thinking about the others in that theater—I'm sure they were as knocked out as I was. I'm thinking of the audience today, the one you've always sought.

It's what I call the forgotten audience, you know? The real intelligentsia are usually people with very little money, and they don't have to be young either. There are lots of people who are teachers and librarians and nurses and people who wait on you in the stores and should have a theater that they can afford to go to. Because they're the ones who really appreciate it. These are the people who use the art galleries, who use the public libraries, who go up to the top gallery to hear music. I mean, they're the people who *really* want this type of theater.

HIRAM (CHUB) SHERMAN

1968

At sixty, he is an established Broadway actor. Much of his time, whether "at liberty" or while engaged in a play, has been spent on the Council of Actors Equity. This conversation also appeared in *Hard Times*.

I learned in the '30s that you could exist on very little. To paraphrase Tennessee Williams, you can depend on the kindness of strangers. When the Depression actually began in '29, I was just on my way to New York. It wasn't any demarcation point in my life. There were no stocks to be lost, 'cause we didn't have them.

There were no jobs in New York. I worked in summer stock and touring companies. I remember also what you'd pick up odd dollars doing. As a jobless actor. There were sight-seeing buses—see Chinatown, see the Bowery, see New York. They were lined up right on Times Square. If you've ever noticed a sight-seeing bus, there'll be a couple of people sitting on the bus. And they'd say: It's leaving right away, guided tour, just leaving for the Bowery and Chinatown. Well, the people inside were usually shills. They're engaged for a quarter or fifty cents to sit there and look eager. I shilled in Times Square sightseeing buses. [Laughs] As people came on, you got off: "Excuse me for a moment." And then you got into another bus. It's a sitting job.

The summer always provided work for actors. I don't know why this happened, I can't explain it. But there was a great proliferation of turning barns into summer theaters. During the Depression, that's when it came.

In 1936, I joined the Federal Theater. I was assigned to Project

891. The director and producer were Orson Welles and John Houseman. The theater we had taken over was the Maxine Elliott. A lot of theaters went dark during the Depression, and the theater owners were happy to lease them to the government.

One of the marvelous things about the Federal Theater, it wasn't bound by commercial standards. It could take on poetic drama and do it. And experimental theater. The Living Newspaper made for terribly exciting productions.* Yet it was theater by bureaucracy. Everything had to go to a higher authority. There were endless chits to be approved. There were comic and wasteful moments all over the country. But it was forward-thinking in so many ways. It antici- pated some of today's problems. The unit I was in was integrated. We did Marlowe's *Doctor Faustus*. Mephistopheles was played by a Negro, Jack Carter. Orson Welles played Faustus.

Our next production was *Cradle Will Rock*, words and music by Marc Blitzstein. And we rehearsed those eight hours a day. We worked every moment, and sometimes we worked overtime be- cause we loved it.

Cradle Will Rock was for its day a revolutionary piece. It was an attack on big business and the corruption involved. It was done à la Brecht. We had it fully rehearsed.

On opening night, when the audience was assembling in the street, we found the doors of the Maxine Elliott closed. They wouldn't admit the audience because of an edict from Washington that this was revolutionary fare. And we would have no perfor- mance. Somebody had sent down the word.

Well, when you have an alert company, who are all keyed up at this moment, and a master of publicity such as Orson Welles, this is just grist for their mills. [Laughs] It's a nice evening in May—late May or April. Balmy evening. An audience not able to get into a

---

*T. S. Eliot's *Murder in the Cathedral* was the most celebrated case in point of this kind of successful poetic drama. The Living Newspaper was documentary theater, based on circumstances and controversial issues of the time: *Triple-A Plowed Under* concerned the New Deal's farm program; *Power* dealt with rural electrification; *Third of a Nation* (a phrase taken from the FDR inaugural ad- dress of 1937) commented on the housing crisis.

theater, but not leaving because Orson Welles and John Houseman were haranguing them in the street: "Don't leave!" They expected to get a reversal of the edict. We're told not to make up. We're told not to go home. We don't know what's going to happen.

No reversal came from Washington. So Orson and John Houseman got their friends on the phone: What theater could we do this in? Somebody suggested the Jolson Theater. An announcement was made to all these people, without benefit of microphone: If you go to the Jolson Theater you will see the show. And we marched. Walking with our audience around into Broadway and then up Seventh Avenue to Fifty-ninth Street, we acquired an even larger audience. Walking with no police permit. [Laughs] Just overflowing the sidewalks. Obviously something was afoot. The Jolson Theater hadn't had a booking for months and was very dusty. But it was open.

Word came from Actors' Equity that proper bonding arrangements had not been made. The actors would not be allowed to appear on the stage. Because now you're not under the aegis of the Federal Theater. You're under some obscure private management. You don't know what, because you haven't found out yet.

This didn't daunt us. We had a colloquy right in the alley. We decided, well, if we can't go on the stage, we could wheel out the piano and Marc Blitzstein could do what he had done in so many auditions: describe the setting and such, and we'll all sit in the audience. Equity didn't say we couldn't sit in the audience. When our cues come, we will rise and give them. So, that we did.

The theater filled.* I don't know how the extra people, who didn't hold tickets for the opening, how they got in. I've often wondered. Did the box office open or did they just say: come in for the laughs? But it was packed with people. The stage was bare, the curtain was up, and you suddenly missed all your fellow actors. You couldn't find them. We were in different parts of the house.

Eventually the house lights lowered a little. Marc Blitzstein came out and laid the setting and played a few bars and then said: "Enter

---

*The Jolson Theater was larger than the Maxine Elliott.

the whore." I didn't know where Olive Stanton, who played the whore, was. Suddenly you could hear Olive's very clear, high voice, from over left. A spotlight suddenly found her and she stood up. She was in the lower left-hand box. One by one, as we were called, we joined in. We turned around if we were down front, and faced the audience. People were scattered all over. It was a most exciting evening. The audience reaction was tremendous. That to me was the most dramatic moment in the theater of the Depression.

When the war broke out, I enlisted in the navy. I had incurred a few debts before the war with high Depression living, and they were still waiting for me after the war. The average actor clings to whatever job's providing money, the longest time possible. I've now come to an age where I can't do that anymore. I find I want very little in the way of possessions out of life. Here we are in a hotel room, and there're unanswered letters piled up on my desk. And that's my life. I don't care. I've got a suit on, and that's about all I want. I'd like to answer the letters before I die. [Laughs] But I don't know that I will.

E. Y. (YIP) HARBURG

1968

Once in khaki suits,
Gee, we looked swell,
Full of that Yankee Doodle-de-dum.
Half a million boots went sloggin' through Hell,
I was the kid with the drum.
Say, don't you remember, they called me Al—
It was Al all the time.
Say, don't you remember I'm your pal—
Brother, can you spare a dime.

Song lyricist and writer of light verse. Among the works in which his lyrics were sung: *Finian's Rainbow, Bloomer Girl, Jamaica, The Wizard Of Oz* and *Earl Carroll's Vanities.* This interview appeared in *Hard Times.*

I never liked the idea of living on scallions in a Left Bank garret. I like writing in comfort. So I went into business, a classmate and I. I thought I'd retire in a year or two. And a thing called Collapse — bango! — socked everything out. 1929. All I had left was a pencil.

Luckily, I had a friend named Ira Gershwin, and he said to me, "You've got your pencil. Get your rhyming dictionary and go to work." I did. There was nothing else to do. I was doing light verse at the time, writing a poem here and there for ten bucks a crack. It was an era when kids at college were interested in light verse and ballads and sonnets. This is the early '30s.

With the Crash, I realized that the greatest fantasy of all was business. The only realistic way of making a living was versifying. Living off your imagination. We thought American business was the Rock of Gibraltar. We were the prosperous nation, and nothing could stop us now. A brownstone house was forever. You gave it to your kids and they put marble fronts on it. There was a feeling of continuity. If you made it, it was there forever. Suddenly the big dream exploded. The impact was unbelievable.

I was relieved when the Crash came. I was released. Being in business was something I detested. When I found that I could sell a song or a poem, I became me, I became alive. Other people didn't see it that way. They were throwing themselves out of windows. Someone who lost money found that his life was gone. When I lost my possessions, I found my creativity. I felt I was being born for the first time. So for me the world became beautiful.

I was walking along the street at that time, and you'd see the bread lines. The biggest one in New York City was owned by William Randolph Hearst. He had a big truck with several people on it, and big cauldrons of hot soup, bread. Fellows with burlap on their shoes were lined up all around Columbus Circle, and went for blocks and blocks around the park, waiting. There was a skit in one of the first shows I did, *Americana*. This was 1930. In the sketch, Mrs. Ogden Reid of the *Herald Tribune* was very jealous of Hearst's beautiful bread line. It was bigger than her bread line. It was a satiric, volatile show. We needed a song for it.

On stage, we had men in old soldiers' uniforms, dilapidated, waiting around. And then into the song. We had to have a title. And how do you do a song so it isn't maudlin? Not to say: My wife is sick, I've got six children, the Crash put me out of business, hand me a dime. I hate songs of that kind. I hate songs that are on the nose. I don't like songs that describe a historic moment pitifully.

The prevailing greeting at that time, on every block you passed, by some poor guy coming up, was: "Can you spare a dime?" Or: "Can you spare something for a cup of coffee?" . . . "Brother, Can You Spare a Dime?" finally hit on every block, on every street. I thought that could be a beautiful title. If I could only work it out by telling people, through the song, it isn't just a man asking for a dime.

This is the man who says: I built the railroads. I built that tower. I fought your wars. I was the kid with the drum. Why the hell should I be standing in line now? What happened to all this wealth I created?

I think that's what made the song. Of course, together with the idea and meaning, a song must have poetry. It must have the phrase that rings a bell. The art of song writing is a craft. Yet, "Brother, Can You Spare a Dime?" opens up a political question. Why should this man be penniless at any time in his life, due to some fantastic thing called a Depression or sickness or whatever it is that makes him so insecure?

In the song the man is really saying: I made an investment in this country. Where the hell are my dividends? Is it a dividend to say: "Can you spare a dime?" What the hell is wrong? Let's examine this thing. It's more than just a bit of pathos. It doesn't reduce him to a beggar. It makes him a dignified human, asking questions — and a bit outraged, too, as he should be.

Everybody picked the song up in '30 and '31. Bands were playing it and records were made. When Roosevelt was a candidate for president, the Republicans got pretty worried about it. Some of the network radio people were told to lay low on the song. In some cases they tried to ban it from the air. But it was too late. The song had already done its damage.

HAROLD CLURMAN

1978

He was a director of the Group Theater during the '30s. Their plays, especially those of Clifford Odets, a member, were regarded as "socially significant." He later became the drama critic of *The Nation* magazine. His memoir, reflections on that decade, was called *The Fervent Years.* During this conversation, there were moments when he took off, and his enthusiasms as well as his indignations added an evangelical touch to the proceedings. At times, he appeared to be addressing multitudes.

The distinction between entertainment as something trivial and theater as something noble and serious is a silly one. The theater is an expression of the deepest feelings of men and the community that you can have and share together. I speak about the theater as if I were a revivalist speaking about morality and God knows, and human love. People always say, why don't you talk about entertainment. I say, "What's more entertaining, more exhilarating and engaging, than the love of the community? The ideas communicated to you by the playwright and by the actors to the audience? That's *entertainment.*"

No theater should depress you. Certain kinds of audiences, they think anything that has tears in it is depressing. But what tragedy does is say life is difficult, but there are men who rise above it, who struggle. And even if they fail, the struggle itself, which is the struggle to make things better than they are, is an exhilarating thing. If there hadn't been people who made sacrifices, beginning with certain religious teachers, and who suffered for them, we wouldn't be the people we are today. The struggle that makes man a very noble creature.

There was fervor in the '30s. I'm very amused by the people saying that it was a period of depression. Of course they're talking about the economics, and that was true. I find now a period of depression, more than then. In the '30s, people were losing money and not getting jobs, but they were fighting it with a kind of sense that they might overcome it. And to a large extent they *did* overcome it. Now I find this dead level of complacency, or indifference, or pessimism, or bitterness, or cynicism, all of which I find depressing.

You said the role of the critic is not to be a wise guy: "A critic's value is not in a summary opinion, but in the quality of his insights and then his capacity to stimulate the possibility of further speculation."

To excite people to think about what they've seen and to question and go beyond the momentary amusement, which is of course the first satisfaction, the indispensable satisfaction. To think more about what they've seen, to question it, to challenge it, to elaborate on it, to argue with it. There are times we laugh at things which are cruel, and we have to say, "I shouldn't have laughed, or if I did it was only the little cruel part of me, which exists in all of us." Every play becomes a statement, even a light comedy becomes a statement. And it's not a statement about the theater, it's a statement about life. Because if theater has nothing to do with life, we don't need it. The theater is there to stimulate our experience of life, to increase it, to make it richer, to make it more than even we understood of it. Because most people don't understand their own experience. It's the artist, whether he be of the theater, or a novelist, or a poet, who enriches our experiences. We understand more about ourselves through having read Tolstoy, let's say, or through having read Emerson's essays, or Walt Whitman's poems.

The arts *are not decorations to life*, they're the *flower of life*. We *live* to create art. We live to create art not only through books and music; we live to create art through conversation, through comradeship, through friendship. All our acts should be a work of art, everything we do should be conceived as art. That is what I think of as art, as being the very essence of what we're here for. That's what life is all about!

People say Samuel Beckett offers no hope, he's pessimistic.

They don't know what they're talking about. He's deeply religious. The whole idea of his most staged play, *Waiting for Godot*, is these people who are derelicts, who are bums, tramps; who are waiting for somebody they call Godot, and he doesn't appear. They always promise that he will appear, come tomorrow, come tomorrow, come tomorrow, he never appears. And finally one of them says, "We're haven't found Godot; Godot hasn't come to us. But we know we're better than most people because we're waiting." What does that mean? We're looking for a solution for the misery of our lives, and we're waiting for some messiah possibly, some redeemer, to answer us with a faith, with a belief that would justify the suffering. But though he hasn't come yet, maybe will never come, we have the aspiration, and that aspiration is a religious aspiration. In another, later play — it's called *Foot Falls* — Beckett has a line where the woman is walking down miserably and she's always walking. [Taps on the table.] And she wants the sound of her walking to be heard. And finally her mother says, "Why are you nervous? Isn't your motion sufficient"? "No," she says, "The motion alone is not sufficient." Which means: Living day by day without any idea, without any feeling it is all meaningful, is not enough. We are looking for more, we are looking for God, if you believed in God, or for something which, whether it's called by any other name, can give us faith.

That's very funny because in your review of Foot Falls, *you thought you had misinterpreted it the first time. And you saw it again.*

I hadn't misinterpreted it, but not completely made explicit my interpretation. As a critic, I was telling the audience to do what I as a critic have done: I had seen the play, I made that evaluation, it was pretty good, and I said I didn't see *enough*, I should have seen more. I am now correcting myself. Very few critics correct themselves. They don't know much to begin with and they never try to find out more after, unless somebody tells . . . Of course *Godot* was completely disregarded by most of the reviewers when it first came. It was considered very unimportant. And as the reputation grew, the critics began to see that maybe they'd made a mistake.

Picasso said art was a lie that tells the truth. And the theater is that way: it's a fiction, it's not true. It's imagination. It's a story, sometimes a cock-and-bull story, but the point is to tell you something that is true and valuable to you. That's what I think all art is, but especially the theater, which is most fictitious. Everything, the scenery is fake, so to speak; the actors are performing parts which are not themselves, et cetera, et cetera. But they're communicating a truth about life, we hope. Hamlet advises the players about art mirroring nature. Often I find, when something hits me, it's because of a play that I saw or a piece of music that I heard. You wouldn't understand the play unless you had something in your experience that it duplicates. Suppose a man or a woman had never experienced love, really experienced it. *Othello* would be meaningless, or *Tristan and Isolde*. It would be a lot of noise. They'd say, "What's this about?" In other words, you always have to have in you a part of the experience which the playwright is expressing. Otherwise you wouldn't understand.

Some people say "I don't want messages in my plays." Every play has a message, including the musical comedies of the Ziegfield Follies. The Ziegfield Follies had a wonderful message glorifying the American girl. That is a point of view. To say, "I have no point of view," is a very devastating, nihilistic point of view. Unless they say, "I have no point of view now, but I will acquire one later on." [Chuckles] I will grow up.

I don't want to go to a play and say, "This show will run for forty years." I don't give a damn how much money the producer's going to make. That's of no interest to me. And so I would encourage playgoing on anything that shows even a *gleam* of some talent, visible talent. The idea that we have to have masterpieces and great men all around us is insufferable, because if we had only great men around us we couldn't live a day either, because the world would be devastated in two minutes.

You once used the phrase, the art of presence.

The physical presence of the artists and actors. Their physical presence is not replaceable by television—and I'm not against television, of course—or radio, or any form. If there were feelies, that you could feel the screen, feel the flesh of the actors, it would not represent the actual presence at the moment of you sitting there and something being created. It's a living art. It's an art of presence. Thornton Wilder said theater was the greatest of all arts because of that, because the community was together with itself. The theater is a means by which society realizes itself, meaning makes itself real to itself.

Ibsen always questioned himself, was never quite sure he was right. He wrote one play in contradiction to another, and if he said you always have to maintain the truth, he wrote another play which said, maybe the truth isn't always a good thing to proclaim. In Ibsen's *Wild Duck*, there's a man who tells the truth, Gregers Werle, and he's very determined, and he's always played like a leader and a prophet. He should be made almost funny because he is a neurotic. He's so fanatically in love with the idea that the truth will redeem people that he's not able to judge anybody, so he's silly.

It would be exciting if he was a clown, who was *also* serious, who can't stop himself. What was Ibsen doing? He was saying, "I'm like that. I'm capable of saying I know the truth, but I think maybe I'm silly, because people aren't as good as I think they are, and if I tell them the truth, I'll just shatter their lives." And so he comes to the conclusion that our dear friend Mark Twain came to. He said, "The truth is like gold: very valuable, you have to be sparing in its use."

Ibsen was sure that he was a great leader, and then he wrote a play saying, "Maybe I'm not pure enough to be a leader, and you have to be a purer person to be a leader . . ." In other words, one has to wake up people's ideas about plays. I spoke the other day and said, "You people didn't understand Shakespeare." They'd seen a hundred of Shakespeare's plays and they don't understand them. And a woman said, "Well, what do you think about *King Lear?*" I said, "I know what you think about it and it's wrong. I said, You think *King Lear* is about how bad children are to their parents." "That's right." "Well, it's not," I said, "because if that was so, it's a very bad play because after two acts you know that isn't the truth. What the play is about is that power inheres in love and not in a crown." That's why, at the end of the play, when he finds out his mistake and realizes the only one who really loved him is Cordelia, he says, "We'll forget about the courts and we'll forget about the palaces." But when King Lear gives away his power, his real estate, so to speak, his crown, then he has nothing. Because he never built an ego on true love, only on the expression, the hypocritical expression of love. It's only in love, and through the love of people for one another that one can have power. Which is also what, ultimately, Ibsen is saying.

People say, "Oh, yes, we know *A Doll's House* is about women's liberation." I say, "No, it's not about women's liberation, it's about man's liberation." Because the last line of the play is the man's, not the woman's. The woman slams the door and she doesn't know what's going to happen, because she doesn't come out saying, "I'm a liberated woman," she comes out, "I'm a bewildered woman. I don't know what I'm doing, what it's all about. I gotta learn." And the man says, "She spoke about a miracle. What is the miracle?" The miracle will come about if he will be understanding enough to let her be free so that they can really have a true relationship, and then they will both be free. Because as long as women aren't free, men can't be free. That's what the play's about.

That's what a critic is for, to say, "You see, you know the story, don't you? But you don't understand the play." You know the story, you can tell exactly what happens in the play. This man shoots who, this guy gets married, this . . . That's not the play, because there are only thirty-five, six plots in all of dramatic literature. Thirty-six plots in all of dramatic literature! But there are hundreds of thoughts in dramatic literature. There are variations, and the insights into effect. Like *Rashomon*, the story of an event and there are six different interpretations of the same thing. So, Ibsen has to be revived with new ideas!

Up through the 19th century, about the middle of the nineteenth century, people believed genuinely or hypocritically in God. But even those who believed hypocritically in God—all those robber barons—believed in churches and God. They still had a sneaking feeling that there was some truth to the old moralities. Anybody went to war in terms of God, right? But there came a period when it was alright to doubt God, but what are you going to put in its stead? Because people need faith. And Ibsen is the person who understood the old morality of the people who profess God, especially in Norway's Protestant community, who professed God, who professed the values of bourgeois society. They were very vulnerable in a moral sense. So he wanted to liberate them. But he knew that if he liberated them, at a certain point they would become free, but without responsibility. That's the point of *The Lady and the Sea*. It's the opposite of *A Doll's House*. The woman says, "I want to go off with this man who's my first lover." Her husband, who's a doctor, says, "No, you shouldn't." He finally says, "She really does want: 'All right, go.'" And then she says, "I don't have to go now. I'm free. But I have responsibility." And so Ibsen was pointing that out. He was saying the old relations were vulnerable; they were falsified. And the new religion of science may not have all the truth either. He was in a halfway house of the old religion and the religion to come, and denying the religion in the middle, which is the religion of most middle-class societies, which is now in despair. That's why we have theater of despair, because they no longer can believe in the old with any firmness, 'cause science seems to deny it, and they can no longer believe in science alone. Ibsen was the harbinger of some future development.

There's a line from Ibsen to Beckett. . . .

Ibsen, too, was waiting for Godot. All education has to be resumed every day, anew, afresh. We are never completely educated. And if we lived a thousand years, we'd still have much to learn, much to investigate, *and much to be extremely curious about.* If I live to be a hundred, knock wood, I shall say, "Gee, I wish I had a little more time to know more, to *see* more, to *experience* more." I say most people are latent human beings. And to become a human being takes an awful lot of effort and determination throughout a long life, because you can die long before you're buried. We all must consider everything, every day of our lives, as prehistory. With a wonderful background of several million years, we're just at the beginning, not at the end as some people seem to believe. Every hundred years people think we're at the end, you know. Good Lord, we've done enough to destroy ourselves, many times over. And nature did things to destroy us: the Black Death in the thirteenth century. Shalom Aleichem said, "There are two possibilities. One positive and one negative. But there's always a third, which is neither the positive nor the negative. There's always another one." We have the possibilities to make ourselves better men in a better world and have a better time. And more fun! [He's on a roll.] What I'm for is more fun! What I'm talking about is all fun. It has nothing to do with so-lemnity and sadness and fears. It has to do with the *joy of life, which is constant even in its struggles*, and I've found it especially in my struggles. I had a *hell* of a time in The Group Theater, and I was in debt twenty thousand dollars. And I came out saying, "This was one of the happiest periods of my life."

4—Chicago Boom-Boom

1981

A farm, eighty miles north of New York. Eighty-eight acres, surrounded by woods. There is a salubrious air to this countryside. It is a balmy afternoon.

He is eighty. Though he moves with some difficulty—diabetes and a series of strokes—he is a gracious host. Despite his health problems, you sense a feeling of "easy does it" contentment. There is a touch of diffidence when it comes to talk of his work.

John McCabe wrote in his biography, *Cagney*, "The reticence about his professional life flowed directly from his deeply quiet nature, his loner instincts, and his honest belief that there was not a lot so say about what was to him 'just a job.' It was a phrase he used—indeed, overused—constantly. But he meant it." I interviewed him for *Esquire* magazine.

After an illustrious career of thirty-one years in the movies, you retired for some 20 years to what I guess was a very contented life. Suddenly, you're back in action as Waldo, the police commissioner, in Ragtime. *How come?*

The doctor.

The doctor?

Yeah, I'm a partial diabetic. He wanted to keep me busy, so he said, "Get this guy working." And they did. It was as simple as that. Milos Forman, the director of *Ragtime*, saw there was a chance to do something worthwhile. He said to me, "How about it?" So we did it.

I'm told by people who watched the shooting that you just dazzled them. Forman says he didn't have a thing to tell you. It was all in-

stinct. What was your immediate feeling when you were back in action?

Just a job. It was easy. Milos was a wonder. We just turned it loose. I didn't feel strange, no. I felt as if I'd done it the day before.

Let's go back to beginnings. [Cagney laughs] You came from a very tough district in New York? On the East Side.

Yeah. But I didn't know it was tough. Nobody knew it was tough. My father was a saloon-keeper. A bartender.

What was your dream? What did you want to be?

A farmer. That is all I ever wanted to do. Can't tell you why. It was just that the country attracted me. My Greek great-uncle and his Irish wife were country people—they had a tiny house in what's now Flatbush, in Brooklyn. It was very easy there. No great strain. There was no great strain for anything, really.

Funny how your approach is so easy-going . . . You lived in a hurly-burly world, turbulence.

I didn't know it.

What about some of your friends?

You mean the ones that went to the chair? [Laughs]

Yeah.

Bootah. Peter Heston. He and I sat alongside of each other in school. And anybody could lick him. But he had a gun. And he did a stickup on 102nd Street, and a cop named Riley came around the corner and saw what was going on. And without saying anything Riley just sneaked up behind Bootah. And Bootah gave him both barrels.

Bang. Killed the cop?

Right then and there. And Bootah went where we always went when we were being chased: down the cellar, through the yard, over the fence, and out in the next street. He had shot himself in the leg putting the gun away, so the cops had a beautiful trail. They found him on the fourth or fifth floor of a tenement house, in bed with the gun. But he was too weak to lift it, he lost so much blood. So they took him in.

I went to Sing Sing to play ball in 1919 and I was catching, warming up a pitcher. And this little voice beside me said, "Hello, Red." I was always called Red. We were told not to talk to the prisoners, so I just said, "Hello, how are you?" He said, "What's the matter? You gettin' stuck up?" Real, you know, New York. And I looked at him, and I said, "Bootah?" And he said, "Yeah." And I said, "How long you in?" And he said, "Five to ten." How he got away with that, I don't know.

Only five to ten for killing a cop!

I was amazed, yes. No, wait; he didn't kill him. Pardon me, I was wrong. He killed a cop *later*. This cop he shot in the neck, I think—a superficial wound. Alongside him was a kid named Red Russell. I used to box with Russell in the backyard.

I'll be damned.

"Hello, Red," he said, and so on—you know, small talk. And so I got up, I went behind the bat, and the first man getting up had white hair. He was twenty-six years old. And this guy Jack—Dirty-neck Jack Dougherty—turned around and I said, "You Jack Dougherty?" He said, "Yeah." He said, "Too bad about your father"; my father had died the previous fall and this was late in September when we were playing ball.

What kept you from being like them?

I had a mother who would belt us if we did anything slightly cockeyed. Stiffened us, really. But we had other interests anyway. We played ball and so on.

What about your father?

A good guy. Nice fellow, you know? Drunk most of the time.

Your mother was the strong one.

Oh, yeah. [Laughs] She was just as tough as she needed to be. A great woman.

We were seven kids. Two died. I was the second eldest.

Is it true that once, when you were a young guy, you enrolled in an agricultural school?

Farmingdale School of Agriculture. [Laughs] One of the profs came over to see why the hell this kid from the East Side wanted to enroll in an agricultural school. He had real clodhopper shoes on, you know, a real farmer.

But you couldn't do it because of the lack of dough, is that it?

That was everything eventually.

Do you think your knowledge of these guys when you were a kid played a role in the characters you created in The Public Enemy, *in* Doorway to Hell?

It all contributed. Some of the things I said in the movies were things people around me said. "Whattya hear, whattya say?" That was one of the lines I put in. There was a gal in the neighborhood, I think she was a hooker—I never found out, really—and she came out with that one day. One of her boyfriends used to use it, so I dropped it in.

You could drop in your own phrases?

Well, I knew more about the hoods than the writers did, for God's sake. They were country boys.

What about "That's the kind of hairpin I am"? You said that in The Strawberry Blonde.

That was my grandfather's line. It was something that he used to say as a kid in Norway.

How did you get into theater? After you were in the neighborhood.

I needed a job, and a fellow told me to go to the 81st Street Theater. That was how easy it was. I walked in, met the stage manager, and I was doing the job the next morning. Dancing, singing, doing female impersonations.

Tough Jimmy Cagney doing female impersonations!

That's right.

You didn't have training as a song-and-dance man?

Oh, no, none at all. But I could dance. They showed it to me, I did it. As we did it, we learned.

How about singing? Did that come naturally to you, too?

I couldn't sing. I never could.

Let me stop for a minute. I come from Chicago. I've got to bawl you out. Wherever I go, people say "Chicago, boom-boom-boom!" They do a gesture with the guns. And they got it from you. Hollywood movies are so strong. I'm talking about Italy, Germany, all over Western Europe. And they see Jimmy Cagney in these movies. Are you aware of the impact?

Never thought of it. Didn't occur to me.

Those were all real Chicago characters in Public Enemy — *Nails Nathan was your boss in the movie, and there was a Nails Martin, a real guy. The movie was so accurate that it even showed how this gangster became a ladies' man, a gentleman riding horses. He fell off the horse, so his confederates killed the horse. That was a real-life story. You killed the horse in the movie.*

Yeah. Had to be done.

I think you must be asked this question a million times. In one of your classic scenes in Public Enemy, *you're with Mae Clarke, but you're in love with Jean Harlow, so you shove that grapefruit right in Mae Clarke's puss. How did that idea come to be?*

It was supposed to be an omelet. Hymie Weiss* had a girl, he was having breakfast with her. They had an omelet on the table and he gave it to her right in the face. But the omelet was too messy, so we used a grapefruit in its place.

I'll never forget the first movie I ever saw you in: Sinner's Holiday. *It was originally a play called* Penny Arcade. *That marvelous old character actress, Lucille La Verne, was the star. You were her bad-boy son. It was the first time I ever saw a movie in which the rotten kid became the central figure.*

I was in a straight play at the time. Never turned down a job, any job. You just damn well did it, did the best you could with it. That was April 11, 1930, when I came to Hollywood.

You remember the date! So when did you know that you were a hit?

Let me see. After *Penny Arcade,* I did a picture called *Doorway to Hell.* We were driving down Santa Monica Boulevard and my name was up in lights. That was the first time I knew.

It's kind of ironic, isn't it? Here you are today, making a comeback after twenty years — and the role you're playing is a man upholding the law, Waldo. But for all those years, you were playing the guy defying the law.

Mm-hmm. Yeah, that's how it goes.

Now that you've come back, what changes have you noticed about movie making?

Well, the directors have changed, of course. Their whole point of view has changed.

Too much money?

Oh, God, yes. Twenty million dollars for a picture. We did *Public Enemy* for $165,000.

---

*A Chicago gangster who was immortalized in a photograph of his dead body in front of the Holy Name Cathedral. He had just been shot. His legs were casually crossed as though he were taking a nap.

Right in the heart of the Depression, too — 1930, '31.

That's right, yeah. But, you see, the people were coming to the theater then in greater numbers. Less money, of course, for admission, but they were coming in greater numbers. And so, what was generally conceded to be the low period financially for everybody was really our prosperous period. I think they slight movies today. They just kind of breeze through the central idea of the picture. They'll cut and then go on to something else. And not make any point of the thing they've been working on before. A lot of things are left hanging.

Some people say that films are more mature today.

I think they're making excuses for what they want to say.

Are you offended by anything in films?

I never see them.

What was the last one you saw?

Let me see now. *Urban Cowboy.* Because John Travolta was in it and I knew him and he ran it for us.

What is it about him that attracts you?

He got us the seats. [We laugh.]

Do you watch television reruns of Cagney films?

Don't see them either. If there's a dance in it I'll look at it, because there's a marked difference between the way we danced then and now. I think we were more precise in what we did. It's a different style.

I've heard that you're offended by some of the current language.

Oh, sure. Don't like it. These young kids, girls, using all those words. And the violence.

What about Jimmy Cagney in Public Enemy? *And* Doorway to Hell?

I got killed.

Ah. In your films, crime never paid.

No, we were knocked off. If not by the cops, then by the other gang.

There was always retribution. [Laughs] You got it when you were pushed through that door with all those heavy bandages on in Public Enemy. *A mummy. Wham! That was a shocker.*

There was a girl who was the head of the sound department at MGM, and she had a very bad stutter. When I met her, she said, "You don't know me, but I know you." I said, "What did I do?" She said, "At the moment when they sent you through the door all wrapped in blankets and bandages, I said, 'Jesus, Jesus Christ' with no hesitation." But she stuttered from then on, too. [Laughs]

When you became a star in Hollywood, what did you do with your spare time?

Paint. I've always painted, though I haven't in a couple of years, ever since I got the diabetes. The one that I did without any model or anything else is an ex-fighter. I call it *The Victor*; he's been cut to ribbons, and he's a winner. You see a hand holding his arm up, and his eyes and everything are just awful. It's out on the wall there.

Do you still follow boxing?

Oh, yeah. But the old-timers are all gone.

I think of you as a lightweight, as a scrapper. The days of Benny Leonard and Rocky Kansas.

Well, now you're talking the best. Leonard could really go.

And Tony Canzoneri. Jimmy McLarnin. Remember him?

Sure. I saw him get the hell beat out of him one night. By a fellow named Lou Brouillard. Brouillard was a southpaw, belted the bejesus out of McLarnin . . . [Laughs]

You like skill and speed, like the kind of roles that you played in films. That fast shuffle. . . . This is the obvious question, of course, but of all the roles you've done, is there one in your mind that was the greatest satisfaction and challenge?

Yankee Doodle Dandy. You see, I grew up with George M. Cohan. I saw him in . . . what the hell did I see him in? *I'd Rather Be Right.* And *Ah, Wilderness!*

Did you ever know Cohan?

Yeah, I met him once. He was casting a play and I went up to a hotel. I said, "Hello, Mr. Cohan." And he looked over at me and said, "I don't think you're right for us, son."

And years later you make the guy immortal as Yankee Doodle Dandy in a film. Cohan was a fink in the early days when Actors' Equity came into being. As a theater manager he terrified, bullied, and fired actors who dared join the union.

Oh, sure he did.

Yet you became one of the early presidents of the Screen Actors Guild.

That's right. You do all the things that happen, one into another.

Yet you're always on the side of the underdog. You even gave dough to the Abraham Lincoln Brigade in the Spanish Civil War. You helped poor cotton farmers. That got you into a little trouble for a while, didn't it?

It's all part of the scheme.

You were bringing big dough into these studios; there's no question you were a draw. Yet they held you, didn't they, for a while, to some cheap contract?

Four hundred bucks a week for two years. They were paying Dick Barthelmess twenty-five thousand dollars a picture. I was getting four hundred bucks a week and doing four and five a year. The first time I walked I was out six months before they finally capitulated. And the second time I was out again six months or more, I don't know. Errol Flynn had his way of doing it. He got his makeup on and sat down and said, "Tell the boys I'm ready to go when they come up with four thousand dollars a week." He got it.

What are your big interests now?

My farm. The horses, the cows.

Now that you're back in action, would you be open to other offers?

You know, it all depends on how things shape up. If there is something to do that's interesting and fun, I'll do it.

Otherwise, the hell with it.

5—War

I was eight when I saw my first war movie: Charlie Chaplin in *Shoulder Arms*. He was a goof-up private in the U. S. Army, World War I. I'm certain that seeing it at such an impressionable age may have influenced my military career. Twenty-some years later, I was a goof-up private in the U.S. Air Force, World War II.

At Jefferson Barracks, Missouri, the authorities lost no time in recognizing my astonishing attributes. The obstacle course and rifle range experiences told them more than they needed to know. It came to such a pass that the drill sergeant from Sevierville, Kentucky, who had so terrified the other recruits, spoke softly to me. He recognized a case when he saw one. He played a fair country guitar and whenever, in the barracks, he sang "The Little Rosewood Casket," he glanced at me with a wistfulness that I interpreted as darkly meaningful.

It was the memory of Charlie in *Shoulder Arms* that, I'm certain, possessed me. As I remember, he wound up capturing a German battalion and eventually the Kaiser. I didn't come within 5000 miles of capturing Hitler.

I was fourteen when I saw King Vidor's *The Big Parade* with John Gilbert. It was at the Garrick Theatre that, for a few years, showed "big, important" films, twice a day, matinee and evening, in the manner of plays. Though, at the time, I may not have been aware of the populist nature of the movie, I remember being moved by the rich young idler's unexpected comradeship with the blue-collar workman (Karl Dane). And how it affected the rest of his life.

From then on, I looked forward to seeing all the Garrick specials. *What Price Glory*, an adaptation of Lawrence Stallings's play of World War I, amused me. I'm less amused now as I try to remember it. All I can recall is Captain Flagg (Victor McLaglen) and Sergeant Quirt (Edmund Lowe) trying to make out with Dolores Del Rio, a French peasant girl. That's all.

I guess you could call *Beau Geste*, based on Christopher Wren's novel, a war movie, because it dealt with the French Foreign

Legion. What a special that one was! The young British aristocrat, Ronald Colman, gets in trouble at home, joins the Legion, and is in turn joined by his two younger brothers, Neil Hamilton and Ralph Forbes.

The opening scene knocked me out. There had been an attack on the desert fortress by the Arabs. A rescue party, led by Percy Maremont (or was it H. B. Warner?) finds all the Legionnaires dead at their posts; rifles pointed outward.

What I remember best is not the courage of the noble Geste brothers, especially Ronnie, but the cowardly Boldini (William Powell). It was some years before Powell's elegant ways were recognized in the talkies. Whenever I see a video of a *Thin Man* movie and there is Nick Charles, witty and off-handedly brilliant, having a martini with his equally witty and lovely Nora (Myrna Loy), I hurry toward the Bombay Gin, pour a drop of vermouth in it, and delight in watching the pair—and reflect on the power of talking pictures, transforming a rotten, no-good being into the William Powell we came to know.

For some reason, I still remember a less touted war movie, *Broken Lullaby*. Ernst Lubitsch, best known for his subtle, witty comedic touch, directed it. A French soldier (Phillips Holmes, the most fragile-looking young actor I've ever seen) having killed a German soldier in battle, is stricken with remorse. He tracks down the dead man's family, seeking forgiveness. Despite the usual constipated performance by Lionel Barrymore as the German father, it still sticks with me.

I was eighteen when I saw *Journey's End*, a World War I play by R. C. Sherriff. It was set in a British dugout at the front, during the Battle of St. Quentin. Later, I saw the movie version, with Colin Clive as the gallant, bone-weary Captain Stanhope. On both occasions, I was deeply moved. Yet, after all these years, when a fleeting reference was made to the film, why did I feel less bewitched; more bothered and bewildered?

A number of years later, I saw John Ford's *Long Voyage Home*, an adaptation of Eugene O'Neill's early sea plays. There in that Limehouse pub, where John Wayne, the young Swedish seaman, was about to be shanghaied, I saw Billy Bevan as the craven cockney barman. He was usually cast in these less-than-heroic roles. Often, he was a knockabout comic, having appeared in scores of Mack Sennett two-reelers. Something clicked. Bill Bevan was Second Lieutenant Trotter in *Journey's End*.

A word about Captain Stanhope's fellow officers in that dugout. Lieutenant Osborne was an avuncular, pipe-smoking schoolmaster, wise and philosophical, who had obviously attended the same proper schools as Stanhope; institutions on whose playing fields, the Duke of Wellington informed us, wars were won. There was Second Lieutenant Raleigh, young, innocent, tragically heroic, the kid brother of Stanhope's sweetheart back home. There was Second Lieutenant Hibbert, of indeterminate class; something of a coward. And there was Billy Bevan, as Trotter, speaking cockney talk. (How in the world did he ever get to be a British officer?)

Two pieces of dialogue tell us as much as we need to know about *Journey's End*.

Scene I: (Osborne is reading a book.)

TROTTER: What are you doing?
OSBORNE: (Wearily) Oh, just a book.
TROTTER: What's the title?
OSBORNE: (Showing him the cover) Ever read it?
TROTTER: *Alice's Adventures In Wonderland*—why, that's a kid's book!
OSBORNE: Yes.
TROTTER: You aren't *reading* it?
OSBORNE: Yes.
TROTTER: What—a kid's book?
OSBORNE: Haven't you read it?
TROTTER: (Scornfully) No!
OSBORNE: You ought to. (Reads)

Scene II: (Stanhope and Osborne, in a conversation, casually touch on the subject of Trotter.)

STANHOPE: Funny not to have any imagination. Must be rather nice.

OSBORNE: A bit dull, I should think.

STANHOPE: It must be, rather. I suppose all his life Trotter feels like you and I do when we're drowsily drunk.

OSBORNE: Poor chap!

STANHOPE: I suppose if Trotter looks at that wall, he just sees a brown surface. He doesn't see into the earth beyond . . .

What would Molly Valakis have thought of all of this? She was an Irish cockney waitress working in London's Soho at the Mandrake, where Dylan Thomas had, in times gone by, sung for his supper. And a dram or two.

I clamber the broken wooden stairs, through dark, dank, Dickensian hallways, toward her fifth-floor flat, where she lives with her small-time Greek gambler husband and four boisterous little kids.

"Some of those slummin' people would come to the Mandrake. The ones who go collar-attached. They want you to pay 'em due deference." Molly does an Upper-U accent. "Oh, my deah, it's absolutely ma-a-velous." "'Ere we go, Dave. We smell of cabbage, they say. Can't they ever think attar of roses?

"They never think in terms of another person. They never think they hurt this person. I've got a feeling for these simple people who just don't hit the nail on the head. They can say it in their own way, but these people don't give 'em a chance."

There is something I want to ask Molly, but I'm not sure what. I'm squinting, nearsightedly, at a picture on the wall. In the oncoming twilight, it is difficult to see. Especially in a dingy flat, where the sun never shines.

"You like Breughel?" she asks me.

"Oh, yeah."

"I always loved Breughel. I always think of him—and us. My oldest sister came home one day very upset. She saw an accident. An old blind man was going across the road. Another blind man came along an' touched him, an' they both walked into the road an' under a car. These poor men, the one thought the other 'ad eyesight. A little later, I saw a Breughel print in school: The *Blind Leadin' the Blind*. It reminded me of this accident.

"In Breughel, I saw *people*. You can only interpret art from yourself. You *know* these people. It's like Dickens. Take Mr. Pickwick. Or Pip's cousin Joe, the blacksmith. When I read about these people, I've *seen* 'em. I know they never died. Maybe they wear a different coat. The coat changes, but these people don't change. You constantly meet these people. You can imagine what they were doing that day. There's life in them."

Had Molly ever gotten to see *Journey's End*, I doubt whether she'd have rated it as ma-a-velous. She would have probably regarded Stanhope and Osborne as obtuse, woefully lacking imagination.

In Jean Renoir's *Grand Illusion*, Captain Boieldieu (Pierre Fresnay) had a somewhat different take than Captain Stanhope when it came to the matter of class. If anything, he was considerably more classy. Boieldieu, an aristocrat, is an inmate of a German prisoner-of-war camp for French officers. The camp's commandant, Colonel von Rauffenstein (Erich von Stroheim), is a fellow aristocrat, who holds his elegant guest in high esteem. The war is an inconvenience (a mandatory one, of course, they both being of distinguished military families). It should in no way affect their class *Kammeradschaft*. As the colonel wistfully reminds the captain, they may have once shared the favors of Fifi at Maxim's.

He can't understand why Boieldieu so inordinately respects his fellow prisoners, who are of a lower class: Maréchal (Jean Gabin) and Rosenthal (Marcel Dalio). In an achingly moving sequence, von Rauffenstein feels impelled to shoot Boieldieu, who is helping the other two escape. The death of Boieldieu is, in effect, the death of von Rauffenstein, and the death of their class.

For me, the most indelibly memorable scene in *Grand Illusion* concerns Maréchal and an elderly German prison guard. Maréchal is put into solitary for causing a ruckus. He's going crazy with loneliness in his cell; he bangs at the wall and cries out. The old German guard shuffles into the room and offers his prisoner a cheap little harmonica. A few moments later, the old boy hears a few tuneless notes coming from inside the cell. He peers through the bars and sees a becalmed Maréchal blowing into the harmonica. He nods, contented; a faint smile plays upon his weary face.

I've lost track of the number of times I've seen *Grand Illusion*, the nonpareil of all war movies. I look forward to seeing it again, whether it be on cable TV or PBS or at a peacenik gathering. It is this one scene that tells me more of war's lunacy than any antiwar sermon.

I saw *All Quiet on the Western Front* when I was about nineteen. It knocked me out then and, surprisingly, has the same wallop when I run into it, on occasion, these days.

Again, it is the encounter between the "them" and the "us" that most sticks with me. It is the scene, during a bloody battle, in which the young German soldier, Paul (Lew Ayres) tumbles into a foxhole. There is a French *poilu* (Raymond Griffith).* In an instant, Paul bayonets him to death. The Frenchman lies in an almost upright position, eyes open, staring at his killer. There is no terror in those eyes, no hostility, simply surprise and some vague disappointment. Why?

Paul frantically searches in the man's pockets and comes up with a faded photograph of a young woman and kids. Paul cries out in remorse, shakes the man and begs forgiveness. None is forthcoming as the corpse simply stares at nothing in particular.

ON SEEING *THE DEER HUNTER*

1979

In 1979, when I was sixty-seven, I saw the acclaimed war movie, *The Deer Hunter*. It dealt with the war in Vietnam. A week before, I had interviewed a young miner, Darrell Vanover, from a small Kentucky "holler." I was so affected by the film, I dashed off a critique late that same night. It appeared in *Chicago*, a local monthly.

---

*Raymond Griffith was one of my favorite clowns in silent films. It was his air of insouciance that came across. "A top-hatted Charlie Chaplin," someone called him. He spoke no words in those old silent films and he spoke no words in *All Quiet*, but he said enough.

FANTASY: I have just seen a movie, *The Fox Hunter*. It is based on the reflections, experiences, and epiphanies of Darrell Vanover, a thirty-one-year-old coal miner out of Stearns, Kentucky. Vanover and his colleagues have been on strike against the Blue Diamond Coal Company for almost two years.

"We're not radicals. We're people that like to fish and hunt," Vanover says. "My father, he's a fox hunter. He enjoys goin' out at night and turnin' these hounds loose and just lettin' 'em run. I honestly thought he was enjoyin' life until I really understood what was goin' on and how coal miners were bein' treated underground."

The quote is from a real conversation I had with Vanover. Now comes the fantasy. But the fantasy is based on truth, too. The town of Stearns, I'm sure, has young men who believed in the American cause, who fought and possibly died in Vietnam. I've a hunch that American flags are furled and unfurled on the porches of some of the homes in Stearns.

The Fox Hunter deals with the Vietnam experiences of a group of these young men who have great affection for one another. It also flashes back and forth to their lives at home and in the mine. Lovingly, it reveals the skill and ardor of one of them, a fox hunter.

The movie has captured the dreams and visions of young working-class Americans who fought and died in Vietnam without once questioning the war's cause. We're told that these were young men whom the hearts of bleeding-hearts never bled for. I am deeply moved by *The Fox Hunter* because it is honest and, in its way, a work of art.

FACT: I have just seen a movie, *The Deer Hunter*. I am appalled by its shameless dishonesty. An altogether wretched job has been passed off as a work of art by critics who should know better. God help us.

Not since *The Birth of a Nation* has a non-Caucasian people been portrayed in so barbaric a fashion. (True, there were several "anti-Jap" films in the forties, but they were hardly considered works of art.) The difference between *The Birth of a Nation* and *The Deer Hunter* is the difference between D. W. Griffith and Michael

Cimino. One was a genius who was also a racist. The other is simply a cheap-shot artist.

Of course, the Vietcong were, on occasion, cruel in their behavior. Cimino's dishonesty was to project a sadistic psyche not only onto "Charlie" but onto all the Vietnamese portrayed. There is *not one* who bears any resemblance to a human being who feels. Coming from an American so hard on the heels of that wretched adventure, such a portrayal is positively shocking. I remember a sweet-faced woman who accosted me during the '60s and said, "Those yellow animals don't care about human life. They got no feeling." I highly recommend *The Deer Hunter* to her; she'd love it.

The tip-off to Cimino the social anthropologist comes in a flash on the screen. There is a wretched Frenchman who makes a buck by picking up victims for a game of Russian roulette. When De Niro returns to Vietnam (it's incredible that the Pentagon would let him go back merely to find a friend) and discovers his beloved buddy (Christopher Walken) in a Saigon dive, the Frenchman reveals his humanity, if only for a moment. Of course. No matter how depraved a white man may be, he's still part of Western civilization. Even Frenchie. It's then that we see, according to Cimino, the profound difference between Us and Them.

We got out five years ago. In the meantime, Vietnam has invaded Kampuchea and China has invaded Vietnam. Now *The Deer Hunter* has invaded us. It is the perfect vehicle to assuage any feelings of guilt we may still suffer. In fact, the movie may actually justify to some audiences, especially the young, our adventure in Indochina. They may wonder, If these gooks and slopes are such bastards, why didn't we bomb the bastards back to the Stone Age? Was Curtis Le May a consultant on this film?

Let's move on to Clairton, Pennsylvania, Steel Town, U.S.A. We see flames burst forth from the open hearth at the mill. (When we cut to Vietnam, we see flames burst forth from De Niro's thrower. Get it?) We see a bunch of young guys coming out of the plant, three of whom are about to take off for Vietnam. One is about to get married. It is a Slavic town, with old-country customs fused with American life.

The guys are horsin' around, but underneath there's tension, y'unnerstan', and sadness because they love one another. So they horse around by throwing beer cans, grabbin' at each other an' pushin' an' shovin'. An' even when they talk mean an' act shitty, it's just a real man's way, a workin' man's way, of sayin', "I love ya." Fuckin' A. (There's a fat buddy in the film who says nothing but "Fuckin' A.") In extended form, this is a portrait of every "ethnic" lout you see every night on TV selling gasoline or beer. Just as the execrable movie *Joe* used a stereotype to put down the blue collar, this equally execrable movie uses a stereotype, ostensibly to put him up. In all the horsing around, interspersed with references to the forthcoming deer hunt and wedding, we hear not one word about work. They have just come out of a steel plant, for Chrissake, but they might as well be astronauts.

The characters can say "fuck" as much as they want in this film, but they can't say "work"—that's a dirty word. Working people talk about work in real life, but in this crock, which we are given to believe is about real life, it's taboo.

The wedding scene runs almost an hour in this three-hour film. I've attended a number of such weddings and the parties that followed—Russian Orthodox, Lithuanian, Ukrainian, Polish, Croat, Serb—but I have yet to attend a wedding as dull, one-dimensional, and interminable as this one. I have seen drunken brawls. I have heard words passed. But mostly I have observed the dignity that hard-working people have on occasions of this sort. At such times, encouraged by a drink or two, they talk of their lives; they reveal themselves, their hidden hurts and inchoate hopes as they rarely do in their workaday existence. Here we have the drunks without the revelation. For almost an hour, we stare fixedly at a banal wedding portrait. It is as though *National Geographic* were offering a portrait of the Watusi people. All detail, no insight.

Dare I mention the stranger at the wedding feast? A clod in a Green Beret outfit enters and sits at the bar. The shape of things to come, get it? You know damn well that De Niro is gonna come back to Clairton in that selfsame outfit. Fuckin' A. Cimino goes big for symbols. German Expressionism, y'unnerstan'. Remember *The Blue Angel*? The sad, white-faced clown appears, intimating the fate of Professor Rath. But there's a difference between Von Sternberg and Cimino. One was a serious film director. The other is something else.

Let's not analyze the choral background as De Niro stalks a deer on a misty mountain. The self-conscious attempt at art is a painfully embarrassing artiness. I've seen too many kitschy German and Soviet films to suffer in silence American kitsch.

In the final scene, Walken's mourners sit at the table. This might have been a moving and effective moment were you to forget all the dishonesty and pretentiousness that preceded it. But no: Cimino spits in the champagne, as it were. One character, heartbroken, starts humming *God Bless America* and his friends join in. Freeze. The end. If it was meant as a touch of tragic irony, it came off as very bad Frank Capra. What was meant, no doubt, as a second-generation American's love of country came off as a D.A.R. exercise. Now, *that* is irony. And the crowning obscenity.*

The Deer Hunter has received critical acclaim and is box-office boffo. (Two days after I saw the movie and one day after I wrote this, *The Deer Hunter* won the Academy Award for Best Picture and Cimino won for Best Director.) It has succeeded admirably in denigrating the American working man as well as the Vietnamese people. Thus, we are all diminished.

FANTASY: One day, we shall see a movie, *The Fox Hunter*. It will be a portrait of young American working men who fought and died in Vietnam, who believed in their cause, who flew the flag, and who revealed themselves. It will be a work of art because it will be true.

World War II was probably more celebrated in film than all of our other military adventures put together. I can't remember one that came within 10,000 miles of *Grand Illusion* in the matter of human understanding. I recall one lovely moment in *The Story of Ernie Pyle*, when, in the north Italian campaign, the young captain (Rob-

---

*Of note: The local newspaper reported a slight disturbance in a theater in Carpentersville, a blue-collar adjunct of Chicago. A couple was leaving the house during the final scene. Several young men in the audience called out, "Ya dirty Commies." Obviously, they were deeply moved by the film.

ert Mitchum) is buried by his grieving men. Aside from that, it had more than its share of clinkers.

Listen to Dellie Hahne, a retired music teacher, whose husband had been a G. I. I spoke to her while working on my book about World War II, "*The Good War.*"

"There were some movies we knew were such bullshit. There was a George Murphy movie where he gets his draft induction notice. He opens the telegram, and he's in his pajamas and bare feet, and he runs around the house and jumps over the couch and jumps over the chair, screaming and yelling. His landlady says, 'What's going on?' 'I've been drafted! I've been drafted!' Well, the whole audience howled. 'Cause they know you can feed 'em only so much bullshit.

"If the guy in the movie was a civilian, he always had to say— what was it? Gene Kelly in *Cover Girl?* I remember this line: 'Well, Danny, why aren't you in the army?' 'Hell, I was wounded in North Africa, and now all I can do is keep people happy by putting on these shows.' They had to explain why the guy wasn't in uniform. Always. There was always a line in the movie: 'Well, I was turned down.' 'Oh, tough luck.' There were always soldiers in the audience, and they would scream. So we recognized a lot of the crap."

PAULINE KAEL

1972

One of the most perceptive and influential of American movie critics, especially during her years at *The New Yorker*. This appeared in "*The Good War.*"

During the war years, the whole spirit of the country seemed embodied in *Life* magazine. Its covers featured G.I. Joes, girls, and generals. The G.I.'s were always clean-cut, wonderful kids. And so were the girls they dated. This was carried through in the movies. Everybody was patriotic and shiny-faced. Wiped clean of any personality. Even after the war, when William Wyler made *The Best*

Years of Our Lives, a sensitive movie, by no means cheerful—even that had the look of a *Life* magazine cover.

A lot of the movies were very condescending to Europeans and Asians. There were films like *Bataan*, with Robert Taylor screaming epithets about "the Japs." I was in my early twenties and was seeing them all. Oh, I hated the war movies, because they robbed the enemy of any humanity or individuality. In all these films you were supposed to learn a lesson: Even the German or the Japanese who happened to be your friend, even the one who was sympathetic, had to be killed because he was just as dirty as the others. Even those who were trapped trying to save American lives were weaklings and untrustworthy. We had stereotypes of a shocking nature. They could never be people who were just caught in the army the same way Americans were and told what to do. They always had to be decadent, immoral, rotten people, sneaks.

In contrast, there was *Grand Illusion*, one of the great war films of all time. It would not have gone over during World War II. It was sympathetic to the Germans in World War I. It showed that not all Germans were behind the war. It had a poetic understanding.

Compare that with the shameful movie Alfred Hitchcock made, *Lifeboat*. Once again you had to learn what the master race was all about. Walter Slezak was the Nazi. It took a tough American workingman, John Hodiak, to deal with him. The other Americans were too weak, too liberal, too pacifistic. That was the message. The German represented everything terrible. He mouthed all the clichés.

Even more grotesque was *Tomorrow the World*, in which a little Nazi boy was the enemy. In *The White Cliffs of Dover* the people know that the war is coming home because two little German children are already warlike. *Mrs. Miniver*—oh, God, that was a disgusting picture. It was about the wonders of the British class system when you really got to it. The church had its roof blown off at the end, but the people gathered inside the roofless church and sang "Onward, Christian Soldiers."

The Clock was a popular movie. But it had none of the nasty quality you got in so many others. It was Judy Garland and Robert Walker as two kids who meet in New York. He's a soldier who has to leave in a couple of days. They meet, they fall in love, and are separated. It was a soft, sentimental romance, charmingly done. That was the kind of thing people could love. I don't think that the big action films were ever popular with women.

Of course, we had an incredible switch after the war. We had those wonderful Russians being tortured by Nazis, and suddenly, we had the Russians as bums. [Laughs] That period was one of the last moments in modern history when Americans were viewed as liberators. It's so interesting to see Italian films of that time, where the people are longing for the Americans to arrive. So there's something a little warming about that period. It was a good time for the country. It believed in itself, despite people who really knew better.

The Americans were stereotyped, too. They were always clean-cut, wonderful kids from the Midwest, who had funny ethnics, Italians or Jews, as buddies, who were from Brooklyn. The films were condescending to everybody. The Americans from the Midwest were always so innocent they didn't know a thing. They were virginal boys. There was a sickly undercurrent.

By the time we got to later wars, there was more of a sense that people knew a little something about what they were about. In the Vietnam stories reported, you didn't assume that all the boys were twelve-year-olds at heart. In World War II, there was still this image of the American G.I. giving candy bars to the European kids he liberated. Of course, American boys did that. [Laughs] Chocolate and gum became synonymous with G.I.s.

Soldiers actually used the techniques they saw in the movies. If you were walking down the street and a guy in uniform tried to stop you and you weren't interested, he would say, "That's what we're fighting for, that's what we're giving our lives for." They tried to make you feel guilty for not wanting to go to bed with them. They were going out and dying to protect you. Soldiers and sailors used the same techniques they saw the smart-guy characters play on the screen. These innocent boys.

There *was* still hope. It wasn't until the world became divided pretty much by the Russians and the Americans and Europeans that the hope had gone out. Now, almost every place on earth is a trouble spot. All the fights that seemed to be settled have started up again. So there's a general sense of hopelessness and powerlessness. You remember the pictures of Winston Churchill? On the cover of *Life*? That bulldog face and that big fat cigar. The idea was there were men in charge who knew something. You couldn't pose leaders in that style anymore. People would laugh at it.

Hope didn't really seep out until the counterculture period in the '60s. Even if you went to see a western, the Indians often looked like Vietnamese and the Americans were brutal racists. So you started to hate yourself when you went to the movies. It satisfied an almost masochistic feeling among the younger moviegoers. I think that's when older people stopped going to the movies.

I've always been a movie person, but the war years really put a strain on my patience. I got so angry. It was so difficult to deal with, because in some intangible way they did represent the essence of war propaganda.

6—O Death

I was fifteen when Frenchy Doran, on his deathbed, grabbed me by the wrist and pulled me towards him. His strength was such that the black-and-blue bruise hung on for weeks. Going into that good night, the French-Canadian strongman was not at all gentle. His rheumy eyes were ablaze; he was furious as well as terror-stricken. I happened to be the closest at hand and that was it.

He was a guest at the men's hotel that my mother ran. Frenchy was a carnival roustabout, who awed his fellow guests with his bull-like power. They called him Sandow, after "the strongest man in the world." Unfortunately, he was a bottle baby. His intermittent attacks of delirium tremens, after a bout and withdrawal, caused the others of us to tremble as much as he did. And then, came, inexorably, that moment as he crossed the lonesome valley. And my bruise.

Years later, as I saw Madame Hortense (Lila Kedrova) on her deathbed grab at Zorba (Anthony Quinn), I thought of Frenchy. As I saw James Bell, at the first act curtain of *The Last Mile*, tremble on his way to the electric chair, I thought of Frenchy. As I saw Paul Lukas, at the second-act curtain of *Watch on the Rhine*, tremble on facing odds-on death, I thought of Frenchy. And as I saw the most gifted performer of them all, Alfred Lunt, at the third-act curtain of *The Visit*, desperately fighting off his violent end, I thought of Frenchy.

LILA KEDROVA

1965

The Russian actress, whose most celebrated role was as
Madame Hortense in *Zorba the Greek*.

Madame Hortense was much older than me. But when I read
the script, I saw the poetry. She is an old woman but she is like a
child. Pure inside of her. It is so marvelous in this woman. When
she meets Zorba, she becomes this young person. Also a little bit
ridiculous.

If I played her like a young woman, it would be no good. So I
played *me* exactly as a young girl. When they put the old makeup on
me and those awful dresses and this hairstyle, it was so sad and
funny the same time. The director gave me a gesture. I am flirting
with Zorba and in the same time my stocking is falling down. And I
try to lift them. Everybody on the set was laughing. Immediately, it
was clear to me how this woman behaves. The other gestures came
from myself because I now understood her.

Afterwards, when she is in love with Zorba and he's not there,
Madame Hortense goes to Basil, which is Alan Bates, the English
actor. Zorba's boss. She asks him to read Zorba's letter and he lies.
He told her that Zorba loves her and wanted to marry her. She is
transformed. She becomes like somebody from a very good family.
An aristocrat, almost, yes. I cried because this scene is so full of
emotion and Cacoyannis* he cried himself, too.

When Madame Hortense is dying, remember? She grabs ahold
of Zorba tight. She wants to say, "Don't let me go. I would like to
stay with you forever." And in this moment she is dying. Her eyes
are open wide, she is so afraid. *Don't let me go.* You know, I saw
somebody on his deathbed. Chaliapin, the great singer.† He was the

---

*Michael Cacoyonnis, director of *Zorba the Greek*.
†Feodor Chaliapin, the most admired basso in the history of opera. His reputation was second only to Caruso's. Her father was the lead of the Kedrov Quartet,
a renowned vocal group. Chaliapin regarded the group as "a miracle of vocal
art."

greatest friend of my father for a long, long time. It was in Paris, not long after we left Leningrad. I was a small girl. He said, "Your father told me you can recite Pushkin. Please say something from him now." And I did. He was very touched and he said, "Come here, near." And he kissed me and he blessed me. A very great moment. And he told me, "Lila, you will be actress, I am sure." He was almost near to dying. I prayed and prayed to myself, "Please, Chaliapin, give me a little bit of talent. I would like to be like this." I think it was his last day.

REFLECTIONS ON *THE LAST MILE* AND *WATCH ON THE RHINE*

Spencer Tracy was the star of the prison drama *The Last Mile*. It was his powerful portrayal of Killer Mears that catapulted him to his movie career. Though Tracy was to become my favorite film actor (with the exception of Charlie Chaplin, of course), it was James Bell, a supporting actor in the play, whom I best remembered.

It is toward the first-act curtain. Bell is the young death-row inmate, who in a few moments will be electrocuted. He is trying to keep from breaking down, joking, after a fashion, with his fellows in the other cells. He is, in a sense, telling the story of his life. Now comes the last walk, with the guards, the priest, the heartbreaking show of bravado: Bell is fantastic. He acts as Frenchy would have acted. He exits; the lights dim, the whine of a motor is heard. Killer Mears (Spencer Tracy) in a rage shouts, "What the hell are they tryin' to do? Cook him?" Curtain.

In *Watch on the Rhine*, Paul Lukas as Kurt Mueller, the antifascist, decides to return to Germany to rescue his imprisoned buddy. He knows he himself may be a dead man, since he is high on the Nazi hit list. He sits in his chair, trembling, as his American wife (Mady Christians) is trying to comfort him. It's the second-act curtain.

I'm in the balcony of the Blackstone theater and weeping. A few days later, I encounter an understudy to Geraldine Fitzgerald, who is in the cast. I tell her how deeply moved I was by Lukas's performance. She laughs. "Just after the curtain came down, Lukas asked the stage manager if he could find out the name of the attractive young woman in the third row to the left and, if possible, her phone number."

Moral: Stanislavsky said to act is to do. Lukas did it, at least for me.

JOHN RANDOLPH ON ALFRED LUNT

1998

Alfred Lunt and Lynn Fontanne, the most admired acting couple in the history of American theater, had for some thirty years charmed and delighted American audiences with their consummate performances, especially in witty, sophisticated comedies. They regularly toured the country, appearing in middle-sized and smaller cities as well as big ones.

They took on as their last costarring adventure *The Visit* by the Swiss playwright Friedrich Dürrenmatt.

The locale is a hard-pressed town somewhere in Europe. The richest woman in the world (Lynn Fontanne) appears and promises prosperity for all, on one condition: they kill their fellow-townsman, Anton Scholl (Alfred Lunt). The people are appalled by the suggestion; further, Scholl is the most respected man in town. However, as a pair of fine leather shoes appears in place of wretched torn slippers, a fancy dress in place of accustomed rags, gourmet foods in place of stale bread, as the sweetness of the "good life" possesses them, the Faustian bargain does not seem that bad at all. They agree to kill Scholl.

Randolph played the town's police chief, one of the chosen assassins. He was an actor schooled in the Method, a technique to which the Lunts paid not the slightest attention.

It is a long-distance telephone conversation, as he, eighty-three, recalls the adventure of fifty years ago. His voice, in the telling, becomes that of a young actor excited about his first performance.

It was the most extraordinary experience of my life. I still can't get over it. This guy's been doing this show for months, England and here and God knows where, and here we're doing an improvisation the very first day of rehearsal. We did it about six times. He was never satisfied, wanted to get it exactly right. Lynn's watching it from the balcony. They watched each other all the time.

He knows he's going to be killed. All the guys are waiting for him to come back. He comes to me of all people. I'm sitting on the park bench. We had the scene down perfect. He'd sit down and say, "Must it be now?" These are the words he had, as I remember, "Must it be now?"

This time he stumbled against the bench. You know when you knock your knee against something and you hear that funny sound. Oh, Jesus Christ! And he falls into my arms. Now I did the only natural thing: to hold him in my arms like you hold a baby, just to catch him. I didn't want him to get hurt—he's Alfred Lunt! He falls into my arms and he starts to play with my lapel. He says, "Is it to be now?" I'll tell you something: all you know is that, Holy Shit, you can't even imagine such a thing like that. "Is it going to be now?" Like a baby. And from then on, every night he did that.

Let's come to the big one, John—where they close in on him and kill him.

Wait, wait. At the end of act one, he's at the station with his suitcase, waiting for the train. Peter Brook directed it. Two people happen to be there like it was an accident. And then two from another direction. Wherever he turns, they're closing in on him. It was a fucking ballet dance. He was so scared and frightened. It was extraordinary.

In the middle of one performance, a matinee, an actor got in his way by mistake and touched him. Lunt screamed. That sent chills down your spine. It was the most horrifying thing, his fear.

I said to him, "Jesus. Alfred, that was pretty exciting when you screamed like that." He said, "I know, but it's too much of a climax. I can't do it."

Give me the scene, John, where they're about to kill him and he—

Are you talking about when they grabbed ahold of him and he's trying to kick them away from him? What you hear only is the pounding of his legs. And they were choking him. They were killing him.

No, no, John. What I remember is — I was in the second balcony — as they're closing in on him, his leg goes up against his other leg, and he's clutching at his crotch, as though he's about to piss in his pants, he's so scared.

If you saw that, you're a better man than I am. What happened is that he falls on the ground, his back is to us and we see his feet kicking out as they come in on him, like a wounded animal, he's kicking and he's scared. And he begins to throw up. Originally, Peter Brook had him just fall on his face and try to keep away from the crowd, but Lunt felt it wasn't right. In Boston he got sick and was put in the hospital. He heard the sound of a guy in the next room vomiting, groaning and throwing up, and he loved the sound of it. He used it all the time. Lynn was watching the scene from the wings at the end of act one. She said, "This is Alfred's Actor's Studio ending."

At the end of act one? John, I'm talking about the end of the play. I still remember the terrified man, one leg lifted —

Whatever you remember, I'll always remember working with Alfred Lunt as the greatest fucking experience of my life. When he died on that stage, you knew that was it.

A PERSONAL NOTE: *I saw* The Last Mile *in 1930. Or was it '31? In 1968, a play I had written was to be produced in Ann Arbor. I was looking for an actor to play the role of an old Wobbly. I remembered James Bell. He had, since* The Last Mile, *appeared as Jeeter Lester in* Tobacco Road. *He was one of the several actors who had succeeded Henry Hull. Among the others were James Barton and Will Geer. They all, I'm happy to say, had some pretty steady work, since the play ran for years and years and years.*

Thanks to Actors' Equity, I was able to locate Bell somewhere in Virginia or the Carolinas. I phoned him. On the other end, I heard the voice of an old, old man. The treble was there, the hallmark of Melancholy Jacques's sixth stage of man. I told him I had never forgotten his performance as Richard Walters in The Last Mile. *There was a long pause.*

"You remembered me?"

"Of course. Listen, there's this guy in my play. You'd be great in the role." A long, long pause. I had a funny feeling he was crying.

"You want me?"

"Yeah."

"I can't believe it. I'm old and am not well at all. I can't."

That was the end of the conversation. Not that it really mattered. The play was a dismal flop; deservedly so. I'm glad I made that call.

7—Kindness of Strangers

TENNESSEE WILLIAMS

1961

The Night of the Iguana was having its pre-Broadway opening in Chicago.

Kenneth Tynan spoke of you and hot climates: your Mediterranean characters being much freer than your fair-skinned ones. In this play it's Mexico.

Puritanism is much more an element in Protestant countries. But out of these Puritan complexes seems to come a great deal of that friction that makes interesting art.

I spent most of my life in a very puritanical background. My home life was dominated by a very wonderful, rather puritanical mother, who was in conflict with a very wonderful but rather profligate father. I first sided with my mother, but after my father's death, for some strange reason I began to see his side better—after they put him away in Old Gray, the cemetery in Knoxville. My fighting spirit comes from them.

May I interject something at this moment? Two biographies of me came out this season. I find them disturbing. They examine my background and dissect my life as if I were no longer living. My God, they must think I'm going to kick off. Well now, I've got to live with it and they've got to live with me, 'cause I'm still living and not about to kick off.

The schism between my parents was apparent in St. Louis, not in Mississippi, where we lived in a small community, grandchildren of the Episcopal minister. So our social acceptance was taken for granted. In St. Louis, there was this money aristocracy. Plutocracy is the precise word for it. If you lived in the wrong neighborhood, you just weren't the right people. We had to live most of the time in the wrong neighborhood because there wasn't the money. We went to the wrong schools. Well, you know what I mean.

Nobody knew my real name was Tom. They just thought my

name was Tennessee because we had lived there before coming to St. Louis. In *The Glass Menagerie*, I called him Tom. The leading characters were the mother and the girl.

When I think of Amanda, the mother, and her sham gentility, I naturally think of Blanche Du Bois and hers. And in your current play, I think of T. Lawrence Shannon, the defrocked clergyman, and of Blanche being in the same boat. He's at the end of his tether and Blanche, visiting her sister, is at the end of hers.

I'm glad you made that point. In the portrait of Shannon, I've drawn the male equivalent, almost, of Blanche Du Bois. I knew I was doing it. I don't know if that's good in the play or bad, but that's what it is, undoubtedly. Of course, there are many differences. Shannon is very concerned with what is going on in society. If you listen carefully, you'll realize his redeeming virtue is a true and deep social conscience.

Even though we see him in a state of deep personal disturbance, you still see the presence of an awareness of social inequities—the starvation and the misery. He conducts these tours and says there's a great deal that lies under the public surface of cities.

Blanche's personal situation seems to eclipse everything else, yet there is a speech in which she says to Stella, "We must not hang back with the apes." That indicates a general philosophical feeling. In Shannon's case, it's on a more broad, social level.

Blanche at the very end says, "I depend on the kindness of strangers." And finds no kindness, really. Shannon does.

I think people always find kindness. I think even in asylums, one can find kindness if one is willing to give it. I have no idea what happens to Blanche when the play ends. This play says that this woman, who was potentially a superior person, was broken by—

Brutality.

By society. And the falsities in it.

I said brutality and you said society.

We were thinking along slightly different lines, though they converged a bit. I think in our time, the condition of society is pretty terrifying.

Tynan spoke of your love for those we call incomplete people.

I've always regarded myself as an incomplete person. Consequently, I've always been interested in my kind of people: people that have to fight for their reason, people for whom their life experience, day to day, and night to night, is difficult, people who come close to cracking. That's my world and those are my people. I must write about the people I know. I'm sure it limits me as an artist, but nevertheless I couldn't create believable characters if I moved outside that world. That doesn't altogether mean I'm a crackpot, because I'm not.

Why do you say this limits you? You created archetypal figures trying to survive the day in a brutish framework.

There's never been any question about that. Blanche had the courage to admit that occasionally she embellished on the truth. She said, "I don't tell the truth. I tell what ought to be the truth." When her back was to the wall, she had courage and eloquence, I thought.

There's Alma Winemiller in Summer and Smoke. *What a contrast to Blanche. She is someone caged by her inhibitions, yet when she busts out, there's a wildness . . .*

There always was, yes. That's what gave her the palpitations. She was caging in something that was quite different from her spinsterish, puritanical exterior.

The pagan versus the puritan seems always to attract you.

It seems to be an obsessive figure with me, yeah. I'm gradually beginning to find other types, too, to deal with in my way. But it's gradual. The question is: will one man's life be long enough to complete the discovery of these other types?

Oh, I'm sure there's more where that came from. . . .

Well, I'm fifty now.

That's a beginning.

Life doesn't begin at fifty, my friend. Don't kid me.

Let's consider Hannah in your current play, Night of the Iguana. A spinster, not too acquainted with the flesh of life, yet very much with the spirit of it. Isn't she a new figure?

She has come to terms, of a kind, with life. She is a very modest person, Hannah. To me, a very beautiful person. I'm still exploring her character. Thank heavens, I have a great artist like Margaret Leighton to help me. After the show and between shows, Maggie and I discuss this woman. Maggie really digs her. That's why she took the part . . .

Yeah, she is a new one in my world. She is still in the process of being created. The first production of a play isn't, for me, the final one. Even if this should close after a short run, I would go on working at it until I created Hannah completely.

For me, the production of a play is only an incident in its life. *Summer and Smoke* was a failure on Broadway and a success off-Broadway. I feel that a play is dynamic and living far beyond the time of the Broadway opening and the press the following morning. As long as I'm living, the play will live in me. And I will keep it alive and do all I can to complete it. No, I will not be limited by its reception, no.

These characters are living beings to me. They are more alive to me than I am to myself. They are my life. And I don't feel their life terminates with a Broadway or Chicago opening. Until I've created them as fully as I can, they will be with me. Then, I release them and they have their own lives to lead without me.

Right now, you're living in Chicago with Hannah and Larry Shannon — a ménage à trois.

[Laughs] And old Maxine Faulk.

Maxine, full of animal spirits. Mexico. Another hot climate. Is D. H. Lawrence an influence?

That's what some people think. Not nearly as much as Chekhov. This was composed as more of a dramatic poem than a play. *Cat on a Hot Tin Roof* was the most realistic play I've done. *Suddenly Last Summer* was perhaps the most poetic.

I remember seeing Suddenly Last Summer *in Chicago with Diana Barrymore as the tragic girl*

Her best role was as Maggie in *Cat on a Hot Tin Roof*. She was excellent as Blanche in *Streetcar*. But when I saw her in Chicago in *Suddenly Last Summer*, I realized she was doing a brilliant virtuoso performance of a part in which she was miscast.

FLASHBACK. *Though it may be presumptuous of me to disagree with the playwright, I'm not so sure Diana Barrymore was miscast.*

The press coverage of her off-stage life has been appalling. It was one scandal after another: too many men, too much booze, too many drugs. The supermarket tabloids and a rag called Confidential *had a field day with John Barrymore's vulnerable daughter. Her interviews on television, radio, and in the press were outrageously alike. It was her troubled private life that had so enthralled these voyeur-journalists.*

I have unfortunately lost the tape of our conversation. It was 1959, the morning after Suddenly Last Summer *had opened in Chicago. The reader, I'm afraid, will have to trust my memory of the occasion. It was hard to forget.*

I raised my voice. I guess I was sore about something, I'm not sure what. I remember reaching for a dead cigar — I have no idea why — during my brief, schoolmarmish peroration: "Your private life is none of my damn business. Nor is it the business of my listeners. I'm interested in you, the artist, and through your art we learn about you." Now, my tongue was really on the loose. "Would I ask Frank Lloyd Wright why he stole his client's wife? Is that how we remember him? Of course, I'd ask about his lieber meister, Louis Sullivan. What he meant by 'organic' in architecture. Why his Imperial Hotel in Tokyo withstood the earthquake of 1923. It's your giftedness as an actress I'm interested in, not those other damn irrelevant things."

She said nothing; shook my hand and left. The next morning there appeared on my desk a box of H. Uppmann cigars from the corner

Dunhill store. There was no note attached. There was no need to guess who sent it.

It was a case of life replicating art: A Tennessee Williams vulnerable heroine on the stage being a Tennessee Williams heroine in the flesh.

There's a phrase you used: "We are all in solitary confinement in our skins."

Oh yeah, it's from *Orpheus Descending*. My people are always trying to reach out to each other. In *Night of the Iguana*, each one has his own cubicle. They meet on the verandah. It's true, they're confined in their own skins, their own cubicles. They must try to find a common ground. Communicating. It's the only comfort they have of a common ground.

I can't think of any better example than my grandparents, who were so close together. They were like one person. What was that old Greek legend?

Philemon and Baucis.

Two people who grew into one tree. It's been a great inspiration to me. On the other hand, my mother and father who were in constant conflict, split violently apart and tore their children apart. These are the two backgrounds I had as a forming person. The gentle Laura in *The Glass Menagerie* was, in a way, their victim. She was an abstraction of my sister, Rose.

Tynan speaks of the two American playwrights, Arthur Miller and Tennessee Williams. Miller is the social playwright, who seeks the attainable summit. Williams, the poetic, who speaks of the unattainable summit.

I like Mr. Tynan. Even when he blasts you, he does it with such wit and eloquence that you enjoy it.

Carson McCullers, next to my sister, Rose, was the one closest to me. Though I may not see her for months on a time, we are one in our attitude toward things in life.

Two incomplete people . . .

I'm afraid that's true. To tell you the truth, I'm sure I've never met a complete person. Many have seemed well-adjusted, but I'm not sure being well-adjusted to things as they are these days is a desideratum, something to be desired.

I'm not sure I want to be well-adjusted to these times. I would prefer to be wracked by desire for things better than what they are, even for things that are unattainable. I don't think the human race should settle for what it has now achieved.

I'm an intensely patriotic American in a sense that I feel a longing for this country to go forward. I'm not satisfied with our complacency. I'm afraid of our thinking the rest of the world is in error and we are totally right. Nobody is totally right and the meaning of all my works is that there is no such thing as complete right, complete wrong. We're all in the same boat and that boat is the world.

It seems you can never be adjusted to what may be considered evil—

Oh, I have plenty evil in me. I'm not a nice person. My business, my vocation, whatever you want to call it, compels me to weigh evil and good and, consequently, I'm always in a state of examining.

You are a highly moral man, it seems to me.

Are you talking about my behavior?

I'm talking about your outlook.

I'm glad you're talking about my outlook because I couldn't make such a claim for me as a person, and my behavior.

Who can?

I don't know about other people. All I know is myself. Yes, I am a moralist. I want to discover all that is evil and all that is good. I'm not a very good writer, but I seem to be a man who has this obsession to explore good and evil.

In Camino Real, doesn't your Baron speak of taking chances and running risks?

"Make voyages, attempt them. There is nothing else." That's pretty much my credo.

1981

It is his seventieth birthday. He is in Chicago for the pre-Broadway opening of *Clothes for a Summer Hotel*, a play about Scott and Zelda Fitzgerald.

What I best remember about our conversation twenty years ago is your prescience. Considering the breakdowns of people we've known, your plays are closer to the present than they were then.

Your voice hasn't aged. Mine has, I'm afraid.

Yours has mellowed.

Mellowed, yes. I hope it's still distinguishable. I can't retract anything I've said, though. I just feel it more strongly.

The violence, the brutality has certainly increased. The assassinations—you must remember you are now talking to a man who experienced what Blanche went through. I've been in an asylum and I've survived. I've come out! Whether I am a crackpot—I said in the earlier interview that I was not—I'm a man who has the San Andreas Fault built into him.

Fortunately, my sister is now outside an asylum. She's living in the same town as I. Key West, Florida. She has her own house there, on a better street than mine. I have a cousin taking care of me and she has his sister taking care of her.

The world has become an asylum. It's just totally irrational. And I'm not confident of the future.

Twenty years ago, Blanche, T. Lawrence Shannon, and Alma Winemiller were generally regarded as outsiders. Today these three seem not so far outside.

So many people you'd never expect to suddenly crack up. They live behind a façade, which society expects of them. They manage to maintain that façade up to a certain point. Suddenly, the pressure shows how thin it is and it cracks wide open.

The complete person is still not around . . .

Perhaps one could be a complete idiot. I don't think the complete form will ever be offered to humankind.

It was a wholly different land, different climate when we first encountered Amanda Wingfield in Chicago, during the blizzard of 1944.

And the spring of '45. We spent three months at the Civic Theatre. A beautiful place. [Wistful] A beautiful, hopeful time. And Miss Claudia Cassidy had something to do with it.

CLAUDIA CASSIDY

She was the drama and music critic of the *Chicago Tribune* for almost forty years. Her yeah or nay was more powerful than that of any critic west of the Hudson.

During our conversation in 1966, she recalled that memorable moment, twenty-two years before.

It was the worst blizzard Chicago had had in years. At that time, the Civic Theatre was remote to most people. They didn't know where it was. And this frightful weather. Nobody knew Tennessee Williams. By that time, not many knew who Laurette Taylor was. She'd been away too long. For years, she had been grieving for her late husband, Hartley Manners. There were stories that she had been drowning her sorrows in drink. To have this play come at you was something extraordinary. And her performance.

It was not only the quality of the work as something so delicate, so fragile. It was also indestructible and you knew it right then. I'm proud to say it still is.

Ashton Stevens and I both knew it was important.* I know that the morning after the opening, something happened that surely never happened to me before, and I doubt had ever happened to

---

*The veteran drama critic of the Hearst morning paper, the *Chicago Herald-Examiner.*

him. Ashton telephoned me and said, "What are you doing to-night?" I said, "I feel a little ridiculous, but I think I'm going back to the Civic." He said, "Good. We'll both go." That's what he had in mind, too. Then Ina Claire† came out here, stayed two weeks and went to every performance so she could watch Laurette.

I always felt she had that quality the play had. She was absolutely unsparing and yet magical. Most women, when they play that role, bore you right out of the theatre. And I'm pretty sure Amanda in real life would. A dreadful woman. But Amanda was Laurette Taylor. There's a not very nice person, yet a great artist comes along and highlights something else within her.

In this weird costume—you remember that blue dress sort of beaten up with an eggbeater? But out of that, you really saw the woman who had seventeen gentlemen callers. You saw her! There she was. And yet you saw the old witch going over blue mountain.

You believed her lies.

You did. There was also something there you don't see in the play very much: beneath it all, this great affection and the likeness be-tween Amanda and her son, Tom.

Tom. Tennessee Williams. You are aware, of course, that ever since that first production, he has had a high regard for your opinion.

I always felt that if he had been just able to go ahead, and pay no attention to anybody, that he could have written even more plays than he did, instead of being so vulnerable.

The greatest artists seem to be the most vulnerable.

They have to be, of course. But they also have to be tough. I feel very sad that he seems to feel he has reached his end. I hope he's wrong.

———————

This play about Zelda and Scott Fitzgerald—I've rewritten it so many times. I carry around with me a great satchel of manuscripts.

———————

†A perennial theatre favorite, regarded as the virtuoso of high, sophisticated comedy—in a class by herself.

I'm rather puzzled that so little of my work is produced in New York anymore. I have much better luck in England and Europe. Even in Japan.

In European theatres, a playwright of your stature, or Arthur Miller's, is always honored, no matter what the play is. They may like some better than others, but there is always that high regard for the playwright. Here, it seems you're often treated as though it were your first play, as though you had written nothing before.

I don't know how to explain that. But it's true. I think every American writer has suffered terribly from that. I happen to be reading the collected letters of Ernest Hemingway. They're heartbreaking. What that poor man went through after his early top works.

I'm a really terrific fighter. I had to summon various allies, but I managed to decline to be thrown out of my hotel suite on the day of this opening.

Battling Williams, weighing in at 145.

Many battle scars. But I'm still surviving and creating, thank God. When I stop creating, I'll stop breathing.

People thought it was presumptuous of me to write about the Fitzgeralds. Yet I felt I had experienced all their problems. I'd experienced my sister's madness, which was like Zelda's. And my own, because I had a nervous breakdown. I had experienced early fame, as had Scott Fitzgerald, and then the humiliation that follows when you fall out of fashion. When you fall out of favor is perhaps a better phrase.

When you are no longer regarded as the kid of the moment.

I hope you're not making fun of me.

God, no. It's a phrase Lillian Hellman once used sardonically. Your track record, no matter how great, means nothing.

Maybe American society just thinks in these terms. I know one thing: when I'm no longer able to create at what I regard as an acceptable level, I'll cash in my chips.

You know what's so funny? In that interview twenty years ago, you said, "I'm fifty." I said, "That's just a beginning." And you said, "Don't kid me, my friend. Life does not begin at fifty."

I'll tell you a funny story if you're in the mood for one. When I was twenty-four, I had my first heart attack. It got me out of the shoe business. I was a clerk in a branch of the International Shoe Company in St. Louis. Terrible job for which I was paid sixty-five dollars a month. I worked at night with black coffee and it affected my heart. I went down to Memphis to see my grandparents and one evening I had a recurrence of the palpitations. The lady doctor said, "You're too uptight. Don't worry too much and you might live to be forty." [Laughs]

So much for doctors, so much for prognoses . . .

As long as you have a certain commitment to a thing, it's astonishing how you can hang in. You're never going to defeat death altogether. No. Although I was out with a black bishop last night, who claimed I'd been reincarnated several times and will be again. [Laughs]

Those people who think they can go through life without a terrific struggle are deluding themselves. Especially when it comes to the world of the theater. You always have to have your gloves on.

You'll survive to live another day, to fight another battle, and to create another play.

You bet. That's my raison d'être, my purpose in being.

You are multidimensional: lyricist, poet, story writer, playwright.

Is it all right to add "son of a bitch"?

I suppose that's an art form in itself.

It's something you learn in show business. It's not that I'm bitter. I just think I recognize life. I recognized it during my early years, when I thought I might drop dead any moment.

I'm less bitter now. I know days grow short as you reach September . . . November in my case. Or maybe late December.

It's very important not to be frightened, as I have been most of my life.

Here I am, seventy. I've lived three score and ten and [a giggle] that's about it.

1981

We had several conversations during the pre-Broadway tryout of *Clothes for A Summer Night* in Chicago. Though Williams was obviously dog-tired, he had been rewriting like crazy—he was resigned to bad notices from the New York critics. (They were forthcoming.) Geraldine Page was Zelda Fitzgerald.

Oh, I'm going to stick with this play till I've made it as tight and as telling as I possible can. Gerry doesn't want me to leave. I'll stay here in Chicago until she says, 'You can go home and rest a little.' I would rather go to Gerry than anyone connected with the play because she has the keenest theatrical intelligence of our time. Gerry Page.

GERALDINE PAGE

1958

This conversation took place during the Chicago run of *Sweet Bird of Youth*.

Tennessee Williams has called on her more often than any other actress. Her performance as the aging actress, Alexandra De Lago a.k.a. Princess Cosmonopolous in the current play, has been acclaimed as one "in grand style."

The tempestuous actress, a bit long in the tooth, is in stunning contrast to the first Williams heroine you portrayed: Alma Winemiller, the wispy, inhibited clergyman's daughter, in Summer and Smoke.

I had played so many shy young ladies who are rather retiring. This was such a leap for me. I was told to open up and go as big and wide, as high and handsome as I could get. After the first couple of rehearsals, I scared myself to death. I thought, "Where is all that noise coming from?"

I get so impatient with people who say that Tennessee writes the same plays over and over again. These two women could never be further apart. And I'm driven crazy by those critics who condemn him for his showing the "sordid" side of life and refer to his "antiheroes."

Isn't that the same way people reacted to Ibsen's plays? They thought he should be lynched or driven out of town. "That wicked man, he shouldn't talk about such awful things on the stage." I think people are unhappy because they get shook up by his plays. They're more comfortable with plays that show what people should do than what people do do.

Sweet Bird of Youth shows us what's so pitiful about our terrible accent on youth. There's a speech in the play, where Chance Wayne, the hero, says he was petrified when he was getting out of the army, that his life would be over, because he might be nearly thirty. I think that's a terribly funny line. It's a sardonic comment on the attitude of too many people. Seldom does that line get a laugh. People nod and say, "Oh, yes." What a futile way of looking at life: when your youth or pretty looks are gone, your life is over. Tennessee attacks that attitude full force.

Chance was fed all these false values when he was growing up. He couldn't accept growing old, plus being a failure because he wasn't getting material recognition. Alexandra De Lago had the same conviction. When she thought her looks were fading, this woman who was terribly beautiful and terribly successful, retired from the screen and didn't want anybody to know who she was. She felt she had died in a way.

FLASHBACK. *I met Marlene Dietrich in 1954, in the green room of the Arie Crown Theatre, Chicago. She is on her first tour as a singer-entertainer. The show begins within a few hours. Understandably nervous, she graciously agrees to the interview. I'm not too sure how this is going to work out in the usual bustle that accompanies opening night.*

She is casually dressed, jeans and no makeup. Though she is still lovely, she's a middle-aged woman. Wrinkles have begun to appear; intimations . . . A wild thought occurs: had she been an opera singer, she'd've been a natural as the Marschallin in Der Rosenkavalier. *Remember the mirror scene? The noblewoman, still beautiful, looks into the mirror, spots her first wrinkle or, at least, intimations of one, and decides to give up her young lover. Lotte Lehmann, one of the most memorable of Marschallins, referred to the Strauss heroine as "the wisest of women, who faced aging more gracefully than any I had ever encountered in art or in life."*

As I fear, the interview is cursory and of no value. There are too many other anxieties. After a polite wiedersehen, *she vanishes. An hour or so later, she reappears, out of her dressing room. It is magic. In a tight form-fitting gown, somewhat more revealing than concealing, she is a ravishing Aphrodite. Not a wrinkle in sight.*

Some years later, I saw Maximilian Schell's documentary, Marlene. *Scene: her Paris apartment. She is an old woman now, though we never see her in the film. There are so many photographs of her as a child and as a young woman, and numerous clips from some of her more celebrated movies. There is none of her as she is now. Nor does she ever appear in the film. She was adamant on that score.*

Schell caught every nuance of this tough, demanding, and, to some extent, forbidding subject. She was the I Don't Care Girl* not giving a damn whether she got the job or the man. This offhand manner had so intrigued Josef von Sternberg that he cast her as Lola in The Blue Angel.

She was, it seemed, afraid of nothing, except for one thing. In her casual command that all the mirrors in the apartment be removed before any shooting takes place, she gave the game away — her fear of seeing herself, or of anyone else seeing her, as an old woman.

On second thought, she could never have played the Marschallin, not in a million years.

Alexandra de Lago, finally, against her better judgment, decides to come back and let the world see her as she is. She is absolutely

---

*Early in the century, Eva Tanguay was an American vaudeville favorite. Her saucy air and her hallmark song made her known as the I Don't Care Girl.

frightened to death because of her ingrained conviction that youth is everything. But she learns in the course of the play that there's something left for her. On the other hand, it's not romanticized so that from then on, her life will be glorious. It's terribly true the way he writes. I'm always annoyed by people who say he's so pessimistic. He's presenting the bleakest aspects of this false thinking: this silly idea that youth is the end-all. This play has a very positive message.

It was a curious thing to see the relationship of Tennessee Williams and the director, Elia Kazan, as they worked on the play. They both seemed reluctant to work with each other. Kazan prefers to work with people who will rewrite as he asks them without too much argument. Tennessee would rather have a director who would just do whatever he said. They go through tremendous upheaval when they work together. But when they emerge onto the stage, they are very theatric and very effective. I think they both wish they didn't have to work together anymore, but they can't quite stay apart. It's terribly interesting.

This role of Alexandra De Lago is so rich and varied and lifelike, it's very hard to get it neat and under control. I once said, "It's like trying to wrestle with an octopus." Every time I think I've got something under control and I think I understand it, another end will start wobbling around. It's a continuous challenge to keep it fresh. It's like playing a different role every night.

When we're amateurs, we all have great freedom, because we don't know what the hazards are. But when you begin to learn what they are, it frightens you so you close up and stiffen a little bit. You have to really master technique to the point where you have the freedom of the amateur again. But on firmer ground, so that you can do it more than accidentally.

MARLON BRANDO

He is on tour, promoting *The Ugly American*. We were brought together by his sister, Frances.

Pretense is expected from all of our public figures. It is par for the course for politicians to act offstage as well as on; and certainly from our actors. When someone appears on the scene who does not quite conform, difficulties arise. Through the years, we've read accounts of you, perhaps our most celebrated actor, as being difficult.

Yesterday, while listening to you facing some 300 high school students, I heard someone who seemed without pretense facing his peers.

When you named those who have pretentions, you left out one: ourselves. It's a universal characteristic. I see pretension within myself. Anyone who examines himself, will realize he is not what he seems. Each of us in his own small way contributes to the aggregate pretension: national pretension. Nobody likes to admit it. He would much rather say: I am always right. Conversely, many people like to say: I am always wrong. Whores, pimps, criminals, alcoholics, unfortunates, psychopaths, those suffering nervous breakdowns: these people pretend to deride themselves in the same way as those oriented to a superior point of view tend to defend themselves. Both act as a result of being terrified of issues and conflicts.

This was said best by Matthew Arnold in his poem, "Dover Beach."

> We are here as on a darkling plain
> Swept with confused alarms of struggle and flight,
> Where ignorant armies clash by night.

We like to think ourselves as pure as Christian soldiers marching onward, braving the rigors of confusion and man's eternal despair and suffering at the hands of ignorance. It is never as clean as that. Usually when you talk to someone long enough, you eventually find that there is an inconsistency between what he says and what he feels. So often people say, "Don't tell me I don't know my own mind." Our minds have a remarkable capacity to rationalize and justify our feelings.

Here in America, we have more advantages than anywhere in the world—we are a living dream—a perfect example of what can be achieved in an industrial society that has all its wants satisfied. Why are we nervous, then?

Here you and I sit, concerned about these things. I can see you're awash with doubts. You're not at peace. Your personality doesn't remind me of some of the peaceful people I have seen, Tahitians, Eskimos. I am not at peace, either. In many respects, we are representative of all Americans, who have every advantage, but not the essential ingredient, which is a sense of well-being and peace.

We really don't know what our goal is. Certainly we don't want strife, yet we seem to desire it, chase after it.

It's much easier to find an external enemy to fight than an internal one. A scapegoat must be found because we simply can't accuse ourselves of our iniquities and inadequacies. The faces of god and devil change from age to age, culture to culture, person to person.

The theme of saint and devil in each of us recurs throughout One-Eyed Jacks, *the film you directed.*

Unfortunately, it didn't come out the way I wanted it to. I wanted to show the good and evil that exists in all people. We have a duty to Caryl Chessman in the same way we have a duty to Dr. Schweitzer: we must understand one another's weaknesses and hatreds. Respecting the nature of hatred, we have to understand it in order to dissolve it. Certainly, we're not going to allow Caryl Chessman to run loose, but he is part of us. Society did something to him.

It occurs to me that you, as an actor, examine the saint and devil in all of us. When you played Stanley Kowalski in A Streetcar Named Desire, *critics Harold Clurman and Kenneth Tynan spoke of your lively imagination transforming what might have been a brutish young man into someone more complex.*

If I may disagree, I don't think it related to that at all. My roles come about as a result of examining myself. It's in questionable taste to use oneself as a frame of reference, but it's the only one I have. When I hear something that unsettles me, I must ask myself, why? I could come up with something clever and adroit, but the irritation may come from some other area at which I cannot bear to look.

Still, I can't disassociate what you say from the roles you've played. In Streetcar, *I watched a brutish, crude, rough young man and a delicate, sensitive sister-in-law. Outwardly, the audience might see the brute destroy the lady's sanity and, yet, because of your intelligent, lyrical interpretation, you may have enriched the author's original intent.*

I'm sorry, but I don't quite understand.

You'll forgive me, but I sense you're slightly unsettled when I bring up Stanley. Perhaps because you had been in the pop mind too often associated with this role. I was referring to the critics who said you added dimension to the role. Tennessee Williams agreed.

What critics?

Harold Clurman.

You used the plural.

Tynan, too, referred to Clurman, saying, "Here is a good critic because he speaks from the standpoint of a director."

Eric Bentley didn't say that, and many other critics said something entirely different. You saw in *A Streetcar Named Desire* what Kenneth Tynan and Harold Clurman saw. Someone else saw something different—it all depends on disposition. To me, this has always been a mystery.

Yesterday, you told the high school students that you would not call yourself an artist, that you were a craftsman.

My remarks to the students were tempered by the fact that I work in a world dealing, in an extremely crass fashion, with dollars and cents. Producing a movie is thought of as producing a product, existing within the law of supply and demand. Great pretension about artistry exists. Perhaps, it is out of respect for what it means to be an artist that I do not call myself one.

In the matter of acting technique. I know that you like jazz. When the Count Basie band or the Modern Jazz Quartet work, the soloist who interprets the stated melody also creates by improvizing.

I don't think that is true. The technique I use is primarily intuitive. It can been seen in many different places and circumstances in the world. Eleanora Duse, whose acting technique used feeling, emotions, and intuitions, contrasted to Sarah Bernhardt's, would be an example of intuitive acting. Another would be Alfonso Bedoya [in his golden sombrero], who gave a spectacular, intuitive performance as the bandit in *The Treasure of the Sierra Madre*, although he didn't know Stanislavsky from a hamburger. And the fellow who played in *The Bicycle Thief* certainly was not a professional actor, but he was intuitive. If what Eleonora Duse did was jazz acting, then what I do is jazz, too, and is perhaps an act of faith.

Now, I want to ask you a question. You sit and ask many questions, and so often we get no impression of you as a person. I think it's not inappropriate that I ask you a few questions about yourself. You have an obligation to describe some of your feelings and point of view. What is it about this particular kind of work that interests you? Why are you preoccupied with these questions? What is the nature of your furrowing-out this information from all manner of people? What kind of contribution does interviewing make to you?

This is a reversal. I don't know. Curiosity, I suppose. The danger of being curious, of being inquisitive, is the voyeur lurking in the shadows. The personal peccadilloes of an actor, a musician, a painter, have no meaning to me. But his concept of art does. That tells me more about him than his drinking or skirt-chasing.

When I asked you simply to describe what you feel about your work, you became tense and concerned, perhaps a little confused, unsettled. When you ask me something, I could give you a glib answer, spieling, but if I want to answer the question honestly, I have to search my mind. When asked a simple question, it's not easy to give a simple answer.

Knowledge in depth about oneself is reserved for a few people willing to journey through the night sea and find one's center. History never indicates, however, that people en masse are willing to make the enormous sacrifice required.

Doesn't life have meaning even for the most "average," the most lowly? This comes to mind because of your answer to the question of one of the high school students: Who were your favorite directors? You mentioned the Kurosawa film Ikiru *in which a lowly civil servant, whose life had little meaning, suddenly finds he's dying of cancer. With six months to live. In that period he discovers a significance to his existence. Why were you so moved by this film?*

I was moved by the display of character this man had—his bravery, his refinement, and how little it was, his wanting to make a recreation park for little children, his glory in his last moments. It gave his life more meaning. All our lives have meaning: your life as an interviewer interested in the common and the esoteric; the secretary across the room talking on the telephone; my life too.

At one time, I was, in some respect, a hero of the young. Now, I am not. Someone else has taken my place because I have gone beyond and am no longer a teenage symbol. There again, the young have their own gods and heroes.

I have outworn my usefulness as a hero to the teenager who wants someone else to state the spirit of rebellion in a different way. Looking down the funnel of the years back to a time when I was eighteen or twenty is strange. That time might as well have been a hundred years ago.

Teenagers today are more cynical, more questioning, assaulted by so many lies each day: the false lies on television, the attitude of announcers, the way products are pushed, the psychological second-story mind. Everybody knows and takes for granted that we live in terms of lies.

Teenagers are so loaded with false values that they become cynical. Theirs is a healthy reaction done in self-defense. The kind of Christian values taught in their churches and the kind of Christian world they meet on Madison Avenue are vastly different. A large schism exists in America as a result of the relentless push for the mother—money.

What do you tell your children in view of this world in which we are surrounded by the big and the little lie?

One of my sons was with me not long ago when some people approached and, much to my discomfort, went through this embarrassing ritual of asking for my autograph—the magical ritual of rubbing the lucky touchstone of the hero, and then looking on full of adoration and worship at this strange symbol of our funny life here in America.

I always sign autographs for children, who don't know any better; but it is so distressing when you see adults indulging this sad seeking of the talisman. Still, sometimes I have to sign autographs because I don't want to be offensive. Well, my boy asked, "Daddy, why do they want your name?" To give him a decent answer, I had to scrape the inside of my brain. "Some people think it's lucky to have it—they own rabbit's feet, little charms—and some people like me and want a memento of having been near me and so they want me to scribble something," I tried to explain.

The task set out for sons of a famous man is an awful, ugly, ugly burden. I only hope to find some way or some place in which I can bring up my sons protected from this thing. In other areas of the world, it doesn't matter who I am: I'm just another two-legged person walking around. When my boys go to school here, they very quickly become aware of the fact that their father is somehow an important commodity in everyone's home and life. This enormous problem I wish I could spare them, but they will just have to bull through it as best they can—with all the help I can give them.

You speak of yourself as a commodity. . . .

In one way or another, we all wear a price tag and are bought and sold. Ideas and political ideals are sold over television. The expression, "I don't buy that," comes from a mercantile invasion of the American mind. Stature can be bought—the Playboy Club, for example—or a person can climb to quality by drinking a certain beer. Absurd, sad, but that is the world in which we live.

As I get older, I become more convinced that a simple way of life directly related to living—getting and preparing of food, work directly related to living, such as you find in almost any primitive community—is more wholesome. In America, we are little islands separated one from another. A starving American for example, who must get help from the state, is considered a social reject. To be poor or unsuccessful is to be thought of as sick. People don't like to be around failure.

You mentioned Tahiti to the students as a place of which you had grown fond.

Tahitians have no sense of what it is to have or have not. Bananas, breadfruit, coconuts, fish in the lagoon, these are available, and when they want a house, they stick together palm fronds and wood. Only when they want something specific do they work.

All this will change, when the invasion of commerce begins. Japanese will flood the South Pacific with television sets, and the marketeers will invade Tahiti, and by teasing, cajoling, and humiliating the natives into wanting material things—saying, "You Tahitians are poor, backward, no good, uncivilized, you have no teeth"—they will force a market.

So often America is criticized as a Tinker-Toy civilization, oriented to gadgets and, as a result, we are the butt of so many jokes. Go to Paris or Germany or Italy, and you will find the same kind of merchandising society and mercantile thinking. Forced markets remind me of the forced feeding of geese: a pipe stuffed down a goose's throat allows corn to be poured in so that their livers will be swollen. Our livers have been swollen, too. This we have done to ourselves, and it will take a little time for us to realize that the rat race, the conniving, raging lust for success, is counterfeit.

Earlier in this conversation, you asked me why I do what I do. Why did you become an actor?

I don't know. I can make guesses as to why I became an actor, but the reason is lost in the tangle of who I am. It's so complex, it's beyond my perception.

During these past few weeks I have been on a 35,000-mile tour publicizing *The Ugly American*, and I have had so many microphones stuck in my face that I often ask myself: "What am I talking about? Why are my opinions asked?" If I were a dentist from Duluth, it might not be my face in which the microphone was stuck. Why me and not you or him? Or my secretary or the hotel waiter?

Gray's *Elegy Written in a Country Churchyard* says, "Full many a flower is born to blush unseen." We never know where we'll find that person. I don't believe that the artist is necessarily *the* articulator of wisdom or knowledge. Such a person can be found in a mason or a shoemaker or a farmer, or an inarticulate Tahitian. It would be interesting sometime to interview a criminal and ask him—

I did. Jimmy Blake. He was something of an American Genet. "I spent twenty-five years in the poky and when I got out, I found the world outside more of a prison than the prison I left. I watched those straight people outside and I wondered: if they are so free, why do they look like that?"

[Laughs] That's wonderful. I think it's a fitting close. During the Sturm und Drang that come my way as a celebrated commodity, it's good to sit down and talk for a change.

I don't think I'm a raging success in my life. I don't think I've achieved certain things I'd have liked to have done. We do what we can. I've done the best I can with my age and life.

ACT TWO

1—Ways of Seeing

FEDERICO FELLINI

1962

Here in this movie studio in Rome is a very weary Federico Fellini. The Italian version of *8½* is being dubbed into English. He says it is something of a chore. Nonetheless, a free and easy air pervades.

There seems to be a reccurrent theme throughout all of your films: the indominability of the human spirit. In La Strada, *the first of your films that came to Chicago, the strongman played by Anthony Quinn reveals, as he sobs on the sand alone at the end of the film, that even a brute is a human being. In* Nights of Cabiria *too, a man tries to push the little prostitute into a lake in order to get her money— she is betrayed again, but at the conclusion, there she goes, marching along. Yet isn't the theme throughout the tapestry of* La Dolce Vita *one of the dehumanization, the failure of indomitability.*

You speak of indomitability of spirit: I believe in human beings and I doubt if one could create a film without a belief and trust in people. Perhaps a man from Mars could make such a film; since I am a man living and working with other men, however, I believe in them.

To take an example: Marcello, the journalist in *La Dolce Vita*, is not dehumanized, although he stands on the verge of disintegration. Even as he stands on the beach at the end, however, nostalgia is evident in his eyes: he is looking for something, although he does not know exactly what. A charge of humanity exists in that look. Whether or not Marcello is "saved," on the other hand, is not important. What is important is to stimulate the public. My films do not attempt to make a moral point; instead, I work by instinct. If I were to make a moral point, however, I believe that it is more moral *not* to end a film with some point or message, which is simply a way of evading the issue by excusing it away, saying, "Well, that situation is solved now."

When the audience in Rome watching La Dolce Vita *cried, "Basta!"* *"Basta!" you must have been happy because the protest showed that they were irked and stimulated. In a way, your attitude seems close to that of Bertolt Brecht, who also said to his public, "Think about this; and perhaps do something about it."*

Although the man in *Nights of Cabiria* was moved at the end by the human message of the prostitute, we really do not know what he will do tomorrow; and the same applies to Marcello and any of my other characters. What they do on the day after the film ends is a problem which concerns them. They do not belong to this reality; they are artistic invention. What is meaningful is that the public is faced with the problem which they create.

About the similarity you suggest between Brecht and myself: Any honest artist, I feel, has this need to stimulate participation on the part of his public. *La Dolce Vita* seemed to stimulate many problems and discussions here in Italy and, I am told, in other parts of the world, too.

I am curious as to why you chose a gossip columnist as the protagonist or antihero of that film.

The squalid society depicted in *La Dolce Vita* is an invented city, of course. Rome happens to be where I live and work. Physical environment, however, is not an essential in my films. The scenes in the movie were created, not copied from life: I have never participated in an orgy, for example, nor been a guest at the home of some prince. That it should find its historian not in a Suetonius or Tacitus but in a gossip columnist seemed right to me. Concerning the unmerciful look at each scene: everything in the film is seen through the same curious, negative eye. This way of looking seemed typical of our time: a tragic or a great event is given the same importance as the election of a beauty queen, all are given the same value.

A perennial question about La Dolce Vita *concerns the suicide of Steiner, the intellectual. Why did such a cultured, seemingly happy man take his own life and the lives of his two children?*

MARCELLO MASTROIANNI

Who can interpret Nowhere Man, shoulder-shrugging, bewildered twentieth-century man, better than he? Between
dubbings of his new Fellini film, *8½*, and patiently trying to
light my crooked Tuscany cigar, he offers his explanation of
Steiner's suicide.

Steiner is successful. He is everything Marcello (referring to the
character he portrays in *La Dolce Vita*) isn't. He's intelligent, has a
happy family, and groups of intelligent people around him. When
Steiner kills himself, everything collapses around Marcello. He
loses all hope.

Yeah, but why did he kill himself?

He was too weak and sensitive. He was sensitive to the problems
facing the world and couldn't cope. He killed himself because he
was too weak to cope. He was not virile enough. Is that clear? [He
shrugs his shoulders, hands held forth pleadingly, smiling wistfully.]

ALAIN CUNY

1962

A dressing room in a small theater in Paris. On the wall are
several pictures of Sonny Liston, the American prize fighter. It
is during the matinee intermission of a Pirandello play. He has
a granite, furrowed face; he blows smoke rings, reminding you
of a Chesterfield cigarette ad, as he thoughtfully considers the
question: Why did Steiner commit suicide? He had played the
role of Steiner in *La Dolce Vita*.

Steiner may be rich, cultured, seemingly happy, why did he kill
himself? The external signs of the richness and culture are false. We
all know what hides behind such a show. A French philosopher
once said what is wonderful in the happiness of others is that they
make us believe in it. I don't believe in it.

Steiner's Swedish friend tells him, "You appear to us as high as a cathedral." He laughs, he sneers, he says, "If you could see me as I really am, as I really feel, you would see me as that small." He knew that his life with his wife, his work, and his friends was a total fake. By the way, my life as an actor is a fake. I'm ashamed of doing this work. It's not for a grown man.

———

I have been asked many times why Steiner shot himself. [Laughs] I fear I cannot give an answer as precise as the question. As a matter of fact, I do not know why he committed suicide. What was important to me as a director was to have an episode that could shock Marcello and make him realize that he had identified a way of living with life itself. Real hell, desperation, and madness occur when that happens.

"I feel so safe," Steiner says at one point. Yet, obviously, so insecure?

All of us feel insecurity, don't we? Actually, I am very optimistic about human beings. I do not feel that I have adopted a negative, judging attitude toward human waste. This wandering around today in search of some truth has a certain value, I feel, and I view it with a sympathetic eye. This sympathy, this solidarity, this participation in everything men do, I attempt to express formally in my work.

Although *8½* is a funeral, in a sense, it is not macabre; the film has a message of hope and of expectancy of something to come: *8½* is a funeral of ruins but I hope it leaves the audience with a quickened sense of a carnival right around the corner. Decay can bring liberation and growth. Men tend to become free through it. The hero of *8½*—the movie director Guido—recognizes at the end that he himself is his own doubts and confusions. Out of the decay of doubts and confusion he recognizes himself. Only by admitting that decay can he start fresh, free of doubts given him by wrong education, and free, too, of the way of life imposed on him by his environment and by the conditioning elements by which he lived. By admitting them, Guido is free to start all over again. He finds a new humanity. At the end he says: "I refuse to try and understand anymore; I want only to believe."

All art is autobiographical. If I made a film about fish, it would be an autobiographical film. No personal identification exists between the hero of *8½* and myself however.

I am happy about what you called the indomitability of the human spirit. What I try to do is to reveal a certain human element hidden in all of us and to vibrate a core in our spirit. I am not only concerned with social implications: I care for the poetry in us.

Poetry certainly seems a key to your films: the Rome of La Dolce Vita *is a poetic city of your imagination; the prostitute of* Nights of Cabiria *is not one girl whom you might have known but she seems to be an element of the eternally human situation; so, too, the clown, the strong man, and the simple girl of* La Strada — *they are creatures of poetry. Every film seems to indicate a growth. You say that only when the director in* 8½ *recognizes his weaknesses can the light come.*

Perfectly right. What happens at the end of that film is an experience of both recognition *and* acceptance. Guido's acceptance is not passive, however: it is *religious*. Guido becomes aware of the value of man as he is. He abandons struggling to understand and discovers some truth, and thereby gives up his conflict with life and the world in which he lives. Man's recognition of his limitations is a way to freedom. Only when a man understands that he is free can he know where he stands and then make a free choice. Only at this point can he jump into faith. This faith can be religious, political, or whatever. That choice exists is the point.

RENÉ CLAIR

1963

Paris. One of the great modern film directors, whose movie, *A Nous la liberté*, may have influenced Charlie Chaplin's *Modern Times*.

I still remember those two men released from prison, now free, in another prison, a factory — your funny, biting take-off on mass production.

It was just before the Depression arrived in Europe. I would not have written such a story in 1933, because then the Depression came. I still have the same point of view, because things haven't changed so much.

I started out as a journalist immediately after the Armistice of 1918. For two years, I was a newspaperman. Then, just for amusement, I played a little part in an amateur picture. So I became an actor, a very bad actor, in serials.

I hated being an actor. But I became interested in motion pictures. So I wrote myself a script and I was lucky enough to direct it, that's all.

My first masters were the French filmmakers of the early comic serials. But the greatest effect on me came from the great school of American comedy — Mack Sennett, Chaplin, and all those glorious names. They were my real masters.

What was it about them that attracted me? It's very difficult for me to answer. Only a motion picture critic can do that. I cannot see my work from the outside. It's easier for me to speak about someone else's work.

I think that the great task of a director is to understand actors. Maybe my own experience as a bad actor helped me a lot. Because I discovered a very simple truth. You should never ask an actor to do something you feel he is not able to do. That's all. I think that's the greatest gift a director can have as far as actors are concerned, immediately understanding his reaction.

I remember, I directed a picture in Hollywood called *I Married a Witch*, with Veronica Lake, and a very good an experimental actor, Fredric March. They were completely opposite, because Veronica was a beginner. She was a very gifted girl, but she didn't believe she was gifted. She was good, especially the first take. Second take, she was not as good. Freddie, as an experimental actor, was good at take five, because then he could correct his style and everything. It became very difficult to find an equilibrium between them both. I whispered to Freddie, "We are going to pretend that we rehearse." And during the rehearsal, I was shooting because Veronica didn't know. I give you that as an example. You must understand actors. Some need a lot of work, for other ones you must use their natural gift and not their talent. Even people who are not beginners, there are those who are better the first take. And some people you must correct, and they like to work and be corrected.

We have a script, but we are always prepared for a sudden turn of events. You cannot change the dramatization of the thing, of course, because you need a set, you need actors. You need a great deal of preparation. But there is always a certain margin, you see, in which you can improvise—No, not exactly improvise, but collaborate with the set, with the players. I call that collaboration, not improvisation. You can't improvise and say, "I want another set or another actor." That's for film clubs, but professionals don't believe in it. You can improvise if you make a documentary, but with a big expense of a shooting, you cannot do that.

I was in America for about five years and made four pictures. There is a basic difference, because Hollywood has changed a lot, as you know. It had the best organization against the possible intrusion of genius. [Laughs] Everything was perfect except the possibility for an individual to express himself. That's why a talent like von Stroheim and all these great geniuses disappeared.

I had never any difficulties with the people over there, and I liked it very much. But I was not working like many of my American colleagues. I was not under contract. If you sell your soul, you have to pay the price. I was working more or less as an independent. That's why I made only four pictures in five years.

You came as a celebrated figure —

Oh, that means nothing in Hollywood. You are good only for your last picture. That's all.

It's much easier in Europe. If you are lucky enough to find the possibility of making a film. There is much less interference from what we may call the producer. Because the kind in Hollywood does not exist here. When I'm the producer of my own pictures here, I have no problem.

I always write my own screenplay. Most of them are my original ideas. I never consider myself as a director. Maybe I would be a very bad director if I had to direct someone else's script. I'm a writer who happens to direct.

Someone wrote about Charlie Chaplin, "Charlie makes the whole shoe, beginning to end." In a sense you do this in films, it's yours from beginning to end. There is a new crop of directors in France today known as the New Wave.

This name was given to young directors by the press. It means nothing. I think there are new talents, but there have always been new talents.

I disagree with some of them when they consider that film can be a sort of individualist medium of expression like literature. Being a writer myself, I was interested in motion picture precisely because it was a *popular* medium. To make an interesting picture for a few people is relatively easy. To make a bad picture for a lot of people is very easy. The great thing, the great problem, and the most interesting and new approach in art, is to try to make great things for the greatest amount of people. That's the solution Chaplin has found, and I would like to see a new Chaplin today. And not new, young directors who just want to be interesting for critics.

What is new in our business, what's fascinating, is precisely this possibility you may have of distributing emotion to millions of people. I would not like to see the motion-picture medium be for the few who consider themselves "intellectuals." The motion picture is a new form. Before the motion picture, the diffusion of art was limited to a relatively small amount of people. The great new thing was this: to make art for the great many. Not in the normal Hollywood sense of the word, but in the Chaplinesque sense. It seems to me the New Wave is working more for critics than for big masses.

More and more movies are being shown at home, small projectors. The time is coming when someone can buy a print of a film and can have it shown at home the way he has a painting on the wall.

Why not? Like you have records. If you were able to buy an old Chaplin or an old von Stroheim picture, that has been successful with the masses, but you would like to have it for your own, as your own property, it does not change.

Doesn't the film call for a gregariousness, a gathering of people in a theater—three, five hundred, a thousand. At home you see it by yourself. It's somewhat different.

You should never see a comedy alone. That's an old rule among filmmakers. If you have a new picture, a new comedy, you should never show it to a buyer or some prospective distributor in a small room alone, because you don't laugh alone. Laughter is a contagious thing.

I'm very, very interested in the TV, pay TV. I think that will happen some day. That's the great revolution of tomorrow. The first age of motion pictures was what we have known, theaters: you have to go to a theater. Second step was television. The third step will happen in five years, ten years, twenty years. But it will happen. Of course, that will change the aesthetic of film. The technique is different. If you make a picture for a theater where five hundred people are seated, it is not the same approach as if you make a picture for millions of people, more or less alone in the room.

Remember *Brief Encounter?* It was a very good picture. It was not a success in the big theaters in the States. I'm almost certain that if *Brief Encounter* had been shown through television to the public, it would have been a much better success, because it called for intimacy. It can be understood by a man and his wife, seated in front of that screen. It would be much easier than in a big theater.

Look at the history of the stage. When you had the Elizabethan stage—Shakespeare, and Marlowe and the others—they wrote their plays for the stage, for the kind of public. They would not, if they were alive today, write the same play in the same way, with the same technique. When show business is asleep, it dies. You must always hope for revolution in our business.

S A T Y A J I T   R A Y

1971

He is the Indian film director, best known for the Apu trilogy: *Pather Panchali, Aparajito, The World of Apu.* He is visiting

Chicago during a retrospective showing of his films, notably, *The Music Room*.

We are in the radio studio listening to a tape of an Indian actress-dancer recalling her experience during the Bengal famine.

"It used to be our practice that after the show, we would come out and appeal for whatever people could give to the starving people of Bengal. On one such day, in a very small village an old woman, maybe fifty-five or sixty—she was bent—was dragging a cow right into the auditorium. Before I could recover from my surprise, she said, 'Take this cow. It still gives milk, you know. My child, I have nothing else to give. Take it. I don't need very much milk. The village will see that I don't quite starve . . .'"

It was extraordinarily touching to hear that. At that time, I had just got my new job as an advertising designer, and I was living in Calcutta. Hundreds and thousands of people, from the villages, were streaming into Calcutta. I remember the railway stations were just jam-packed with refugees. People were at the point of death, or would have died in a few days time. We would come out of the house on our way to work and step across dead bodies, just lying all over the place. Ten, fifteen years later, I read this novel by a writer whom I admired greatly, Banerjee. He was actually living in a village at the time of the famine, and he had written the book from his own experience. This was around 1958, '59. And I decided immediately to turn this into a film. I couldn't find the right actors to play the parts, and all sorts of things happened. I went on to make other films. Finally, 1972, I decided that I had to make the famine film: *Distant Thunder*.

I feel my roots are very deep down in Bengal, I've been trying through my films to explore the history of Bengal over the years: the British period, the nineteenth century, independent India, the end of feudalism. The death agony of a particular class fascinates me. There's a poignance. One has to take a sympathetic attitude to something which is dying after so many years. *The Music Room* is a film which shows a sympathetic attitude to even the noblemen, who

were useless people, really. But to tell a story about such one character, one has to take an attitude of sympathy.

From his point of view, it's a major tragedy. It's the folly of trying
to cling on to something which is inevitably going to vanish. And
the new class, which certainly hasn't got the finesse, the culture as
we know it. These noblemen, though idlers, were great patrons of
music and the arts, and that is all gone now.

In this film, I was able to use the top musicians, classical musicians of India. The subject of class has fascinated me all along. The
fact that such contrasts could exist side by side, even today. This
conflict between the old and the new has been one of the major
themes of my films over the last twenty years.

Days and Nights in the Forest is about money, what it can do and
what you can do with it. And the small moral lapses that money
leads you into, that sort of thing. There is a very intelligent, beautiful
girl, who teaches this rich, young idler about civility and thought-
fulness toward those who serve them. At the end, he, hopefully,
becomes more conscious. It is a film of nuances, really. I enjoy doing this kind of thing. It's all half-shades and all between the lines.

This girl—by the way—has records of Mozart, Ravi Shankar,
and Bach . . . She's a mixed culture. This was very common with
the sophisticated class, you see. They buy things from the various
cultures, West and East.

I myself am a sort of product of two cultures. We've been ex-
posed to Western literature, the cinema has done a lot, the radio,
BBC has done a lot. You can't help it. You're part, not just of India,
but of the whole world now; the world has shrunk.

That matter of identity, that double consciousness appears again in
the movie about that mountain resort. The name of the film was*
Kanchenjungha.

Kanchenjungha. [An incredulous laugh] Where did you see that?
Very few people have seen it. It is about an ordinary middle-class
boy who needs a job very, very badly. He meets this aristocratic

---

*"Double consciousness" was a phrase W. E. B. DuBois used in reference to
African Americans.

chairman of five companies and he rejects his offer of a job, because he has found out this man was fond of the British, fond of his British title and of looking down upon revolutionaries and all the struggles for freedom. He just rejects that offer, saying that, "I would probably have accepted it if I were sitting in Calcutta in this man's office, across the table. But here, surrounded by these enormous mountains and the Himalayas, I felt like a giant."

The influence of place on character, of atmosphere, of surroundings. In your normal surroundings, in your humdrum, everyday surroundings in the office, in an employment exchange, you would be behaving in a certain way. But up in the Himalayas, where you feel big, you feel like a giant, you can do things. Maybe you'll regret it afterwards, but you'll still do it, as a gesture. It makes you feel good for the time being.

The trilogy: Pather Panchali, Aparajito, The World of Apu. *I remember seeing* Pather Panchali *for the first time, and I was bowled over. Aside from the story, it's your use of music — Ravi Shankar.*

He was a very close friend of mine. When I offered him the job, he was delighted, but he was too busy as a concert artist so that he could only come over for a day. He saw half of the film and composed the music at one go and recorded it.

Here is the universal theme. As the village life declines, there's the move to the city: This is everywhere in the world.

The village is coming closer to the city also because there are some city elements moving into the village. Now, in the village you find little radios, wireless sets, and a little shop where people gather. Maybe in about ten years' time, there will be a television set somewhere; one, maybe, in the middle of the village, and people would come in the evening. In fact, it would be very difficult to make a film like *Pather Panchali* today. It is only ten miles out of the city limits. I was there some five years ago and I couldn't recognize the place. It has been electrified, brick buildings have come up, everything has happened to it.

I have found working in the village at the time that some of the values have not been corroded, they're still there. The extreme generosity to a guest, for instance, a guest from the city. . . . You can go to a village, anybody's house, they will offer you a meal. On an hour's notice you will get a meal there.

They have very little themselves. A guest is treated as a god. This is in the Indian scriptures. In *Distant Thunder*, a very old man appears at the height of the famine, and the wife says, "We must give him a meal." The husband is changing gradually; he's clever now. He says, "No, he's a scrounger. I know he's come to beg, so we must be very cautious, we must think of our own meal." She says, "I'll go without it. I'll go without lunch, I'll go without dinner, but let's give him a meal." The husband is a priest, he's a schoolmaster, he's a doctor. He knows nothing very well, but he has status because he's the only Brahmin in a village of peasants. He goes to perform a ceremony to ward off cholera; but before he goes, he reads his book on hygiene and he performs the ritual. He says, "By the way, don't drink the river water, don't do this, don't eat food where flies have settled," you know, that kind of thing. He believes, in a way, in what we call progress and science.

Fine, excellent. But in the beginning he is a bit of a racketeer, because he's exploiting the ignorance of these poor people. At the end, when death, through the famine, comes to an untouchable woman, and nobody would touch her dead body, it is the husband, the Brahmin, who says, "I'll go and do something about it. I'll perform the cremation myself." So he is liberated enough to be able to do that. His humanity then emerges.

Back to Pather Panchali, *and that one stunning moment — it's with me even now, as we're talking. Apu, the small boy, sees it all. His beautiful little sister dies in her mother's arms. The father has come back with a piece of cloth, for a sari for the girl. The mother screams. We don't hear her voice. We hear Ravi Shankar's instrument. Not the sitar —*

No. It was a bowed instrument. A sitar is plucked.

It was a scream such as I never heard. Something out of a Francis Bacon painting. It was that lithograph of the Norwegian, Edvard Munch, The Scream. *I saw that as I "heard" that mother.*

It was a cry. We selected a particular raga for this moment. We made the instrument cry instead of the woman actually doing it. Sometimes it is more effective to do it that way. Otherwise, it would be too horrifying. It is more heartbreaking, raised to another level.

RAVI SHANKAR

1992

When Satyajit Ray asked me to do the music score, he wanted me to take three or four days at least. I said I'd like to see the film just once. I was so moved, it got me so deep in my mind. [He demonstrates on the bowed instrument.] This, it came to me spontaneously, the whole theme. We started to work from ten o'clock at night. I had everything in my mind. I told my colleagues, there was no need to write anything down. Only three of them—the flutists, the drummer, and the bowed instrument. We did the whole film in four hours and fifteen minutes.

When the little girl dies, the mother is keeping all her sorrow bottled up, but when the father appears, gives her that piece of cloth that he brought from the city for the girl, she breaks out. [He plays a brief passage. There's that damn catch in my throat again.]

Mr. Ray, in the second film of the trilogy, Aparajito, *there is another death.*

Apu's father dies in Benares, where he has been practicing as a priest.

At that moment, I remember those pigeons. They just flew—whoosh! As though life flew.

Yes, yes. At the beginning of the film, I show the pigeons assembling at a certain place where they're fed. You give them little grains and they start pecking away. The moment the father's head falls back on the pillow, whoop, the pigeon's go up flying. And it's the end of a chapter. It's also the end of a life, flying out. . . .

We come to the last of the trilogy, The World of Apu. *He is now on his way to becoming a writer. In Calcutta, he meets a girl, they marry. She dies in childbirth. His grief is overwhelming, as her love was. There was a matter of class here, too. Intellectual class. She, who had appeared so childish at first, has that understanding heart. He is lost.*

His grief. He abandons the son, doesn't even bother to find out whether he's living or dead, and then he abandons the novel. He wanders around, and then he takes a job in a coal mine away from everything, his normal surroundings. His friend finds him out and says, "You must go back and look after your son. There's no one to look after him." He says, "Oh, I've got a son? How old is he?" "Five years." "What's his name?" et cetera. He comes back home, finds the boy. An immediate sort of filial affection, a paternal affection grows. The boy rejects him in the beginning. And finally, he accepts him as a friend who's going to take him to his father. He comes back to responsibility. I believe in that. I don't believe in denunciation. The acceptance of responsibility. I believe in that very strongly myself.

2—Ways of Doing

FRANÇOISE ROSAY

1963

A well-appointed apartment in Paris.

When the elderly cabbie, hip and wise-cracking, realized whom I was visiting, he chortled. "I thought you were seeing Brigitte Bardot. Rosay. Oh la la." He rattled off the names of some of her films he had seen. Only Arletty, the beloved Parisian *titi** he admired more.

Rosay achieved international renown for her role as the mayor's wife in *La Kermesse Heroïque (Carnival of Flanders)*. In a Breughelian setting, it concerned the invasion of a Flemish town by the Spaniards in the 1600's. Intentionally or not, it was one of the earliest feminist movies. Her knowing, witty performance established the tone.

Even though she was coughing incessantly ("a bad cold"), her vitality and enthusiams were astonishing.

We did *La Kermesse* in German, too. I am glad you saw the French version. The German actor who played the Spanish duke was absolutely great. He dominated me. The French actor was good-looking, a good actor, but not great.

You know you never act alone. In life, if you have a strong husband, you don't react—or act—in the same way as with a weak husband.

My mother was very clever, much wittier than I am. But she was not a mother. She was an actress, my dear. My father was gone.

I was pretty much alone. I went to so many schools, in Germany, here, elsewhere. Every year, she changed her mind. One day it had to be Catholic, another time it had to be a rich one, then it was a very poor one. I saw quite a lot of school and I hated it.

Long ago, when I went to the acting school, I had to bring my

---

*Argot for a "child of the Paris streets," the most celebrated being Edith Piaf.

papers showing where I learned. When I had to go get them from the very Catholic one, I remember the feeling. You won't believe it, this place had that same smell, that same attitude. I could have set it on fire. Of course, I did not. I got my papers.

My childhood was not a very happy one, but it was full of fantasies. Of make-believe, you say? I liked being alone. I had dreams of being in a fantasy forest where nobody had ever been. I think you're born with a gift for acting, imagining. We had servants all the time. When my mother was away, the servants met in the big kitchen and I used to act for them. I was six. I would put on a show for them in the drawing room. One day my mother returned and found carrots, potatoes, and onions in her lovely drawing room. That stopped my acting career for a moment. Everywhere I went, the servants were treated like animals. When I was all alone with them, I saw how they drank tea. There was a piece of hard sugar hanging on a string from the middle of the ceiling. They had no sugar on the table. They put the sugar in their mouth, sucked it and then drank their tea. It was always on the string. Hygiene didn't exist at that time, you know. I found that really exquisite.

The sharing of sweetness.

Exactly. I went everywhere, hospitals and all that, and I was appalled at the way people were treated. In other countries, too. I loved Spain, yet in spite of its beauty and the kindness of everyone, I saw so many thin animals, thin people, sad people. I was ashamed of the steak I ate in that fancy restaurant when they looked through the window glass.

When I was five years old, I went to St. Petersburg with my mother. A French theater. It was owned by the czar. The businesspeople spoke German. In the shops in St. Petersburg, they spoke German. But the high-society people and the learned people spoke French, so they had to have a French theater. I went there later by myself when I was twenty. I played in the same theater as my mother had. We did a different play each week.

My mother worked for the great director, Antoine. Twenty years later, I worked with him. He taught us — I don't know how to say this in English — *rhythm* first, does that sound right? It has to feel very natural. He didn't want you to *look* like eating or *look* like you were making love. Everything had to be, to feel, like you really were doing that. When I was young, I had tremendous rhythm, maybe too much. The first time I acted for him, I showed so much rhythm, I destroyed the whole decor, the set. I pushed and the wall came down. He liked it. Without rhythm, it's no good.

In jazz they call it swing. "It don't mean a thing, if you ain't got that swing"—a Duke Ellington song.

In talk, it's the same thing. A form of energy. Some people don't have it. They shouldn't be actors. It's the same with music, of course.

I loved music. I played piano and I always wanted to sing. But my mother wanted me to be an actress. At sixteen, I went to drama school. I was there six years. First for acting, then for singing. I did some opera, too.

Music helped me a lot for film. Some actors say that cinema is difficult because you have to be in the mood right away. You have that, too, in singing. If you sing a melody of Schubert or Schumann, you have to be dramatic right away. Film is like that.

I prefer films to theater. Oh, I like the rehearsals for a play, but when you do it a hundred times, the same role, you are fatigued. I don't mean you're bored—just worn down. Not tired in a good way. In a picture, you do your best, work hard for three, four months, it goes everywhere and you have your own life.

In a play, you always have to prove yourself. Every night. You can be loved in one play and if you are bad in another one, you go down, you're nothing. It's an extraordinary métier, isn't it? Once a painter proves that he is great, anything he does thereafter is accepted. The snobs, or those who decide he's great, like anything he paints, even if it's not very good. On the stage, you must be a success every time. Especially when you're abroad, where they don't know you. I heard an English workman, backstage, say about me, "She's a pro." That was my greatest compliment. Then I know I can go on.

[I indicate an old photograph on the mantelpiece.] Is that Sarah Bernhardt?

It's Sarah Bernhardt in *Frou Frou*. She was very beautiful. She had lovely eyes. When I was a small child, five or six, my mother took me to see her. She knew my mother. It was during intermission, after the first act. I was touched by one of the old actresses—they surrounded Bernhardt, because she helped lots of them when they couldn't work. They were looking after her. She was in a wheel chair. At that time, the theater of Sarah Bernhardt was full of perfume. There was perfume everywhere, even for the audience. The old lady who attended Bernhardt told us to wait. My mother said, "Try to find something nice to say. Don't be stupid, as usual." I was completely dizzy from the perfume. Suddenly, the door opened and the old lady said, "Madame Sarah Bernhardt is waiting for you." Imagine. I was so dizzy, I tripped on the carpet and fell onto her lap. I never got to say the words. She smiled and said something nice to me in that wonderful rich voice.

When I saw her, she was very, very old. I attended a big gala in her honor. She arrived on stage in a wheelchair. She was surely seventy, seventy-two, in a blonde wig, with violets on her lap and furs, looking wonderful. She was pushed by a young nurse, who was at most twenty-eight. No makeup, no nothing. A good, but pale face. Bernhardt, of course, had much rouge and powder, which she applied so expertly. A little boy in front of me asked his mother, "Who is the woman who pushes her?" The mother answered, "Sarah Bernhardt's mother, of course."*

Since you were well-known in Germany, how were you affected by World War II?

Oh, yes, but you know then, at that time I was horrified because that was new to me. I acted in German pictures until '38. I was horrified by all that was happening. When I heard a French traitor, on the radio, speaking of collaboration with the Nazis, I was so furious. He used an assumed name. I walked up and down the rooms of my

---

*George Bernard Shaw, as a young drama critic, was asked his opinion of the two great actresses of the epoch, Bernhardt and Duse, who never used makeup. He said, "I prefer the Italian. Her wrinkles are her credentials of humanity."

house answering him. "Why don't you use your real name? Why are you hiding, you swine?"

My husband* said, "If you feel that strongly, why don't you say it on the radio? They know you in Germany." So I wrote my speech in French and Max Ophuls, the director, translated it into German. I didn't want it to be considered just anti-German propaganda. If you say, "You are disgusting, you are nasty," the people won't listen.

I spoke to the German mothers. "I'm the mother of three sons and my name is Françoise Rosay. Perhaps you have my photo on your table. As a mother, I speak to you." I told them what I had seen in 1918. I pitied them for their children who will be killed. For what? About Polish children being blond and Goebbels being black-haired. As for Aryan blood, how do you know who you are? I told them about the Jewish children and mothers in death camps. The insanity. The horror of it! "You'll pay for it. Your children will be killed. Why?"

I prepared for my talk like I prepared for a play. This may have been the most important role I ever acted. And it was *real.* The reaction was enormous. I was condemned to death by Hitler or maybe it was Goebbels. [Laughs]

When I was in Switzerland, during the war, I received a letter from Germany. It said, "Madame Rosay, stop talking to us. We are very happy." The friend, who delivered the letter, said, "Look under the stamp." We did. It said, "Bravo Rosay! Go on doing it!"

I made a number of such talks on the radio. After the war, I was invited by the German press in Hamburg to make a speech. I gave them some of my papers. It was an extraordinary feeling, being in Germany. But most astonishing was to hear what I had said a few years before being read by a Jewish woman who had been in one of the camps. She was a very good director of a theater in Hamburg.

During the Occupation, we had very little work and very little money. Fortunately, I remembered seeing Ruth Draper in her one-woman show in Berlin and in London. This was before the war, of

---

*Jacques Feyder, who directed *La Kermesse Heroïque*. He was Jewish.

course. I thought she was wonderful—doing all those different characters. So I tried it. I did it in France, in Algiers, Tunis. I escaped from the Vichy government there. I did it in London and for the Red Cross. It was a challenge, reflecting all the different personalities in one person.

Alexis Carrel, the doctor, said we are born with seven personalities and only one lives.* This is wonderful in the theater when all these other personalities come out. Actors are always a little mad, aren't they? We take the words of authors and say them as though they are our own. There's something crazy about it, don't you think? And I love it.

We're always playing our own life, but our own life is sometimes not rich enough, so we have to watch other people—to see how they live, how they think, how they react. Acting is believing what you do. You have to become inside somebody else. If you play the wicked person, you have to find out why she's wicked. You have to believe it, or you're not that other person. You are not really an actor.

At the same time, on that stage, you have to be two people. You have to become that other person, but you also have to be you, yourself, watching that other person. Because you have to be heard by the audience. If you cry, you have to think of your makeup, so it won't run down your face. Otherwise people won't believe in you. They'll laugh. You have to watch all the time.

In a New York theater, I was to play a hundred-year-old woman. I'd never met one in my life. The makeup man fixed me up. I had a white nose. I had black everywhere. It was not real. I was like a clown, like a Chinese warrior in the Peking Opera.

Luckily, I knew a French doctor in a New York hospital. I said, "You must save my life. Could you find me a woman a hundred years old?" He said, "Easy." When I saw that woman, she was wonderful. She was shouting like mad when I arrived in her room. She

---

*A French biologist who won the Nobel Prize in medicine in 1912. Later, his pronouncements and works, including one with Charles Lindbergh, became controversial.

was very bossy, very intelligent. She had been a doctor herself. Imagine what a fight it must have been for a woman, so long ago, to have become a doctor. Because the men didn't like this idea, did they?

She was so funny. "No, I won't wear that nightgown. It chokes me. It does not become me." She was marvelously furious. I told her, "What lovely hair you have." She said, "Too much." She had such wonderful eyes, she could see right through you.

Then I saw how age shows. She had wrinkles, but not much more than when you are seventy. Not going out much from that clinic, her skin was like parchment, gray. You could see the bones a little more on the arms, because then there is no fat there, no muscle. So skin and bone. Well, I was saved because I knew how I had to look. I knew then it was the real thing. In the film, *Le Grand Jeu*, I was an old tart and I had to be very slow. I said, "This part is written for a fat lady." I was thin at that time. I can't move slow as that, unless I have a reason. I said, "She has to be very sick or she takes dope." So the director gave me a little box of pills, little black things for a cough. The kind I'm using right now for my cold. I played the role very easily, because I made myself believe it was dope.

I also have to know how a person moves. What she does with her hand. A waiter doesn't handle money in the same way as the man who pays the check. The postman doesn't handle a letter like the man who sends it or receives it. The man who owns the pub doesn't pour your drink the same way you do at home. The work you do all day with a certain purpose gives you an attitude. This attitude has to be found.

And costume is of great importance to me. If you have wonderful shoes and sit comfortably, you probably have money. If you have ugly shoes with holes underneath, your attitude is completely changed. Your body changes, too. The way you move.

Adapt the dress of the person you play, adapt it to your body. Put on that dress, watch her behavior, then learn your lines. Then you believe and become the person.

I always remember the man who made my shoes. I was in an opera at the time. I gave him seats. When he came backstage, I asked him if he enjoyed it. He said, "Yes, it was good. But what terrible shoes!" Every one of us watches what he knows. The pianist watches you play piano.

Geraldine Page told the story of her dentist. She gave him tickets for Sweet Bird of Youth. *When he came to her dressing room after the show, she asked, "How did you like it?" He said, "Fine. But when that man opened his mouth in the second act, his bridge work was terrible. Who's his dentist?"*

It always comes back to reality, doesn't it?

There's something you once said about an actor: "He must be gifted, but not necessarily intelligent."

A gift has nothing to do with intelligence. I knew a wonderful actor who was perfectly stupid. One day a well-known actor died. We went to the church for the services. We were all standing outside. I remember it was raining. Suddenly, this man arrived. He was very important looking, white hair, a handsome sculpted face. He began to talk about the deceased and in two minutes everybody was crying. I said to him, "Monsieur, I see you liked him very much." I could hardly speak, I was sobbing so much. He said, "Me? I never saw the man in my life." [Laughter]

When I was young, I admired this wonderful actress. She looked like a queen and when she played one, you believed it. In real life, she was quite ordinary. She could hardly read and write. But she had a gift for being noble and wonderful. Of course, if you have intelligence and you're interested in music, painting, literature, all that, it is much better. You have so much more to call on.

Now, I'm spending my old age teaching young people. I like young people. It helps you to get old with some grace. When you're old, it's sad to have the feeling that you're not necessary anymore. Then you lose the reason for being. You say, "Why am I here? Nobody needs me." But when you give lessons to your young pupils, you help them not only in acting, but in life itself. Youth is not easy and life is difficult. I know, I've been through it.

RUTH GORDON

1971

In 1935 — or was it '36? — I saw her as the high-spirited, tragic-bound Mattie Silver in *Ethan Frome*, Owen Davis's adaptation of Edith Wharton's novel. She and Pauline Lord, as Zenobia Frome, knocked me out; Raymond Massey, as Ethan, considerably less so.

She has a distinguished track record on stage in *A Doll's House, Three Sisters*, and her British triumph in the Restoration comedy, *A Country Wife*. She created the role of Dolly Levi in Thornton Wilder's *A Merchant of Yonkers* (the basis for the musical, *Hello, Dolly*).

She is most celebrated, however, for her movie roles in *Where's Poppa?* and *Harold and Maude*. She is on a national book tour, promoting her memoir, *An Open Book*. She speaks at a breathtaking pace, one thought tumbling onto another.

I have to take you apart. That's all right, isn't it? You called me distinguished. I've lived the latter part of my life to prove that I'm not distinguished, damn it. When I played *The Country Wife* at Old Vic, the London critics called me, "a distinguished actress from America."

That's the most damning thing you can say about anybody. It's a kind of a poor soul who has struggled along, done everything right and just lived a sort of circumspect life. A distinguished actress!

So, how can you live that down? Well, you get in a film called *Where's Poppa?* When you do that part, no one *ever* calls you distinguished again. The scene where my son, George Segal, is trying to get in the house and put me out — I just say, "Oh, you can't do that, you have no idea how adorable he is." While I'm saying this, I pull down his pants and give him a good nice kiss on his bum, and the girl runs out absolutely terrified. That was a very nondistinguished thing to do.

You call yourself a visceral myth.

That was Thornton Wilder's phrase. He said, "The world believes in the visceral myth. They believe in fables of trouble and disaster, but something happens and it comes out all right in the end." So I said, "Maybe I'm a visceral myth." I've been doing this—since 1896 I've been alive—and I've been believing, and I've had troubles, worries, and horrors, and it all came out right in the end.

Beginning with a hard time, the whole of my life has been ups and downs, probably more downs than ups. I was born in Quincy, Massachusetts. I had a hard time because the doctor said I was dead and threw me away. Then I gave up a little cry and he said, "Ho, ho, ho," gave me a few slaps and they could hear me at the Congregational Church across the way.

The interesting thing about downs, once you've lived through one, once you've conquered it, you know you can do it.

I'm a very conceited person, I *believe* in myself, I think I'm always right. I'm so astonished in this book to find I've made mistake after mistake.

Thornton Wilder, who's played a big role in your own life and that of your husband, Garson Kanin, once said, "Get up early in the morning. So other people don't breathe up all the air."

Oh, no, he says—this was in Stockbridge—"I didn't say that, you did." I said, "No, Thornton, you said it." And he said, in a not-very-complimentary way, "Well, it certainly sounds more like you than it does like me."

In Quincy, they call me their best ambassador, and they're damn right. It's the 350th anniversary of Quincy and I'm invited to speak at the banquet. I can also act when I stand up in public. My father, not a theater person, said, "When you get up in a meeting, you've got to deliver the goods."

I'm sitting next to the master of ceremonies and ask, "When do I go on?" He says, "Right after the superintendent of schools." I think that's a good spot, they'll be ready for a little entertainment. More and more people come up and are introduced. I thought I'd speak about three quarters of an hour because they said, "We want to hear your memories of Quincy." Now heads of wards, heads of libraries, heads of so forths. It's getting late. I ask the emcee, "How long do you want my speech? He says, "As you can see, it's getting late." So I thought, just for a joke, "How about five minutes?" I thought he'd say, "Don't be silly." "Oh, my God," he said, "Would you really, would you really?" There was the look like a basset hound in his eyes, just despairing relief.

So now, a lady who's a very distinguished doctor from Quincy gets up and tells her story and everything. My husband said, "She wasn't very interesting." I said, "How interesting do you think you'd be on child diabetes?" I said to the emcee, "How about my taking two minutes?" He got right down on his knees on the dais, right in front of everybody. So my great speech was cut down to two minutes and, true to my father, I delivered the goods.

I reminded myself of Quincy. I was asked if the people of Quincy weren't worried when I decided to go on the stage. Didn't they think it would be wicked? I said, "No. Nobody except my Aunt Ada, who said to mama, 'For Ruth to go on the stage is just the same as for her to be a harlot.'" "Oh, that's horrible, that's dreadful," someone said. I heard myself say, "Listen, if you haven't tried it, don't knock it."

That was my two minutes of Quincy. And they *knew* they were in touch with show business.

In those early days, wasn't the actor regarded as something of a gypsy, someone not to be trusted by the townspeople?

Oh, yes, those one-night stands. Like Vermillion, South Dakota, population 2,000. I played hundreds of 'em. When you'd go up to the hotel desk to register, they'd ask, "Are you with the theatrical company." I'd say, "No, I'm traveling with Arnex hose." Saying "I'm from Arnex hose" was better than saying I'm in *Fair and Warmer*. Arnex hose people were supposed not to steal towels. There was a girl in our company who had a towel from every state of the union except Vermont, and she'd have had one from there, but they didn't have a theater in Vermont.

You, through the years, worked with some of the greatest. Edith Evans in The Country Wife. *Albert Basserman . . .*

Oh, yeah, in Eddie Robinson's film, *Dr. Ehrlich's Magic Bullet.* I played his wife. I had never heard of Basserman, though he was the sensation of Europe. He was a German actor who fled Hitler. He had the small part of the great Dr. Koch. Edward G. Robinson was Dr. Ehrlich, who discovered the cure for syphilis.

We *all* came to the studio that day to see Basserman act. I wasn't scheduled but I didn't want to miss this guy. Every once in a while there's a scene—it's what I call opening the window. Think of the greatest scene you could be tested in. I'll never forget that scene from *Ethan Frome*, when Mattie said to Ethan, "Let's die. Let's go down the hill together. Let's die, let's die, let's die." That was a test moment. Bernhardt couldn't have had a greater test.

At that studio, we were all waiting for Basserman's test moment. Ehrlich says to him, "Look through the microscope." You see, he's isolated the germ. Here's Basserman in a frock coat, wing collar, handsome, elegant, bearded. He looks in the microscope—does he believe this is it, or doesn't he? *What* do you do, looking in a microscope to show that a miracle, one of the wonders of the world has taken place? Do you say, "Oh, my God, oh, oh!" Do you remain silent? What *do* you do? Basserman stepped up, and he looked a long, long time into that microscope. And then he gave a sigh. He just went [a deep sigh]—and he knew—and *we* knew—that the cure had been achieved. You go to drama school, you have drama coaches, but only through life and the creative urge and a sense of genius can you do what Basserman did. That sigh said it all.

There's what I call Broadway acting. You learn how to do it and you do it fine and they laugh and they applaud—and two years later, they forgot what they saw. They don't remember a thing. Then there's acting that creates memory. I have a memory of Maude Adams in *Peter Pan*. That's the kind of acting nobody can teach ya. You've got to learn, you've got to learn, you've got to learn, and then you've got to forget what you've learned, just like you forget you've got a nose and eyes and a mouth.

How can I ever forget Pauline Lord? They Knew What They Wanted *was the first play I ever saw. 1925, I think. She was Amy, the young waitress who answers the ad of the old Italian wine grower who's looking for a wife. Richard Bennett was the old guy. I was about thirteen. It's about sixty years ago, but I still see this young woman appearing on that stage. She didn't do anything but just appear. And I was—*

You were knocked out.

And then, ten or eleven years later, I see her with you and she's the bitter, furious Zenobia who's making life so miserable for you and Ethan. And you both knocked me out.

Pauline Lord was the end of terrific. She could speak in a voice that you would think was monotonous. But it would reach the last corners of the gallery and wring your heart. I saw her the opening night of *Anna Christie*. She's drifting into the barroom in this brown, shabby velvet dress. All girls who were prostitutes in those days wore either black or red. You didn't believe what this girl created with just that . . . just that. Pauline Lord did nothing like anybody else in the world. And she had a great sense of humor in the middle of all that.

I don't value humor all that much. What I value is courage. How to hang onto it, how to get by the terrible moments everybody goes through in life every other day and how to live through it. If you call that humor, OK. I see the funny side thirty or forty or fifty years later. Believe me, at the time I wasn't seeing the funny side.

I always wanted to be an actress from the Year One, never thought of anything else. Once I asked Brooks Atkinson, the great critic, "What did you really want to be?" He said he really wanted to be a critic. I said, "Nobody really wants to be a critic." "Yes, I did," he said, "Because H. T. Parker was on the *Boston Transcript.*"

Me, I just wanted to be rich and powerful and sexy and have a lot of fellas and a lot of fame and I didn't know how I was going to do it on no money. When I saw *The Pink Lady* and all that dazzling going on, I knew I wanted to be an actress.

SIMONE SIGNORET

1963

Paris. One of the oldest buildings in the city. When you ask the woman sweeping the sidewalk where Simone Signoret lives, she cheerily indicates a French basement: 15, Place Dauphine. She lives in back of a bistro, with her husband, Yves Montand.

Hair in curlers and a plain wrapper in no way diminish her grace and womanliness. There are plenty of cigarettes and coffee; there's a memento from a friend, Picasso. In a couple of hours, there's a rehearsal of her translated-into-French version of *The Little Foxes*.

This house is almost 500 years old. It was originally a shop; we transformed it into a flat. That's why it looks so. . . . [Laughs softly]. François Villon may have lived around here.

You live with history.

It's true. Not only the way we live, but the way we think, also. The Italians live even more with history, and the Greeks even more than they. You Americans can't, because you came from somewhere else. You all had reasons and sought happiness in a new country, and so you are a newer people.

Though you had a fine reputation as an actress in Europe, it wasn't until your role as Alice in Room at the Top *that you became celebrated in the United States. Especially by American women.*

The men also, strangely enough. You can live perfectly well being unknown, even being an actress, but when I suddenly discovered people knew me through that one picture, I was very moved.

Why do I think it has such appeal? Alice was not very young. Alice was not very elegant. Alice was not very handsome. Alice was like a lot of women are or think they are. Alice had a love story, which a lot of women may have or dreamt they had.

I was stopped in the streets by middle-aged women who saw Alice as themselves. I guess I was reassuring them because I wasn't young any more. And there was hope.

Why did you choose Lillian Hellman's The Little Foxes *to translate and perform?*

To me, it's more than a family play or a money play. It's much deeper. It's about two kinds of people in the world. The Hubbards, a terrible bunch, who are going to get big at the expense of others, and those gentle ones, growing up and trying to stop them.

It's the attitude as well as the money. It was an environment I lived in as a child. We didn't belong there. We didn't have much money, but we had music, books; we were more inclined toward culture than our neighbors. The flat was a mess, the maid was always leaving, bills were coming in — the people in the building despised us because they were all very well off.

They had the same maid ten years. They had country houses. They had all that we didn't have. I was ashamed of it because it was not like the houses of my schoolmates. But it was a funny house. I discovered to my surprise only last year when I met some of my old schoolmates that they *loved* that house, its ambience. But I couldn't stand it.

When my mother went to pick me up at school, she looked just like the maid. She just did not care how she dressed, just anything. I didn't like that. I would have loved her to be more unnoticeable. I guess children want to have gray parents, gray and unnoticeable. Like the others. To conform.

What influenced me to change? Oh, just a little detail — the war. It was enough. [Laughs] It changed my views about conforming and everything. [Sighs] My God, we were asked to shut up and do as we're told and be very gray. That's when I discovered to conform was all wrong.

In Occupied France there was a very simple line between the bad and the good. It was as easy as that. It was a horrible time, but on one level it was wonderful because everything was so clear. Among the good there was an extraordinary mixture of people coming from all kinds of society — working-class up to the aristocracy. All kinds of political opinions were heard because there was a common enemy. For some people with out-of-fashion, passé patriotic feelings, there were the Germans, the enemy. All that crap. For some of the others, there were the Nazis, which was much more precise. On the other side, there were the bad ones: those who were Nazis and deeply, profoundly fascist. Or those who thought, "Well, they're here. Why not take them the way they are and try to buy and sell? Make money and live."

Now that I'm working on the *The Little Foxes*, it's obvious that the father of the Hubbards would have been one of those who collaborated. He was a man who would have lived very well during the Nazi Occupation.

If you think of the way some of these people in North Africa think, the way they've treated the Arabs during a hundred and thirty years.* I met a good number of them here. The way they talk, they sound just like Ben Hubbard explaining how their father and grandfather worked and made their money and were tough and hard in the place where they had just arrived. New Orleans. How good things were—low wages, no strikes. These natives happy to work for you.

I was about to say—somewhat melodramatically—that out of this crucible, the war and what followed, you emerged. Free association: I saw you and Yves Montand in the movie of Sartre's adaptation of Arthur Miller's The Crucible.

We first did it in Paris as a play. It was an enormous success. It was a tough, quick, fast, horrible story. All kinds of customers came. We had snobs and working-class people. We had the middle class. We had the young, the old, everybody. It wasn't only for the highbrows.

It was so wonderful, the sold-out houses, because this wasn't exactly a musical comedy. It was about life and death and conscience. It ran to full houses for a whole year in a huge theater. People came to see the play who hadn't been near a theater any time in their lives.

People who were used to seeing Montand singing and jumping and laughing and joking were curious to see him in a serious part, in a tragedy. They'd come after the show to talk to us and say, "This is the first time we saw a play." It was very moving.

---

*This conversation took place during the Algerian crisis in France.

They were sharing the action with us so much that on some nights, they were whistling. In France, whistling is not a sign of admiration—it's a sign of disgust. They were whistling at the judges, the villains. Poor Abigail, the bad girl, they almost whistled her off the stage.

Oh, that play was a wonderful experience. I'm a little annoyed to speak about the picture because Sartre did a wonderful job. Apart from the fact that he's so talented, he may be the most intellectually honest man I've ever known. Almost to a fault. That was the trouble with this movie. He wanted you to understand the reason why somebody does something. He wants to be fair even to enemies. I think the picture was too rich in this and in a way it was so complicated that the message wasn't clear.

The challenge to Proctor, the hero of the play, is to say yes or no. During the Salem witch-hunt, right? If he says yes, OK, his life will be saved, but his name will be dishonored and his children bear the name of a man who's cheated his conscience and his friends.

Françoise Rosay, an actress you admire, once said: "Acting is a gift and does not really require intelligence."

Sure. I know people who are great actors and are completely stupid in life. If you have talent and intelligence, you can have a very good career. But I agree with Mme. Rosay: intelligence isn't necessary. I'm stupid about some things. In mechanical things or in mathematics, I have no curiosity. For other things, I am not stupid. It's a relative matter, who is intelligent and who is not. Sure, there are some people who are complete idiots, but that's something else. Some actors are intuitively good, but off stage nothing is there. They may have things in their head, their heart, dreams they can't express in life and suddenly *phsst!* it bursts out and makes you say, "My God, where did he find that? Where did that come from?"

Actors are often told not to have opinions about things outside movie work and theater. You mean, I have no right to express my feelings? I'm not saying an actor *should* do this or that because everybody's got his own ways. If you can live without any interest in the outside world, that's your privilege. It just doesn't fit me. I was on a TV show called *Small World* with Ed Murrow. Miss Hedda

Hopper, and—a wonderful woman—Agnes DeMille. We were having a hot discussion. Miss Hopper said actors could have opinions as long as they had good ones. Miss DeMille said she agreed with Miss Hopper completely. I don't think they had the same interpretation of what was good. [Laughs]

I was in the middle, not being American. I made my own statement about what French people of my generation may be like. I wasn't born thinking about right and wrong. But it was brought to me during the Nazi Occupation when I was nineteen. So I got into the habit of thinking ever since. I don't think Miss Hopper quite made out what I was saying.

When I was in New York last year, I saw a lot of actors starting a big protest about the bombs. They were suddenly aware of the dangers of atomic bombs and they were organizing meetings. Of course, they were mostly criticized.

Most of the time you're told to shut up and just learn your lines. Don't get mixed up with these other things. Leave it to the people who know. But the funny thing is, when there's an election, they all come with cameras and want to photograph you while you're voting.

Just the other day, I said, "Why do you want to photograph me voting? Most of the time, you tell me, 'It's none of your business, learn your lines.' I don't see why twice a year you want to know my opinion, while the rest of the year you tell me to shut up." There's a slight confusion here.

3—Ways of Seeing II

IAN MCKELLEN

1986

He is in Chicago as a member of the National Theatre of Great Britain. It is a two-week run of several classics.

His one-man Shakespeare program, first performed at the Edinburgh Festival and subsequently on television, was regarded by critics as "a revelation."

My mind was full of Shakespeare and I thought I'd try an experiment before a hopefully indulgent audience. Not what Shakespeare is to the academics, but just to a working actor. To explain why I'm so fond of the man, who he has been revealed to be through his plays.

There are many problems about doing Shakespeare and getting in touch with the language, which is not modern-day speech. It's something you can train yourself to do. You've just got to sit down with a paper and a pencil and start marking the script and understanding how the rhythm goes and that sort of thing.

What's more difficult is utterly believing that Macbeth ever existed. How could that man exist? At some point in the play of human frailty, of self-disgust, of the essence of evil, what finally impels this man to say, "Tomorrow and tomorrow and tomorrow. . . . ?" What I try and do, in playing this character whom other actors have played with enormous success, is just try and think: Is there anybody alive today like him? Nineteen eighty-six, not 1604, when it was written.

Is there anybody in my experience, a friend of mine, perhaps, someone I read about in the newspaper, who has the elements of Macbeth? If there is that modern person, if he exists, then I can believe Macbeth exists. Therefore, I can make him exist through me.

Immediately, I had the not-very-original idea that Macbeth was

Richard Nixon. It didn't seem so far to go after all. The director said, "That's absolutely wrong. Macbeth isn't that man you wouldn't buy a used car from. Macbeth is John F. Kennedy, the golden boy, the man with the wonderful wife, the civilized people surrounded by beautiful people. The people who run a marvelous court, who you long to go and spend the weekend with."

Macbeth is rightly ambitious because he's clearly a good man. The play opens and people can't stop saying wonderful things about him and his wife. And his wife! She's delightful.

What you don't expect when you go to the Kennedys, of course, is to wake up dead in the morning. Macbeth and Lady Macbeth are like the Kennedys, only they went wrong. The Kennedys didn't go wrong, as far as I know. Macbeth's ambition overwhelmed him. He was the Kennedy who became president through evil means.

Who was Coriolanus? Who is the modern man who I can just latch onto as Coriolanus? He is a privileged man who comes from a patrician background where things are expected of one. He clearly was sent to the right school and protected from the realities of the world. This has turned him into a brilliant fighter. But fighting is rather a lonely job. It doesn't fit in particularly to be involved in politics. This is where we find him at the beginning of the play, just about to leave the world he knows fairly well to become a politician. What is it that makes this man who seems to despise everybody want to be involved in society at all?

I thought of John McEnroe, who earns his living as a great athlete. He doesn't kill people, he slaughters them. Or did at the time we were rehearsing *Coriolanus*. He appears in public in front of thousands of people. He clearly enjoys that. But he despises the people he's entertaining. That's rather like Coriolanus: he wants to be out there. He wants to be the star. But there's something in him that says, "I hate you all for making me a star because if I'm a real star, I don't need your approval because I know how good I am." I think that's behind all McEnroe's outbursts.

I get a kick out of the way your mind works. Most of us would never think of connecting Coriolanus with a tennis player, the one they called the brat. We're more literal-minded. Immediately, I'd think of a warrior, a war hero, entering politics. Eisenhower would never do. He, easygoing, trimmed his sails to prevailing winds. Precisely the opposite of Coriolanus.

You've got to be careful with that, though. If we reduced the play to the story of John McEnroe, it would be a libel on him and Coriolanus. It was just a little aid to me as an actor to make the leap of imagination and say, "Well, McEnroe exists, therefore Coriolanus exists."

Coriolanus can be and has been played as a right-wing play, with a pro-fascist attitude. It can be played as a left-wing play. In fact, Brecht wrote his own version of *Coriolanus* to prove just that. Our version in London was directed by Peter Hall, who is very middle-of-the-road in many things, including politics. He insisted on seeing it as an SDP play—the Social Democratic Party, midway between Labor and Tory.

As each generation goes by, different things become of interest. It would be intolerable in the 1980s, or, indeed, the twentieth century, to present *Coriolanus* without giving the tribunes, who are the elected representatives of the people, proper airtime to express their point of view. And to be taken seriously. In the past, I think those characters have been rather reduced, and therefore the balance of the story between the patricians and the people has been slightly knocked off kilter.

It may be hard to draw a political figure today to parallel Coriolanus. De Gaulle, perhaps, in the matter of stiff-necked pride, but that doesn't quite do it. It is so much easier to find opposites. Ronald Reagan comes to my mind immediately. Avuncular, charming, full of bonhomie, yet appealing, some would say, to the baser impulses of "the people."

And that's why Coriolanus has to die, because society cannot tolerate somebody who speaks the truth. [Laughs] Coriolanus's mother, a wise old bird, who has brought him up to be the man he is and has spoilt him outrageously, says, "Darling, you've only got to pretend. Just bow the head. Pretend."

The miracle of Shakespeare is the breadth of his humanity. That must always be an encouragement rather than a salve on troubled minds in the audience. I think you ought to come out of a Shakespeare play feeling uplifted, not pessimistic, even if it's been a tragedy. Usually there is some resolution at the end of the play which looks forward to the future.

I feel optimistic at the end of a Shakespeare play because, I think, my God, there once was a man named William Shakespeare, who knew it all. We as a people haven't changed that much since Shakespeare's time, we've hardly changed at all—if he can encompass in his mind all that we are, well, then, perhaps God exists. We do have the chance by reading his plays and seeing them to find out a bit more about ourselves. I feel the more we know about ourselves, the kinder we're going to be to one another.

What was that world Prospero envisioned? Forgive me for trying to exploit you at this ungodly hour in the morning in this radio studio, but [sighs] I'm part of that species he so understood. Taking advantage of you. . . .

[Laughs] Ahh. "Our revels now are ended . . . These are actors, as I foretold you, all vanished into air, into thin air. And like the basest fabric of this vision, the cloud-capped towers, the gorgeous palaces, the solemn temples, the great globe itself, yea, all which it inherit shall dissolve, and like this insubstantial pageant faded, leave not a rack behind. We are such stuff as dreams are made on. And our little life is rounded with a sleep."

I sometimes think that that's a description of the end of the world. Imagine a great city like Chicago, gorgeous palaces, solemn temples—the great globe itself, the name of Shakespeare's theater—shall dissolve, melt down, leave not a rack behind. And yet after that concept, Shakespeare takes hope. "We are such as dreams are made on." And here's a promise: our little life is rounded with sleep, you know. Perhaps it was Shakespeare's farewell to the theater.

JONATHAN MILLER

1968 and 1970

Trained as a neurologist,* he took to the stage in the satirical revue, *Beyond the Fringe*. His colleagues were three fellow alumni of Cambridge and Oxford: Dudley Moore, Peter Cook, and Alan Bennett. He has since become a theater director, notably of Shakespeare plays, among other classics. Since the time of these conversations, he has directed operas in unconventional ways, to acclaim as well as to controversy.

I moved into this matter of directing quite casually, really almost by accident. I enjoy it very much. It is totally absorbing. There are so many demands on your time and on your attention that you never have to think about what you're going to do next. This has always been a trouble with me. I've got a very low threshold of boredom. (I very easily become disturbed about what I ought to be doing at the next moment and I become very indecisive about which is the more worthwhile pursuit.) But as soon as you get involved in directing, all decision is taken out of your hands, because you suddenly realize that you have a play ahead of you in a month's time and you have a mass of problems, which have got to be solved.

I've been directing at Nottingham Playhouse, about 120 miles north of London. It's an industrial city with a long history: D. H. Lawrence, Robin Hood. Its actors are practiced journeymen, who are skilled technicians, who speak verse, who move well, who are well trained, who've been through the canon of the classics. That's the one thing I think which acting has in Europe, that it doesn't have in America — a sense of antiquity, of an enduring tradition. It goes back to the idea of troubadours touring in trucks and putting up their stands in marketplaces, performing for a populace. This sort of rough, tradesmen-like feeling about acting gives a certain ruggedness to the English theater, which is lacking in the American.

---

*His book, *The Mind of the Body*, had been adapted as a BBC-TV series, of which he was the host.

The audience is largely middle class. The whole tradition of the theater in the last hundred years has been very much a middle-class one. It must have been different in Shakespeare's time. It's very hard to say. There probably was a bourgeois, aristocratic majority, but there were always the groundlings, the townspeople. Shakespeare obviously wrote in a great deal of comic stuff which would satisfy them. And during Restoration, Drury Lane was quite a raucous, bawdy, turbulent place.

England and Europe have a tradition which goes back through the earliest days of Christianity, back to paganism. There's no feeling of paganism in America, no feeling of that rural primitivism, going back to a pre-Christian era. In America, it's primitive puritan rather than primitive pagan. America started as a rural Christian community. They were people who came from Europe. Nevertheless, they blew like seeds across the ocean and planted a refined form of Calvinist Christianity. Christianity has grown *around* the pagan oak like ivy. In England, you feel the old shadow of the golden bough, which goes back long before Christianity.

You have a feeling of strange, sort of shaggy-thighed, hoofed figures as phantoms on the European scene. America starts out as a modern country. There's the bright light of theological rationalism shining on your country. There's a marvelous description somewhere in Hawthorne, I think it's in his preface to *The Marble Fawn*, about the absence of dark, mysterious shadows in this country. The fact that everything is lit by the common light of day. There is no sacerdotal mystery about this country. Not enough shadows. One of the things about the English actor is that he's much more content to go along with the mystery of his own talent. He accepts it and allows it to bubble out on the stage, perhaps in deference to this pagan origin of his own craft.

There are no mysteries in the American theater. The marvelous thing about drama is the fact that it doesn't ever leave you in a state of *explained* enlightenment. I love the darkening mystery of the experience of a stage play. There's a programmatic feeling about American drama, that it poses problems which the play in some way proposes to resolve. The lovely thing about the traditional roots of the European theater is that it's not a question-asking maneuver. It doesn't set out to do anything. It's a demonstration of the mystery of being alive. It doesn't propose to suggest that this mystery can be solved in any way. It is a ritual. But it's a ritual which is intended to produce some sort of enlightenment. At the end of a play one should have a sense of rest, of state of settlement, of improved or enlarged understanding.

The bother when Americans do Shakespeare is that they are so subordinated by the reputation of Shakespeare, they're so impressed by him, that they put on great sententious, sing-songing voices. Rather as the English did, until, in fact, Peter Hall's company revolutionized the manner of doing Shakespeare. If Americans could rid themselves of that slightly vicarious respect that they have for Shakespeare, it's quite possible that they could do it in a way which would be very shattering and disturbing indeed. But at the moment, they have a hideous, ponderous reverence for it, and it ruins almost every Shakespearean performance I've seen. There are rather marvelous Shakespearean actors in this country, but they're not well known. The famous ones are, in fact, deplorable, I think — especially in *King Lear*.

I don't think age is the important thing about King Lear. In fact, if you play him too old, it blows the whole plot. If this is simply an old man who in his feebleness surrenders his kingdom, then it is just an enforced retirement. There's no tragedy in it except the very generalized tragedy of senility. What I think is interesting about *King Lear* is the idea of a man at the very end of late middle age, just approaching old age, who voluntarily, in the prime of his power, suddenly abdicates. The reasons he does this are very obscure. I suspect that he abdicates in order to buy love. I have a feeling that in some way this is what Lyndon Johnson was doing. And I see Lear very much as Lyndon Johnson's age. A huge, powerful figure, who has had gigantic political power all his life. Who's been able to manipulate the machine and bend people to his will. Who suddenly discovers, towards the end of his life, or towards the end of his effective, powerful life, that people no longer love him. And there is this sudden crisis that often occurs in late middle age associated with deep depressions, when people suddenly feel a withdrawal of love. And abdication sometimes becomes a desperate crisis gesture through which an attempt is made to purchase love, perhaps as pity. I will abdicate because you dislike me so much. Therefore, through pity, love comes. But then, following on from that, I will abdicate and then I will buy your love by giving you portions of the kingdom over which I held sway. And by this, I will purchase your love, which I feel slipping away from me. Now I think if one plays it in this way, quite suddenly Lear starts to vibrate and become very interesting.

If someone in the prime of his power unexpectedly abdicates his power, it shatters the whole social structure, the political structure. So long as a man is in power and is expected to be there for some time, there's a state of settlement. Envious perhaps, but nevertheless a state of settlement, of envious settlement. The fabric holds. All the lines of force are under control. It's in a state of tension. People are wishing to see the person deposed, but so long as he has the grip on the position of power, at least the position holds. [His speech quickens in excitement.] Quite suddenly, he lets his grip go, all the lines of force, all the threads, all the chains suddenly relax, and sudden, catastrophic disturbances of mutual position-holding occur. It's as if someone was holding a very, very heavy weight over a cliff along a rope—a very strong man—and quite suddenly he let go. Hundreds of climbers all in different positions on the other side of the cliff, all on this rope, and he just releases this. Of course, some fall, some grasp, some clutch at others. And in this sudden release of the political tension sustained by one man, you get a gigantic upheaval of social structure. This is exactly what happened in America. Within hours of Johnson's abdication, you saw this sudden catastrophic realignment of loyalties, of affiliations and alliances, and the whole thing produced a social earthquake.

Lear is also of the tragic failure of the purchasing of love. Of the fact that love cannot be purchased. Cordelia expresses this very, very early on in the play. The other daughters are not evil women at all. They are women who just simply follow the inexorable laws of nature and of the succession of generations, which shows that if you start to purchase—buy—love, you're doomed.

It's traditional to think of Lear as mad. His madness, in fact, is very short lived. What's much more important is the madness of his children. Regan and Goneril are the mad ones. Think of the extraordinary behavior of Regan and Goneril, both of whom descend, as Albany says, into the behavior of beasts that would devour themselves. I think that they are in fact frozen, emotionally locked people.

I remember you saying, speaking of Lear, that out of a certain madness, out of a certain topsy-turviness, a new kind of awareness arose.

Elizabethans realized this perhaps better than we did, possibly because they hadn't yet fallen victim to the straightforward clinical distinctions of the twentieth century in which madness is seen as something on one side of a certain line, which puts you beyond the pale, or into care. I think at that time, madness was like melancholy, was one of the conditions into which human beings could lapse, through which some sort of insight could be achieved. Melancholy could be an undesirable illness, but also possibly the prelude to inspiration. Olivier represents that. He used that as Orsino in *Twelfth Night* to some extent. I think they were interested in madness, they saw it as possibly being something which was a prelude to a higher form of insight. Obviously, they also saw it as something dangerous as well and risky and perilous. The nineteenth century saw madness as something intriguing and interesting. It's only now, or certainly until the '50s in this century, when we've dubbed madness an illness, a disease. And we therefore tend to dismiss what goes on in madness.

There's absolutely no indication to show that Lear was a great monarch at all. His status of power had nothing to do with a raging, magnificent creature at all. Goneril says early on in the play, at the end of Act One, "The best of his times have been but rash." This is a man who probably had no particular personal nobility of any sort. Certainly none to match his status as a monarch. This is what the play is really about, ultimately. Lear himself talks about it in the great mad scene on Dover cliff: robes and furred gowns hide all. But, and as he says, dogs in office are obeyed. The office makes the man, it doesn't necessarily alter him. It elicits obedience from those who surround him simply because the office was a sacred office. And people were impressed simply by the anointed officer.

What's the role of the fool, the man who can speak truth to power because he wears the mask?

There are all sorts of official statuses which can give a man authority to speak the truth. One is superior authority. He can say absolutely anything because he carries the sanctions of his office. Kings can speak the truth, scientists can speak the truth, heads of departments can speak the truth. The other way of speaking the truth is to have absolutely no authority at all, which allows people to ignore what you say, and therefore you're in a position to say what you like because it can be taken or left. The fatal position to speak the truth is in the intermediate zone where people are frightened for their jobs.

The clown has nothing to lose, and the king can never lose what he has—heads of departments can't lose because they're at the top of the pyramid. The fatal place to speak the truth is in the middle of the pyramid where you can tumble to the position of fool, while trying to get to the position of king. Therefore, you keep your mouth shut. This again is what Lear is about. Lear is about the two ends of the social pyramid. In the first mad scene, Lear crawls outside the hut and asks himself to feel what wretches feel. Then he looks at the bare, naked Edgar, and sees that this is what man really is, a bare creature. He's constantly debating with himself how on earth does this puzzling situation arise, such that an ordinary man can simply get into a smart-looking set of robes and with a crown, and be obeyed, and strip them all off himself and be neglected and mocked. The fool is really just another way of making the same point. It's interesting that the fool vanishes from the play once Lear is on the road to understanding these things. The fool is necessary as a device in the play to make Lear understand this.

There are different ways in which one can be at the bottom of the pile, and therefore speak one's mind freely. If one is to have the official status of being at the bottom of the pile, which is to be a fool who has no wits, which is a way of being allowed to be neglected, and therefore being allowed to say what you like—but really having the wit in an underground fashion.

There's nothing more shallow than dressing up Shakespeare in modern clothes. If a play is good, it is modern in its antiquity. I very much approve of shifting periods, but it must always be done with some attention to the effect you're going to create by doing this. Using the chess analogy for a moment . . . If you make your moves like the moves of the queen on the board, you have almost total freedom; you can move eight squares at a time and at right angles. You have too much freedom. If you're going to change time, it should have that rather cramped, limited, unexpected, quirky move of a knight: one forward and one to the side. The limited but unexpected move sometimes produces very dramatic results.

It's very hard, for example, to say what period Shakespeare's plays are set in, because, if they're set in any period at all, they're set in Shakespeare's period. *Antony and Cleopatra* was about a period of which Shakespeare had no direct knowledge, or even any indirect knowledge. Egypt had not been excavated. He had no idea what Egypt looked like or felt like. It should be played not in Roman and Egyptian costume. It should be played, I think, in Elizabethan costume, and I think it should be a masque, rather like Veronese's *Mars and Venus*. It should be perhaps slightly Venetian. And Cleopatra should be a great Venetian courtesan, a dusky lady. Also, it would be close to the core of what Shakespeare was doing. This thing is a great Renaissance masque on love and war and on the fading autumnal love of middle-aged lovers. This is a very Renaissance theme, the theme of the decay of youth. And these enduring figures that run through the renaissance of Greek mythology transformed and crystallized in the Renaissance imagination.

Your forthcoming production of The Merchant of Venice, *with Olivier as Shylock, calls for a nineteenth-century setting.*

Usually two sources of ideas determine how the play is going to be done. One is a fairly large-scale moral notion—this is a play about whatever. Like in *King Lear*, this is a play about rank, authority, and parents and children.

Here, in *The Merchant of Venice*, of course, I'm very anxious to avoid a dramatic stereotype which has crept into the play and ruined, in the end, accuracy, and dramatic effect and cogency. Shylock has always been seen as a shuffling, gabardined, ringletted, mittened figure, rubbing his hands in glee over his ducats. With the result that he becomes almost a figure out of a medieval morality play, or out of pantomime: something carved on the underside of a choir stall. A completely medieval demon, really. And while this is useful in a medieval morality play, in those curiously rounded, robust, and substantially real plays of Shakespeare, that sort of character has no place at all. One has to try and find some genuine Jewish character. There's the additional problem of trying to find a character that is not immediately, outrageously offensive to a Jewish audience. In the light of the persecution of the Jews, they've turned him into a sort of shiningly virtuous character, simply the victim of anti-Semitism, which of course he is, but as all victims of any persecution are, they often become nasty as a result of it. And virtue is not his only characteristic. His greed is relatively unimportant. That's part of the stereotype of the Jew. I think that in his particular case, the interesting thing about him is his insularity, his patriarchal tyranny, his absolute failure to understand that his daughter could possibly marry someone outside his own community. Shylock himself is tyrannous in this connection, and I think this is part of his vindictiveness in court, wishing to finally get his pound of flesh. . . . I believe it does start as a joke. It starts as the rather pathetic attempt of an outsider to wager and be in with the jockey club aristocrats, but becomes a grim, serious thing when he sees his daughter robbed and taken away from him by the gentile community. A more accommodating intelligence would have let him understand that this wasn't robbery.

You see Bassanio and Antonio as a couple of sharp operators.

I don't see them as operators. I see them as a homosexual couple. They're very much really like Oscar Wilde and Lord Alfred Douglas: this treacherous young lover, who could go anywhere and this rather sad, middle-aged crypto-homo, agonized and pained by the infidelities of his young lover.

I don't like changing the period of Shakespeare enormously, but I think in this particular case it's a shift that works rather well. I think if one sees it in the Venice of the 1890s, you get the overtones of the Dreyfus case. You get the drab, dingy feeling of industrial capitalism, of fortunes that are based on dingy, oppressive factories in Milan and Turin, and of money made on the backs of the nineteenth-century European proletariat. It is a play not just about the Jews and gentiles, but about money and about the exclusiveness of the status conferred by money, and the even greater exclusiveness of the status conferred by aristocracy, which would exclude that conferred by money. The way in which the parvenu is looked down upon by the person of noble birth. The way in which, for example, the Rothschilds had to struggle to gain acceptance, simply because their money was new. Money has to be brewed for several years before it's accepted.

To pick up on the chess analogy, you made that unexpected, quirky move, setting Shylock's Venice in the turbulent nineteenth century, yet it seems appropriate. And so in your forthcoming production of The Tempest, *your Ariel is as black as Caliban. . . .*

This idea is based on the work of the French anthropologist Lévi-Strauss. There's a description of the fatal impact between European civilization and the primitive civilizations of Africa and South America. It seems to me that the beauty of *The Tempest* lies in the accurate way in which it describes this impact. It isn't just, as it were, a neocolonialist or anticolonialist tract. That would have been an awful way of doing the play. It seems to me that it's got all the beauty and weird mystery of trying to describe the collision of two incompatible cultures, one of which finally destroys the other. I think that both of these figures, Ariel and Caliban, represent the two forms of indigenous native culture. For example, the reference to Sycorax, Caliban's mother, is only as a figurative mother. It's a reference to the mythical mother of all the natives of that area. In fact, all myth systems refer to the great mother, or the mother of the tribe. It's a totemic reference and not an actual lineage.

As a postscript—something seemingly unrelated, yet, I've a hunch, related—your BBC film version of Alice in Wonderland *caused a stir, pro and con.*

I saw the book as a prose version or a gloss upon, although obviously not conscious, Wordsworth's immortality ode and on the sense of the fading vision of childhood, and of the sense of the transcendental which the child still has and which fades with old age. Wordsworth makes this very poignant, of course, in the immortality ode when he says that "the glory and the freshness of a dream and the things that I have seen, I now can see no more." He gives the impression that everything was once bathed in a dew and a radiance which as the hot sun of maturity comes up somehow dries out and becomes sapless and worthless.

Alice was a Victorian child of a certain period, yet the music you used was Ravi Shankar. There was a lazy, almost dream quality to it.

That was why I chose Ravi Shankar as the composer. I'd always had in mind something about this drowsing, insect-laden air of the English summer. A sense of almost overripe heat which is just before the autumn comes. And the leaves fall.

The end of innocence, too.

It's there, if you read it. It's there in Carroll's poems written before and after the book. People don't attend to these things at all. People are very careless in the way they read the text. They think it's just a jolly fairy story, so why tinker with it? People should read the text and read things carefully. And not assign things to rigid categories. Things are not what they seem. Works of art are not what they have been settled to be. The text should be read, and all the attendant texts should be read, and the period should be consulted. And quite suddenly, the thing will appear for what it really is. And quite clearly it is a lonesome academic bachelor's cry from the heart of the loss of vision, the loss of innocence, and of the horror of approaching middle age and then death. *Lear* and *Alice*. There is a common denominator in that both of them are concerned with growing old. In both of them, there's the same sort of structural theme in that a curiously disheveled odyssey takes place. Lear wanders across the blasted heath of his own imagination. And Alice wanders through this dreamland in order to discover herself, and lands up in the trial. In the end, Lear has to make the same journey through the storm, through the turbulence of the blasted heath, in order to discover the folly of what he's done.

As I'm about to take off and catch that damn plane, it's one man's vision we're talking about, yours.

In the end, that's all that one can ask of an artist. Whether he sees something that no one else has seen before. We're all looking at the same material: we've looked at it a million times before. The fabric of human consciousness and of human existence. This stuff passing in front of our eyes every day.

I can't help but think that you're a doctor schooled in medicine. Neurology was your interest. Do you see a connection?

I never felt that this was very much of a diversification. I think that medicine is very much the same sort of thing as the arts. The practice of medicine, of course, is a concrete task that has to be carried out, and you have certain jobs to do: therapy has to be handed out and patients have to be rehabilitated and so on. That makes it very different from the arts. But underneath it all, there's a common factor in that they are both concerned with just the strange, rather mortal material which comes into existence, has a brief span, and then rots. And both the arts and medicine are concerned with this rather perishable material. So I don't really find any sort of a dichotomy at all. The science of medicine is concerned with analyzing the perishable material, finding out why it perishes, finding out if you can delay the perishing. Art simply comments on the perishability and on the agony of the perish.

4—A Touch of Shaw

SYBIL THORNDIKE

1962

We're sitting in a dressing room at the Hippodrome Theatre. A cold, drizzly Saturday afternoon in Brighton-By-The-Sea, some sixty miles out of London. Dame Sybil, a doyenne of British theater, is making her debut in a musical, *Becky Sharp*. It is a pre-London tryout, set for the West End in two weeks.

I was eighty, week before last. I don't think actual years make that much difference. Oh, I've done some odd bits of singing in plays, but I've never been in a musical since I was an amateur. [Laughs]

Sense of discovery? Well, I'm a very strong, healthy person and that gives you a certain kick in life. I'm interested in so many things. My work is my main interest in life. I come from a family that was always trying to find out about things. Naturally, I'm going to keep on finding out and I'll keep searching a lot more when I've passed from this earth—somewhere else. [Laughs]

In a way, all of life encompasses theater. What everyone does in life, somehow you express in theater. If I hadn't all these other interests, I think there are certain roles I couldn't play. I would never have been able to play Hecuba in *The Trojan Women* if I hadn't been passionately against war. The very big plays belong to contemporary life. *The Trojan Women* was against one of the most unjust and terrible wars. And yet something heroic came out of this cruelty. I've been a pacifist all my life, ever since after the '14 War. I'm very much against force and violence. There was a funny thing in the paper the other day: Isn't there a cause for which you'd be willing to die? Yes, lots of causes for which I'd be willing to die, but there's no cause for which I'd be willing to kill, to commit murder. That's an entirely different matter.

Oh, yes, I was one of the women's suffrage body. I was never chained to any railings, because I was working all the time. [Laughs]

It was my husband that twisted me to that.* When I joined the theater in Manchester—it was the first repertory theater in England—in 1908, I met my husband. He was a flaming socialist and women's suffragist and everything. He was shocked and horrified to find that I wasn't interested in politics. My goodness, I had to pull up my socks because I rather fancied him. In three weeks' time, I was taking the chair at suffrage meetings. [Laughs]

Before I met him, I was an ordinary young woman, brought up as a good old solid conservative in a clergyman's household. I was always interested in religious things, because, naturally, we were brought up in that atmosphere. My father was a parson and I absolutely worshipped the ground he walked on and thought whatever he said was straight from God. I wasn't interested in politics at all until I met Lewis and he was so frightfully keen and I fell for him, bang. [Laughs] We were married a few months after we met and I've never looked back. I'm a socialist now. [Laughs]

Of the many roles for which you have been celebrated, we immediately think of Saint Joan. And your association with George Bernard Shaw.

Joan was an extraordinary creature, wasn't she? Her passionate faith, her passionate Christianity. And yet she was this amazing general. Oh, I've got no sympathy with her violent military things, but she was a pioneer in her age. As one of the generals of the time said, "She wants us to use the artillery in a way we never thought of before." It's the way they use it now. She was a great military inventor as well as a mystic and a saint. *Saint Joan* was the greatest thing that ever happened to me in the theater. And for my own life as well. She said and did so many things that I felt so deeply about. I think that's probably why Shaw chose me. He wrote the play when he found that I could do what he wanted.

Was it the passion of Joan that caught your fancy because of your own passion for life?

---

*Sir Lewis Casson.

I think it was. In a way, it symbolized everything I'd ever felt. I felt to get inside a person like that gave me an enormous stimulus to *doing* things.

Shaw directed every one of his plays that were done for the first time. Always. He was a *wonderful* actor. He could act all the parts better than any of us. In reading the play for the first time, he would act out all the roles. It's an extraordinary thing, he knew the tune of every sentence. It was like conducting an opera. I could go through *Saint Joan* now and know the exact tune of every sentence: where he made his pauses, where he went up, his inflections. He knew exactly what he wanted and he wouldn't pass it until he got it. As though it were a piece of music.

The theater is a musical thing. I'm a musician myself, a pretty fair musician. I wanted to be a concert pianist. I would still rather be a concert pianist than anything I can think of.

Outside of being an actress. . . .

No, I'd rather be a concert pianist than *anything*.

I play a bit of Bach every day when I'm home. I can't do it in Brighton because I haven't got a piano. At home, when I wash up the breakfast things, I go and do a half an hour of Bach. It does something for me mathematically. Its precision. Its wonderful construction. Its solidity. I think Bach is the nearest approach to God Almighty I've ever met on this earth.

No wonder Shaw chose you for his Joan. I understand he tried something revolutionary with dialect.

No, it wasn't really revolutionary. He knew that she was a country girl and couldn't speak in the elegant language of the period any more than he wanted me to speak in the elegant language of London—which is not all that elegant, anyway. He said, "I want you to be a country girl. I should prefer it a North Country girl." So I sort of made a dash at it. I know the north very well—some sort of not quite Lancashire, but a broad northern country accent. Shaw saw the French Joan as the universal country girl. She would not have spoken in the elegant French aristocratic way.

The new playwrights? Osborne, Wesker, Pinter. I think they're terrific. Pinter has written a classic in *The Caretaker*. He cares for every syllable to be just right. He's as meticulous as Shaw was. Oh, Shaw wouldn't let a thing pass. If you missed a comma, a metaphorical comma, he'd be after you. He liked you to use a lot of notes. And *clarity*. He hated muddled speech. He was such a magnificent speaker himself. That's the only thing I do regret in our modern times. Our theater is *very* alive, tremendously alive, but the speech of the younger generation . . . they want to sound so much like the man in the street.

Theater must be larger than life. I think we're finding new forms for the theater. Shakespeare's theater was a new form after the Greeks. We're all built on what came before. We should build on the Greeks, we should build on Shakespeare, we should build on Ibsen and the fine early twentieth-century writers.

In theater, you have to play all sorts of people that you wouldn't want to know in real life. You've got to find out why you're like them. You've got to *be* like them. You've got to find out how, given other circumstances, you might have been them.

There's a fine spirit of growth in young people today. I think it's an exciting new generation. Stupid ones do violent things, but that's only an excrescence. A lot of them haven't fervor because they came from tired parents, who were tired of wars. I wouldn't mind leaving the country to them. They might do better than the old ones.

[A voice is heard at the door.] That is the half hour. I'd better go now. Perhaps, one more question.

Is it true that your husband is teaching you chess these days?

Yes. I just learned chess this summer. And it was partly because my husband's eyes have really gone bad. I read aloud to him, but his hearing is going. He's having a rather stupid time with hearing and seeing, though his mind is so alert. He said, "What shall we do?" I said, "I'd like to learn chess." I'm *thrilled* with it. It's the most *exciting* game. I shall never be an expert, but I love to do it. There's always such search and discovery. I think search and discovery of new things is the most exciting experience in the world. I'll go on searching and discovering new things. Then, when we come to die, we'll find something else, I hope.

ROBERT MORLEY

1986

Now, where else would Robert Morley be but in bed? Where else would he be trying to make it through the day, when life, though for the most part amusing, may be, at times such as this one, a bit tiring. While visiting Chicago, "flogging" his book, *A Reluctant Autobiography*, he caught a cold. He is best known (aside from his British Airways television commercials) for his roles as Sir Andrew Undershaft, the wealthy, aphoristic munitions maker in the film version of Shaw's *Major Barbara*; and for his portrayal of Oscar Wilde.

I have enjoyed my life. Something will, I suppose, go wrong. Yes, it's been lovely. It's no good pretending it hasn't. I hope that if things go wrong now, I'd have the grace to admit that for sixty years, at any rate, the sun shone at my back. Today, as you see, I'm frightfully brave giving this interview from my sick bed, because I've got a bit of a cold. I believe in cossetting myself unduly. If I have a cold, I go to bed for three or four days.

I love bed. I had an arm twisted in bed for seven years, and then got up and went around the world. Of course, in those days there were more servants to bring you the food and things. But it was nice, wasn't it? Just went to bed for seven years.

You're not opposed to an egalitarian society, are you?

Ah, now. Egalitarian means an equal society. I'm a Labor boy myself. I'm very left, you know. I know you see me in this beautiful suite. I'll tell you a secret. It's not paid for by me. It's paid for by my publishers. So I thought, well, there's a bed, why not go to bed in it.

For a moment, I thought you said deathbed, because at the very opening of your autobiography, you said, "What a pity we can't start with my death."

If you read a book about someone who had all these marvelous things happen to them, or they made a fortune, or they climbed

Everest, or sailed around the world, and then they're dead when you're reading it, you'll feel a little bit better. But I can't die just to improve the sales of my book; that would be unfair.

My mother was a conformist. She believed in the status quo. She believed that a good servant of God was a good servant about the house. He was a middle-class God. My father was a gambler. I've inherited, I'm happy to say, his gift for gambling and his love of it. He did teach me that. It's a useful thing to have.

Your book is dotted with aphorisms, Morleyesque aphorisms. It's good out-loud reading.

Do you know I believe I'm better. I really am better. My cold seems to have gone. I think I'll get up, walk around the town.

There have been considerable changes in England since you first broke in as an actor —

It wasn't a happier country when I was young. I would go round the provinces of England and see a lot of misery and unhappiness and children without shoes. I was talking to a fellow who had been all his life a teacher in the East End of London, which is the slummy part. He said, "In the old days, I used to look at them coming to school and wondered if they'd had a meal. Now, under the health service, if they look at all peaky, I can take it up with a doctor, I can send them away for a month, I can see they get special food. And the consequence is they all work hard." I'm not a great believer in education, but I think it's nice to know that when they're sitting in class they're not hungry, don't you think? I like socialism, you know. I suppose we mustn't say so!

Is it all right to sip a little medicinal breath? We're not in a dry state, are we? I went down to Richmond, Virginia, you know, and got into deep trouble.

Is it all right to wrinkle up my nose and force a little brandy down my throat? For my health, you know. It's very important to keep fit.

I'm not really fond of schoolmasters, are you? When I became an actor, and got a bit well known, they asked me back to school. I said I'd only go back to lead a revolution if I was assured the troops were within the citadel. The man wrote back and said, "I'm sorry you feel such antipathy toward our school because I taught you French, Morley." I was able to close the correspondence: "I know you taught me French and I still don't speak one word of it!" It wasn't really his fault at all. But still, I had the last word, and that's a very important thing to have.

No, it wasn't brutality, but of course corporal punishment was a great thing in British schools, and still is, I'm ashamed to say. Do you know that the British teachers voted the other day to retain the birch? This is the sort of people the school masters are. Given half a chance they'll beat the children into insensibility. Disgraceful, isn't it? You don't hit children here, I hope.

It was Shaw who said never strike a child except in anger. He's absolutely right. If you lose your temper with a child, giving him a great clout on the ear doesn't harm. The schoolmasters in England very often were sadists, a lot of the schoolmasters were. I went to British public school, which is really a British private school. In the theater you had to talk like me when you were young. If you didn't talk like me, you didn't get a part. Now the last thing they want is anyone who speaks what they call "posh." You have to have a dialect or an accent, a regional accent to get on, and preferably from Liverpool.

You quoted Shaw a moment ago. You were Sir Andrew Undershaft, the witty munitions maker in Major Barbara. *Did you know Shaw?*

Yes, I did. He was a god to me. He taught us at the Academy. I remember the first day I ever saw him. He came into a room full of nervous students. He looked at us all and he said—he had a beautiful brogue which I can't imitate—"I want you to watch very carefully while Bernard Shaw, the great Bernard Shaw, takes off his overcoat." He was sort of setting himself up and us. He was, like all great men, a very simple man, a very enthusiastic man. He overpraised our efforts to act his plays. Of course he was really funny, really funny. And when you sometimes see the plays that they put on now containing a message, you'll remember how Shaw always wrapped it up in a delicious plum or a sugar-coated something. Take *Major Barbara*, what he says about poverty. "The greatest of all sins is poverty; it forces us into our natural cruelties." It's a marvelous speech. It should be blazoned across America on road sides because it's what's wrong. He's absolutely right: it's fear of poverty that makes people unpleasant to each other.

It forces them into unnatural cruelties, the rich. Oh, it's a marvelous speech on poverty; it's a marvelous speech and it exactly sums up . . . This millionaire when he went to the slums and saw it all, he said, "Well, I'll take the people and give them a good job and an income for life, and their children will be pounds better and heavier, and they'll be Methodists before the year is out." It was rather good, that. Undershaft may have been clever, but I don't think he was truly intelligent. Actually, Shaw saw if you give a man a house and a certain amount of security, he will stop beefing about his lot with the people above him and start bullying the people underneath. In a way, what he said was true, but he was rather wicked, too. I don't think Undershaft is a philosopher; he's an arms manufacturer, and he takes the world as it is. His great thing is not to be shocked by human behavior. I don't think Undershaft was a very admirable character.

I may have a little medicine now. Will you share some with me?

It was Oscar Wilde who said, "I put my talent into my life." Of course, he put his genius into his life and made an awful mess of it, which is rather sad, really. I think I was influenced by his remark. I thought, have a good time while you're at it, otherwise there's no point in doing any of it.

I loathe people with their briefcases hurrying about. That's the only moment I'm unhappy in America; when I get into the elevator in the morning and there are five grim gentlemen with their little briefcases. I wonder what they're thinking about. They're looking as if they're going to sell something improbable and work too hard all day. It's eight o'clock in the morning and they resent stopping at a floor to pick somebody up. You can see it in their faces. They didn't want to stop at the ninth floor. They wanted to shoot straight on and get on with their boring, laborious, and hopeless tasks of whatever it is. ·

Did playing Oscar Wilde influence the manner in which you talk?

I was a very sort of unattractive, fat child, who couldn't protect myself in any sort of field of play or work, and I developed a waspish, rather unpleasant tongue. I found I was more accepted by the community. I wasn't quite so unpleasant when I talked. I think I learned conversation as a sort of weapon, and it's not a bad thing for a child to do if he's unhappy, because it's really good to be able to strike back with words. If people want to insult me I can get in and insult them right back.

I'm never worried about children who are unhappy at school, but I am worried about how unhappy they are in their families. As long as my children haven't liked school, I've always smiled, because the child that conforms to school conforms to life, and there's nothing more gloomy than somebody who conforms to life. You should be constantly protesting and shouting and making a nuisance of yourself. I love difficult children. I love the British child who grows his hair and says, "I'm not going to look like my father. I may look more like my mother, but I don't mind that." I like children to protest. This awful way that parents always want to try and teach their children things. For instance they say, "I'm going to teach my child the value of money." There's no value in money. The only place where money is no good is in a bank. You should never save a penny; it's a great mistake. I come of a theatrical family. We spend everything we've got. Because if we haven't got the money we go on working.

Do you remember any of your encounters with Hollywood tycoons?

It was marvelous being in films in those days. Norma Shearer, the star of the film I was in, had a private orchestra on the set. Five musicians who would play any tune that anyone wanted. Fancy going to work at eight o'clock in the morning and having this string orchestra and you'd say, "Play me that bit that goes dum de dum de dum." Or "Play me 'Tea for Two,'" or something. They'd always play it. Then if the director thought you weren't acting very well, he'd have some sad music if you had to be sad. Oh, it was super.

When I had finished the film I was given lunch in great splendor in the executive dining room. And I thought, I own this studio. Louis B. Mayer said, "Now, Mr. Morley, we've given you a great break and you owe it to us next time you get an offer to let us better it." "Yes," I said, "Uncle Louis." I didn't call him Uncle Louis, but he's an amusing man. The best thing he said to me was, "You know, this industry has only given one artist to the world—Greta Garbo. Unless you count that goddamn mouse." He said, "Let me know if ever you want to make a picture in Hollywood."

When I finished my play, I said to my agent, "I'll write Uncle Louis and tell him I'm available." And he said, "Are you raving mad?" I said, "We don't have to play hard to get with Uncle Louis." I wrote him a letter saying, "Dear Uncle Louis, you may remember, you did ask me to let you know. Well, I am now available for a film." I didn't hear for three months, and then we got a letter from the assistant to the assistant to the casting director saying, "If there's anything, Mr. Morley, that we can offer you in the future, rest assured we shall not forget you." My agent was right, you see. I learned never to play it cheap. When I used to put on plays myself, if the actor came in and said, "I think this is a very silly play, I couldn't possibly do it," I tried to get him always. When one came in and said, "Oh, what a marvelous play; I'd play it for nothing," he'd be out at once.

I enjoyed Hollywood in those days. Well, who couldn't? We ran the place. We were the kings of Hollywood. We had little numbers—we rang our people whenever we got into trouble. Oh, it was lovely, lovely.

I wrote my first play when I was quite young—and miraculously, it was accepted within two days. It had Rex Harrison, Margaret Rutherford, A. A. Matthews, and Sybil Thorndike in the cast, and it ran three weeks. It wasn't a very good play. *Edward My Son* was for me a lovely play. I based it on a man who was head of Imperial Chemicals in England, a great industrialist. I had met him and I was rather fascinated by this jolly extrovert who at the same time was a little bit of a robber baron. I wanted to show up the fact that these great tycoons didn't have time to bring up their children properly. But, of course, when they saw the play, everybody wasn't worried about the child. All they wanted to be was the great tycoon. So as usual, when I give a message in a play, it goes undelivered.

I think this is a business in which actors either age overnight or don't age at all. And I'm lucky in my mother-in-law, Gladys Cooper, and in Sybil Thorndike too; they never got any older. They stay about forty when they are seventy-five. They've goth got a lively mind. This is absolutely true. They never look back, never say, "I was a great star once." It doesn't interest them. What interests them are things that are going on today.

Leonora Corbett said something wonderful to me once. "There's one thing to be said for getting on; it enables you to drop your old friends." I knew what she meant. You've known so many people, but once you're a success you're so boring that they refuse to come up to you. Success and failure, as Kipling said, are two impostors.

Poodle, I remember, was a taxi dancer. I was in love with her. We drifted apart. I didn't hear of her for eight years and then I was going up to Scotland with my first play. I'd become respectable, a great playwright, no longer a touring actor who went to nightclubs. Poodle rang up, and I thought, "Oh, my goodness, she's going to try and blackmail me. I must pretend it isn't me." So I said, "Oh, no, no. This is not the Robert Morley you knew. He was an actor. I am a playwright." At the first night, there was Poodle, beautifully dressed. She came up to me in the theater and she said, "Are you Mr. Morley?" And I thought, "Well now, that's funny. She doesn't remember me. I having refused to remember her." She said, "If ever you meet the actor that I used to know, will you tell him how glad that I am that he's had a great success, and that he never forgets his old friends." Her husband, who was a doctor, looked at me and said, "Game, set, match." I stood there feeling really a fool. I hope I've changed.

Once, when I was a touring actor, a woman came up to me and said, "What are you doing?" I started to give her a long list of my recent engagements. I said I've done this and that and I was going on tour with something else. I looked at her and I thought I must have known her at the Academy of Dramatic Art. I said, "What are you doing?" She said, "I'm trying to earn five pounds. Do you want to come home with me?" She must have been awfully annoyed with me, in the middle of the afternoon being so silly. But in those days, London streets were full of all those girls who picked you up. New

York's full of them now and it never used to be! There used to be a rather elaborate call-girl system. Now the poor girls are back on the streets. Whatever you may think about morality, you must not think it's a good thing for the girls to be on the streets. It's very bad for them; they get terrible colds in the heads if the weather's at all like it's been in New York for the last month.

[He reaches toward the side table.] Isn't it time we had a little medicine?

[We did. It went down quite well.]

It's been very kind of you to come and visit the sick.

5—Bert and Sam:
Brecht and Beckett

KENNETH TYNAN

1963

Kenneth Tynan has been acclaimed as the most perceptive drama critic writing in English today and the best since George Bernard Shaw.

In one of your essays, you take to task a 1958 editorial from the London Daily Mail which had bemoaned the fact that in modern theater there was too much message, lecture, and sermon, arguing that theater was really diversion, entertainment, pastry?

Theater as entertainment is the kind of attitude about which we have all been getting progressively more furious in England and in Western Europe for the last twenty-five years. American theater— Clifford Odets, the Group Theater people—got furious about it in the early 1930s.

Here in England, we haven't had the privilege of anything even approaching a classless drama: for 100 years, about ninety-five per cent of English plays were concerned exclusively with the life of only five percent of our population—the people who could afford fast cars, mink coats, and who could tell one cocktail from another. Drama about this sort of life ended with the election of the Labor government in 1945. At least, we fondly hoped so.

When the Labor government was out in 1951, we found to our surprise that everything was unchanged: the fast cars, fur coats, the two kinds of cocktails were still predominant in British drama and films. The young people of that time, who had been promised a completely new society and art after 1945, felt themselves betrayed; so they stood on hind legs and made a loud, booing noise in the form of plays and films. John Osborne tore down a few of the old walls in *Look Back in Anger*.

Since then, a whole group of young playwrights have developed an approach to drama which says, "What happens to ninety-fiue percent of the population counts." Now, this probably seems a very, very naive statement—obviously it ought to be the case in all of the performing arts but, in fact, it hardly ever is.

Drama began in ancient Greece as the art of a community. Since communities multiplied and became more complex and industrialized, however, drama became more and more a minority, almost aristocratic, certainly an upper-middle-class, art form. Which it still is in Paris, Rome, and in contemporary Athens.

Here in England, on the other hand, with directors like Joan Littlewood doing Brendan Behan's *The Quare Fellow* and *The Hostage*, the John Osborne plays, and Arnold Wesker being performed at the Royal Court theater, we, in fact, have theatrical representation for people hitherto never treated seriously on the English stage— people who work with their hands on farms and in factories and who, suddenly, with the spread of education since World War II, became outspoken, literate, and, having things to say, needed a platform.

The ancient principle held that drama was political, expressing what the *polis*, or city-state—the community—felt and thought. That was only possible in a tiny community, however; with the growth of commercial theater, plays appealing to big-spending audiences had to be staged. What we are trying to return to in Europe is the idea of theater subsidized by either community or government.

Since Jimmy Porter exploded on the stage in Look Back in Anger, *has this new theater, more closely related to the life of the great majority of people, broadened or altered the nature of the middle-class audience?*

I am afraid not. That is the awful thing. Although a great many of these dramas have played successfully in London and on Broadway, they haven't created the new audience yet. When building a new approach to drama, there comes a point at which you say, "We must now rebuild and remake the audience." Something but not enough has happened to the structure of English society. Basically, England still has the same society that it had in 1945. True, one or two industries are nationalized and there is a national health service—but England is still the most class-ridden society in the world with the exception perhaps of Japan and certain tribal societies of Africa. British still judge one another by accents. I am not now speaking to you, for example, in the accent to which I was born, I was educated out of that at Oxford to aspire to the kind of job that I now hold.

This matter of accent is beginning to break down in the arts, however, partly because of the determined push made by our young playwrights. Our drama schools no longer teach that it is an obscenity to have a north country accent: you can become a star—like Albert Finney in *Saturday Night and Sunday Morning*, and Tom Courtenay in *The Loneliness of the Long Distance Runner*—with what would have been regarded a vile provincial accent ten or fifteen years back. In the civil service, bureaucracy in general, and the upper echelon of the Tory Party, an accent is *the* definite handicap. Eton or Harrow would never employ a teacher with a provincial accent. Half of the parents, horrified, would immediately withdraw their boys.

Only two main developments exist in European drama. One, the Brechtian epic, the social play with political content, has had a very powerful influence on English authors like Osborne, and on French directors like Jean Vilar of the Théâtre National Populaire. The other school, the Theater of the Absurd, is the complete opposite, the introspective drama of fantasy in which the author sees man as a puppet crushed by fate, destiny, death, and whose only possible rebellion is the cry of despair—the plays of Samuel Beckett, Eugene Ionesco, the early ones of Arthur Adamov, and half a dozen others.

I feel, however, that the mainstream will be the drama as handed down by Bertolt Brecht because it is more international in scope and aimed at the large audiences, which drama essentially ought to be. The drama of the Absurd, on the other hand, strikes a note of privileged despair exclusive to the Western European intellectual who, seeing the whole world changing overnight, gives up, hiding in the attic, his head under the bedclothes.

Any author under forty who is in despair makes me impatient. Despair is something you have to grow up to: Beckett, the best of these playwrights, didn't begin to write plays until he was forty.

Then it is permissible. For people living in an affluent society—high employment, nobody starving, men earning decent livings—then, too, it would seem permissible to look at the cosmos and ask, "What is the point of the earth?" But the first job of an artist today is to bear at the back of his mind that, no matter what his subject, he is in danger if he only writes for his compatriots or for the privileged of his part of the world. At the end of World War II, Cyril Connolly said: "It is closing time in the gardens of the West." From now on, he argued, a man will be judged on the resonance of his solitude and despair. Well, that may be true of the gardens of the West, but it is opening time in the gardens elsewhere. Our Western artists ought to keep that firmly in the back of their minds. Other people all over the world must be given the opportunity to share our despair.

I wouldn't pretend to write like Brecht's knotty, compressed, concise style where, in almost every sentence, you can tell that enormous stress and pain has gone into the formulation of a thought so precise, as if he achieved simplicity in the way that rocks, by terrific pressure, produce diamonds. Constant strain, self-questioning, and doubt is evident in any sentence of his; I couldn't live in the amount of doubt that he always lived in. Brecht was looking for certainties, a more hopeful quest than looking for uncertainties, which is the other Western habit that asks, "What don't we trust? What can't be believed in? What have we given up and what lost?" More important questions than these would be, "What can we look for and discover? What can we be sure of?"

Strangely, we are used to thinking of Brecht as the harsh one, yet you present him as affirmative. When I saw a college production of Mother Courage *in Chicago, I was tremendously moved by Mother Courage, her fate, the loss of her children at the end. Martin Esslin said that, in this instance, Brecht's drama was better than his ideology. Did Brecht really mean for us not to be moved by the fate of* Mother Courage?

Concerning Brecht's intention in *Mother Courage*: I sometimes wish Brecht, who died tragically early at fifty-six, were here to tell us not to take his teachings so seriously. Stanislavsky once said, "If you can't use my system, forget it; use your own." Brecht formulated some thoughts about what he called the alienation effect, which asks the audience not to identify with the characters but, by being detached, to judge and criticize them.

What must be remembered, however, is that he addressed these remarks to German actors, who have a tradition of overemotionalism and bombast—the sort of approach to acting that produced great actors like Adolph Hitler. (When I saw the Berlin production of Brecht's *The Resistible Rise of Arturo Ui*, that jagged, raucous parody of Hitler's rise to power, I was assured that Hitler did take speech lessons from an old actor, but I have seen no authentication of this.)

Coming home to Germany after World War II, Brecht laid great stress on the opposite sort of acting technique: play it cool, be detached, don't try leading the audience but let people make their own decisions. This was an attempt to create democratic actors and audiences in a country that had forgotten both.

If he had been directing British actors, I am sure he would have said *more* emotion. On all factual matters Brecht was an extremely empirical man. When the American director Sam Wanamaker came here and saw British actors, he exclaimed, "You are all detached, Brechtian, throwaway, casual, cool—for God's sake, warm it up!" Brecht, I am sure, would have said something of the same.

He regarded his basic purpose as didactic; but then, so has every other great theater: Molière thought of himself as a teacher and satirist of behavior, conduct, public and private morality. Religious and civic lessons were certainly the aim of Greek drama. To teach is the entire corpus of medieval drama, too. Shaw had no other end; Ibsen very few other ends. Even in Chekhov, you will find that strain of uplift, which I am afraid we neglect in our productions of his plays but it is certainly there in his letters and texts. Didacticism should not be the exclusive purpose of drama—Heaven forbid!—but it is a mistake to think that it has ever been absent from drama.

The Theater of the Absurd, on the other hand, will be the minority theater of our time and perhaps for a great many years to come. One certainly welcomes it for its wit, fantasy, inventiveness, use of new technique. Its eventual fate, however, will be something like what has happened to the double bill of Ionesco that has been playing for six years in Paris in a little theater seating about two hundred people. Every year, a new university generation fills that theater; these plays will probably run for another twenty years, and more power to them. But I should be very surprised if Ionesco and his school become the majority theater of the future.

What is in the air is a new sort of total theater involving dance, song, mime, speech, bits of opera—a drama that includes rather than separates the arts. Brecht always borrowed from others: Chinese theater, classical, and Indian—the use of mime, dance, and song. Hints of this exist also in *West Side Story*, even in *A Funny Thing Happened on The Way to the Forum*, with the use of vaudeville techniques on the musical stage. The big drama form during the next twenty years will be this sort of mixture, this melee, this hodgepodge. To make hard and fast rules for drama, however, will be very difficult since we are in the middle of a rule-breaking era.

In some of the German towns, the theater is supported by the state but it is also civic supported. Towns compete with each other; it is a matter of pride: Düsseldorf wants to have as good a theater as Hamburg, Cologne, or Berlin, and so on. Regional rivalry is good. It *must* be subsidized because it is impossible to put on six classical or first-rate, serious productions every season, alternating them so that one can see six plays in a week, and still make a lot of money. How can you do *Peer Gynt* without a permanent company of sixty actors, which no commercial theater can afford? That is the reason why American or English playwrights do not write plays like *Peer Gynt*. They are perfectly sure they will not be commercially produced. Large-scale plays like those of Schiller or Brecht are only written in countries where there are subsidized theaters. Some of the directors and actors in subsidized German theaters are employed annually; others on the five- or ten-year contract. Obviously, if these dramas continue to play to empty houses, the local government will say, "There must be something wrong with our directors, we must get somebody else." In fact, however, the German theaters perform such plays to ninety-seven percent capacity houses.

Visiting the Berliner Ensemble is like taking a cold shower after having been in a Turkish bath. Our theater tends to be—at least in its serious aspects—extremely overemotional and overtense—what one might call the Elia Kazan syndrome, where the higher the intensity on stage, the higher the quality of the drama is supposed to be. Brecht's attitude, on the other hand, is that while it is perfectly easy to hypnotize people into a state of emotional trance, this has nothing to do with the purpose of acting. Actors, he felt, should commune with an audience as equals; they shouldn't try to scream audiences into submission or woo or charm, but chat to them. Brecht encouraged this by allowing outsiders to attend rehearsals—a thing unheard of in Western theater where rehearsal is a secret, holy ritual conducted behind closed doors until the play is ready to be shown. Nonsense, Brecht said: if you, as actors, can watch somebody digging a hole in the road, then the ditch digger should be allowed to come and watch you create your work. He would always warn actors, "What you are doing is not something holy or separate: it is a social activity, like driving a truck."

Anybody sober and not noisy could come and sit in on rehearsal, which gave actors a remarkable lack of self-consciousness because when opening night came it was no surprise to them to have an audience since they had been playing to total strangers for ages. This is really treating drama as just an ordinary, social function rather than as something that you attend in order to be thrilled, exalted, taken out of yourself. Instead, you go to be introduced to yourself.

The German actors are not trying to impose themselves on you. Quite often, they will step out of character and address you as the audience; there is no pretense that you are not in a theater: a stage is a stage and they are actors in costume. Of course, this degree of casualness and relaxation and underplaying is only possible with the very long rehearsal periods they have, sometimes as long as six months. Following that is a trial of opening night with an invited audience; then one or two other trials; then maybe the play gets rewritten. This group activity is encouraged by the fact that they do not have one director for each play—they may have two, or even four sitting simultaneously. England's Old Vic, by contrast, spent only four weeks rehearsing *Peer Gynt*, a four-hour show—and this is about as long a rehearsal as you get here—whereas in Germany they would rehearse that play not less than four months.

In these years, British drama has had the Osborne breakthrough, a minor revolution, and we now have the best young actors, in fact. I say this with great qualms: I am not a patriot but I think ours are the best young actors in the world—Albert Finney, for example, who is a symptom of an enormous epidemic of actors of his kind. Older, middle-order character actors tend to be rather bad here because they are a little bit out of date, still acting in a pre-war style. When our new school grows up, it will be as good as any theater in Europe.

When it comes to older actors, Russia, you said, has an attitude approaching reverence.

There is a sort of hierarchy in their leading theaters. You graduate from drama school into small parts. You very gradually reach leads. Then you tend to hang on to leading parts until you're a bit too old for them. You get actresses of fifty playing young girls of twenty. It's awful. And it's very hard to dislodge them until they stay long enough to earn their pension, which is a handsome one.

They are regarded as venerable figures, sages. If you walk down Moscow streets with a senior member of the Moscow Art theater, a small group will follow you. Not asking for autographs—they never do that. They just want to be close to this great man, this hero of the Soviet Union. It's an extraordinary feeling, the reverence for acting instead of adulation. I found that extremely reassuring.

PETER HALL

1962

He is the director of the Royal Shakespeare theater in Stratford-upon-Avon.

In 1958, I did *Twelfth Night* with Dorothy Tutin. We took it to Russia. The Russian reception was extraordinary. They're not used to seeing young people playing young people. I think we carry it too far. I don't believe anybody of twenty can express twenty on the stage. I think it takes thirty to tell us anything objective and really artistic about twenty.

Julie Harris, thirty or so, playing a thirteen-year-old in Member of the Wedding.

Indeed, indeed. But on the other hand, the Russians carry the matter of age too far. Our Mariah was played by a girl of nineteen and when she met Leningrad's Mariah, who I should think was about fifty-nine, their looks of mutual astonishment were very amusing.

For a long time there were two schools of classical acting, one led by Sir Laurence Olivier, the other by Sir John Gielgud. Grace, deportment, and verse speaking were emphasized by the Gielgud style, which hasn't moved with the times and during the past ten years has become more and more out of date, especially as far as Shakespeare is concerned. Olivier, who is terribly clever, has always been able to adapt more. Far more of a chameleon, he can smell out a new movement and take on its protective coloring . . .

His role of Archie Rice in Osborne's The Entertainer. . . .

Exactly. Olivier also brought to the classics increasingly in the last fifteen years a more contemporary, earthier approach in which you play, say, tragedies almost as if they were history plays rather than poetic arias. Sir Laurence is far more capable and malleable — it may be a self-protective instinct in him — to general trends than is Sir John Gielgud, various as his contribution has been. Comparing them, one would have to say that Olivier was burgundy and Gielgud claret, or, the latter plays in the minor key, whereas Sir Laurence plays a major chord.

What used to madden me about the American theater was that I had never seen so much talent put to so much ill use. But I don't think that the amount of energy, talent, and exuberance in the American theater can be enslaved permanently to the tyranny of the box office. Sooner or later, somebody is going to stand up and say what was said in England in 1880 by the poet Matthew Arnold: "The theater is irresistible; organize the theater!" Arnold said this in an article advocating a national theater subsidized with a permanent company where actors could develop a style.

That is what I missed in the American theater, where I would see actors come back to New York ragged, nervous breakdown cases after an exhausting out-of-town tour involving seventy-five rewrites, new directors, and everyone changing lines that might not appeal to Brooks Atkinson and adding lines that might appeal to Walter Kerr. That was not the way to handle talent; it seemed cruel. The more I saw playwrights and actors whom I knew being put through this mincer, the more I felt that the legitimate theater on Broadway was a dwindling art suffering from a bad case of commercial shellshock.

When you do get the odd adult play like *Who's Afraid of Virginia Woolf?*, it is a rare oasis. Gradually, I felt that I was becoming more of an obituarist than a critic. Four out of five of the plays I reviewed would be closed before my notice appeared in the *New Yorker*. One hates to write about a living art in the past tense, which I found myself doing more and more, feeling at the same time that, for purely economic reasons, there were more chances for experimental drama in Europe where it simply costs one quarter what the same production does in America. Risks can be taken, therefore, and that essential privilege to flop kept, which the commercial theater in the States is losing. Slap-up, expensive productions can be given in Europe to experimental plays, whereas in the States such dramas are produced off-Broadway rather cheaply with perhaps not quite first-rate actors. If there were more theaters in America like Tyrone Guthrie's in Minneapolis, this could change overnight. Here is the old contrast between private affluence and public squalor.

Much the same thing inhibits American playwrights and actors: after you have made a smash hit in, say, *A Streetcar Named Desire*, you are scared to come back in case you don't top yourself—so you become a Hollywood actor instead. To expect playwrights to go on improving is a mistake. Writers must have the right to be at less than their best sometimes, without meeting an all-out critical assault.

During his entire creative output, Eugene O'Neill had hit, flop, hit, flop, and nobody particularly minded. Nowadays, every Tennessee Williams play is either pounced on or adulated as if everything must, like the gross national product, go on getting bigger and better. This is not necessarily true. If Shakespeare had to operate under that sort of searchlight of publicity, he would probably have turned out only a third of what he did. A man can't work under the constant scrutiny of 1,000 people with hatchets.

What has kept Arthur Miller from Broadway for so long is the fear of not living up to other people's expectations of himself. There is also the tendency among playwrights to feel that if you once had a hit with one kind of play, you should go on repeating it. This has happened, I think, to William Inge, a talent in a blind alley created by its own early success. I hope he gets out of it, but it doesn't seem to me that Inge has developed since *Picnic* of ten years ago.

What I don't want to see is any more exploration of depth analysis in playwriting and acting: we have gone far enough with the couch and the couch school. Nor do I want to see a deliberate attempt to return to poetry in drama because of the assumption that poetry can express things that prose cannot. Nor do I want to see prettiness put quite so high up the theatrical scale as it has been during the past twenty years in France and England. Finally, I don't want government expenditure under any circumstances in any country to be cut down one red cent without a revolution.

LOTTE LENYA

1963

She is in Chicago on a tour of *Brecht on Brecht*. We are listening to her recording of the "Moritat" (Mack the Knife) that opens *Threepenny Opera*. Book by Bertolt Brecht, music by Kurt Weill (her husband). Both men have since died.

Margot Asquith spoke of your voice as that of a "disillusioned child singing outside a public house."

I'm still doing it, still singing outside public houses. If somebody asked you to describe my voice, what would you say?

I hear the loneliness, the lostness, the squalor of a city, all this. Also a street smartness. I can think of only two other singers who had this quality: Edith Piaf and Billie Holiday.

I think that's why they wanted me. Their first collaboration was *Die Kleine Mahagonny*, way back in 1927. It was just a collection of songs. Some were used in their big opera, *The Rise and Fall of the City of Mahagonny*. This one was just based on five poems by Brecht. It was written for one of those festivals that we have here in Tanglewood. So highbrow, you know. Where the so-called serious composers, Schönberg, Hindemith were played. Brecht said, "I don't think this will go over right away in a highbrow festival like this." So he supplied us with little whistles. Whistling in Germany means disapproval—not like here. He foresaw that. He stood there with his stogie in his mouth and said, "If you hear whistles, whistle right back. Don't let them win. We must win that evening." So it happened: half the house applauded like mad, because it was so unusual in such a festival. All of a sudden the stagehands set up a little boxing ring and two girls, prostitutes, appeared with little suitcases and straw hats and sang something that sounded like "un fella Alabama," in pidgin English. Brecht didn't speak a word of English and he thought this would become the universal language of the world. It was at the time they invented Esperanto. Brecht thought everybody would speak it. He was Bavarian.

You were Viennese.

I still am!

Your dialect was different than Brecht's.

Viennese is a little softer. Brecht's rolling "rrrs" are a little stronger than mine. Of course, with his sharpness in appearance and in his way of talking, he exaggerated the harshness.

There was a touch of gentleness in your voice—

It's still aggressive, just a little bit gentle.

There was tension here that made your voice very exciting. The slight gentleness against the harshness—the combination, the voice of a lost child.

My voice has been described in so many different ways. Critics have disliked my voice, others have praised it. One critic called it, "a bleak, sour voice," another said it was "irritable." If I had listened to everybody, I'd have gone completely crazy and couldn't sing anymore. I never intended to be a Callas. So I sing it the only way I can and this is it. It's not a voice that "comes out of no-man's land," as one critic said. I resent that. I know exactly what I'm singing, of emotions any human being goes through in life.

My husband, Kurt Weill, wasn't just a songwriter. He had studied twelve-tone with Busoni. His first opera was atonal. He wasn't that interested in "serious" opera, though he was serious about his music. He was losing interest in chamber music, too. That's when he met Brecht.

He said, "I want my music to be sung by people." Some say he didn't care about posterity. That's nonsense. Any creative person thinks about that. What he meant was he'd like to live long enough to hear his music played and sung. He was lucky. He was a *theater* composer. At the same time, he said, "I don't want to hold back my horses." In German, it sounds so much better. [Laughs]

He lived in two worlds, the world of musical theater and opera. He fulfilled his dream in America, when he wrote *Street Scene.**

ARNOLD SUNDGAARD

An American composer, he wrote the libretto of the folk opera, *Down in the Valley*. Kurt Weill wrote the music.

I had written folk songs in a somewhat Brechtian style. That's how I met Weill. I know it seems strange that a German refugee could work on something so indigenously American as *Down in the Valley*. We know that so many European writers were fascinated with America and wrote about it even though they may never have been here.

Kurt said he loved the American sounds. Names like Susque-

---

*An American opera based on Elmer Rice's Pulitzer Prize–winning play of the same name.

hanna and Monongahela. He told me that he and Brecht both thought that Alabama was pronounced "Alabamee" because they had heard Al Jolson sang it that way.

———————

One of your most celebrated songs is "Surabaya Johnny." There's a recitative in it; you both talk and sing.

Sprechgesang, we call it in German. This is the eternal cry of the creature who gave everything she had and he deserts her. She knows it from the beginning. It's very difficult for young singers. If you get too emotional in the singing, it carries over into the speaking. And the other way around. The bridge is difficult. Brecht adored Sprechgesang.* Oh, my God, he loathed traditional singers. He loathed opera. Very unjust, a fanatic on that. When actors audition, some feel they have to prepare themselves emotionally. This one actress drove him crazy. She stood there with her back to the audience. Brecht asked, "What is she doing?" The stage manager said she was getting ready for the audition. Brecht said, "Send her home and let her come back when she's unemotional."

In Brecht's theater, you had to be ready any time. Never mind "preparing." Never mind "putting myself in the mood." An actor has to be able to create any mood any time, wherever he plays, whether it's in a barn or in the street, on A or on Z. It's just being in complete control of the moment. You make the *audience* feel the mood.

A young actor, who uncritically follows the Stanislavsky technique, known as the Method, would have a hard time with Brecht.

Oh, my God, yes. He'd throw him out. Wasting too much time. That's why I'm in love with making movies. You have to concentrate on the spot, on the moment. They may start the scene from the last or from the middle, so its instantaneous concentration. I like it because it's easy for me. Brecht trained me that way.

———————

Addio del passato, Violetta's aria in *La Traviata*, is especially moving because it was preceded by her letter reading, spoken-word scene. Hearing Claudia Muzio's recording never fails to knock me out. Call it Sprechgesang, Italian style.

Speaking of controlling the moment, there's a scene in Threepenny Opera *where you, as Jenny, betray your lover, Macheath, the crook-hero, to the police. There was a certain gesture you used—a flick of the wrist against your forehead and a snap of the fingers. Didn't this become a symbol among young people in Germany during Hitler times?*

Yes, whenever there was a betrayal, people didn't have to say anything. They didn't have to say, "She betrayed him." They just used the gesture I made in *Threepenny Opera* and they knew. It was a gesture in Berlin for a while until it wore out.

Aside from Threepenny Opera, *the most provocative of all the Brecht–Weill works may be* The Rise and Fall of the City of Mahagonny.

Mahagonny is an invented word. *Das is kein Ort.* There is no such place. It's an imaginative American city during the Gold Rush. A no-man's land. Everything is allowed in Mahagonny. You can kill, you can rob, you can do anything. It's OK. There's only one crime which you pay for with your life: being poor, running out of money. Brecht is a moralist.

Some of the songs in Mahagonny, *like the Alabama song, have a sweet, sentimental pop quality.*

It's a take-off, joking, those kind of songs.

Alabama rhyming with mama, so "we've lost our good old mama." And sweetly singing, "We must have dollars, you know why." Harsh ideas sweetly sung. Am I assuming a great deal here?

You're assuming in the right direction. It's a take-off on Al Jolson with "Mammy" also. There are many things that sneak in.

The song, "As You Make Your Bed," I'm saying this to my lover in *Mahagonny,* Jimmy Mahoney. He is so drunk, he's asleep on the billiard table. They are both so drunk, they think they've sailed away to Alaska. The music stops, they're still in that bar. The owner says, "Pay your bill." He said, "I can't. I've run out of money." She turns to Jenny. "Can you help him out?" Jenny says, "I? That's funny what they ask girls to do. No, I haven't any money." Then she sings to Jimmy, whom she loves, "How you make your bed, you lie in it." Love is love, but money is money. So Jimmy dies for lack of money.

[We are looking at a photograph of Brecht, Weill, Hindemith, Lenya.] I'm sure this question has been asked of you many times. Berlin, at the time, may have had the most creative artists in the Western world: Schöenberg, Reinhardt, Klee, Kandinsky, Jannings, you name 'em. Yet, fascism was just around the corner.

It was very strange. Zero hour for freedom in Germany. Yet we were still undisturbed by Hitler. When *Mahagonny* was done in Leipzig in 1930, it caused such a riot. Such turmoil broke out, whistling and applauding and throwing chairs and fistfights. They had to turn on all the lights to finish. The next day when it was repeated, there was a policeman at every exit. The lights were on the whole time, so they could arrest somebody if he started a riot. Eventually, they had to cancel it. The Nazis were already around the corner.

Strange, you know, when you're in a time like that. When you're young and ambitious and excited about your work, you're less concerned with the outside world. You're thinking about what you want to achieve with your life. We were aware of what was happening around us, but we were actors. Stupidly so. That was our profession and that was what we did. So all those disturbances from the outside didn't affect us very much. In looking back, no.

Brecht and Weill had something to say. That made us ten times as courageous because we believed in what we were saying. Playing Brecht now, when you listen to these songs and what they say, it's as true now as it was then and probably will be true a hundred years from now. I think the things he was attacking are still around— corruption and poverty. What do you think?

You're asking me?

Yes or no?

[Laughing] Yes.

[We are listening to a Lenya recording of "Surabaya Johnny," a torch song of a love betrayed.]

Whenever I've sung these Weill songs and read Brecht's words to young people in America, I've found it fascinating. College students, a lot. At first you think they don't understand it. Then comes this thunderous applause. A teacher wrote me: they are too shy to ask when they come backstage. They just look at me with their big eyes and ask for an autograph. But teachers tell me it's had a terrific effect on them. . . . I hope.

JOAN LITTLEWOOD

1964

Several years before this conversation, I had seen her on television.

Malcolm Muggeridge was having a hard time with Joan Littlewood. And when her tam, perched precariously on her head, fell off, as it had been threatening to do throughout the BBC television program, she scrambled under the table to retrieve it. It was all so discombobulating to poor Muggeridge, who seeks a preordained order to things. At home in Chicago, watching these two, I was enjoying the best theater in years. The born-again Christian, solemn as a periwigged judge, didn't know what the hell the exultant pagan was talking about. It wasn't really his fault. She was a visitor from another planet. Or was he a stranger to earthly delights?

I was bound to run into her, I know.

New York. A small dressing room, backstage. *Oh! What a Lovely War*, Joan Littlewood, director. Not really. Kenneth Tynan said it: "She doesn't direct a play. She creates theater." Same thing with Brendan Behan's *The Hostage*. She didn't direct it; she was its midwife.

We pick up the conversation where we had left off. The fact that I have never met her before is of small matter. I had just come in to get out of the rain and was curious.*

---

*This interview appeared in my book, *Talking to Myself*.

What are you trying to stir up?

I have nothing to do with it. It's lying all over the shop, like gold and rubbish and diamonds.

What is?

People. I'm sick to death of all these silly old political and social and educational systems which have got in the way of human expression. You've got a parliament—your Congress—our parliament that represents a frizzled old excrescence from the past. With life bursting out all over the place, you've got a Broadway theater, like a calcified turd, where people line up in black dresses and gloomy faces. Here you have this great country, and, my God, what a mess you've made of it. [Laughs—the sort of laughter that so bewildered Malcolm Muggeridge. Suddenly gentle] Except for the people you bump into on the streets. There's a million Brendans out there. And yet there's nothing geared to human delight.

Here we are on a planet, life's short. For a few times in human history, there's been a crossroad and there's been great theater, like Shakespeare's. Now we're at a crossroad again. We can move forward out of prehistory and we can pull down the walls of these terrible blocks, where the posh people and the poor people are trapped alike. And open the door to having perhaps more pain in our life and more delight. Rilke said it: Every day, a woman locked in her little flat is for one moment a poet. All along the back streets of this world.

FLASH FORWARD. *Walls had been pulled down in a Chicago neighborhood back in '61, but not in the manner Joan envisioned. An old neighborhood, pulsating with the life she was celebrating, was demolished by the mayor, realtors, insurance companies, and banks. It is now a cold complex, euphemistically known as Circle Campus, University of Illinois. It is surrounded by ribbons of cement, called expressways. No people. Observing the scene, Joan, some three years after our first encounter, said it was a historical sport, a throwback to another time. When medieval armies invaded a town, they drove out the inhabitants and made it a fortress. She painted the portrait in such live colors that I actually saw the moat and drawbridge some fifty yards away; and those young soldiers, euphemistically called students, dutifully going about their chores. Separating this fortress from the civilians, driving by, was a stone fence. It was a portcullis I saw, thanks to Joan Littlewood's sense of history. And when, that evening, she chose Louis Sullivan's Testament of Stone from the bookshelf, was it an accident? He had visions, too. Tall ones, too. "He was cut down, Joan. And his visions with him. He died on skid row." She knew that, too. But it doesn't appear to stop her.*

[The cast is waiting outside the dressing room for a few words from her; it's all right, they're laughing and having a good time. It's Brendan Behan she's thinking about.] Life was a bit too much for him. He didn't die of drink, he died of love. He was not a tough man. He was a very shy, gentle loner. The old woman on the corner, the penniless old tramp, the outcast, the prisoner, these were the people he made laugh. These were the people who followed him to his grave. Not the rich and powerful, the politicians, the stars from show business. I didn't see them. But thousands and thousands of the poor of Dublin that always followed him like the Pied Piper, and who stood as he went by and said, "Oh, Jesus, he may never get there." Because he gave them laughter, apart from sharing every penny he got by throwing it around every bar. And by the fish market early in the morning when the dead fish were laid out on the marble slabs and giving them all the last rites after a night of booze. [There's that laugh again.]

Poor old suffering Jesus. Hanging up there, having a miserable time that we've had to live by. There was another theory, you know. Kit Marlowe said He danced with the apostles. They had a ball. [The laugh, again. And the vision.] And we are that side of the penny, the clowns. That's what theater is, love, communion.

I'd like to see people realize their full height. Did you ever see people who never danced dance? They become so beautiful and alive. A little boy at home is told he is dull. He's an A, B, or C. How dare they judge? We know we're all chemically different. How dare they judge the unique genius, these so-called educators? How dare they put up these buggery cloisters from the Middle Ages and call it a place of learning?

Each man, each woman is part bird, part fish, wishing to fly, to dance, to fuck well, to eat well, to think. And we will. We've got to risk as artists. More pain, as Brendan knew it, but isn't it worth it? Who wants to be a vegetable? The woman who's shut up in her room parades as Cleopatra, we know. We only have to say, We're good enough. Let there be war, but *real* war between man and man over an idea. We've slapped the backside of the moon, yet we know nothing about you and me.

We're part of the herring fleet, we're part of this flight of birds across the planet. Life is short. But there's more joy than we know, more brains than we know, more ability to learn. But learn for what? We learn quickly in times of war and disaster. But in life, there's a disaster all the time. The waste of human possibility. And we don't face it.

I pick up what's in the wind. All these things I love and believe in. It's easier to cling to the past. Now people are so lost, it seems, so barren. But the time must come when all those funny old freaks of distinguished politicians and kings, queens, presidents, who tread their paranoid way through dreary corridors—their time must come. We've jumped into the future without knowing it. And we're gonna win!

Should I bet on it, Joan? Didn't Blake sing out of a new Jerusalem during the Industrial Revolution?

Yes. Raleigh, the intellectual, and Marlowe, the poet, dreamed of a republic of clowns. Of laughter, of bringing the stars to man's knowledge. Later came Hasek, the Czech Brendan, and his *Good Soldier Schweik*. He made war laughable and the soldiers threw down their rifles and went home. Before I die, I'd like to push open the door, so that people can see the absurdities of the calcified turds and recognize the genius in themselves.

[As the young clowns of her company file into the dressing room, I ask Joan to call upon Blake's vision again. We sure could use it. She looks past me, way, way out there, somewhere out there, and she sings it:]

Bring me my bow of burning gold!
Bring me my arrows of desire!
Bring me my spear! O clouds, unfold!
Bring me my chariot of fire!
I will not cease from mental fight,
Nor shall my sword sleep in my hand,
Till we have built Jerusalem
In England's green and pleasant land.

That's what he said. Poor old bugger. [She gets up to go to work with her young clowns.] It's not a rehearsal. It's a renewal.

ALAN SCHNEIDER

1969

The director who introduced the works of Samuel Beckett to American audiences, beginning with *Waiting for Godot*. Since then, he has directed all the plays of Edward Albee.

I have an idea that all modern plays of any serious importance in the twentieth century say opposite things on this issue of truth and illusion. There's one kind of playwright, say, Eugene O'Neill, who says you can't live without illusion. And there's Edward Albee who says you can't live with illusion—you gotta face reality. I think they're the ultimate positions of modern life. O'Neill in *The Iceman Cometh* says, "Don't destroy a man's pipe dreams." And Edward is saying we've got too many pipe dreams and we've got to face up to them or they lead us into trouble. Of course he's writing thirty years or more after O'Neill, in a different society, and certainly our pipe dreams are different. He's saying we have certain illusions about ourselves, and unless you face up to that you get into trouble.

That's what's obsessing Albee: the sense of false values on which so much of our lives are now based. He doesn't do it in a taciturn manner. He has great wit, he has scorching humor, very funny. That's the test of appreciation of Albee: because we must laugh as he makes us laugh and wants us to laugh; but we must also see ourselves, see our truths, our foibles. I think that's the function of comedy anyhow, isn't it? Any great comic writer is fundamentally satirizing or poking at society.

I think Albee is a serious writer who writes comedically. I think Molière's a serious writer who writes comedy. I think Aristophanes was a serious writer who wrote comedy. Albee is in the tradition of Swift. That's how I got into Beckett. I came from Beckett to Albee, so I relate them very strongly. Beckett is a very Swiftian writer.

To some, Beckett is the chronicler of man's despair.

I don't think that he is concerned with despair, at least in the conventional sense. I think Sam is saying to us in the same way that Edward is, unless we face up to certain truths about the nature of our lives on earth, we cannot really live as human beings. Most people think of Sam as kind of a gloomy Gus, who wanders around hitting his head against concrete abutments. I've wandered with Sam through the gardens of Luxembourg eating grapes that we bought off an open market, looking for a Ping-Pong parlor. He was a tennis player, he was a rugby and cricket player. I've never met a man with as great a love of life as Sam Beckett. He's a genial, lovely, Irishman, with great wit, great sensitivity.

Is this story true? It's probably apocryphal. A marvelous young actor said he heard the story of Beckett's father. When he died, he grabbed Beckett from his dying bed saying, "Never give up. Never give up."

Apocryphal or not, it's a good story. I don't get any sense from Sam of giving up. He has an intense love of life. There is a story which I know is true. Years ago, when Sam was relatively unemployed—not exactly Joyce's secretary. He read to Joyce as Joyce was getting blind, the way a great many young writers or artists in Paris were hired by Joyce to read to him. He may have answered a letter, which gave rise to the myth of being his secretary. During this time, knocking around the Sorbonne, he was walking up the Boulevard St. Michel and he was approached by a beggar, a *clochard*; Sam reached into his pocket and handed the beggar a few coins. The beggar turned on Sam and stabbed him in the back with a knife, a great big knife. Sam was taken to the hospital, and for a while it looked as though he weren't going to live. But they fixed him up. He was asked by the Paris police to prefer charges against this guy. Sam said, "No, I can't press charges against this man. To have done a thing like that means that he's suffering enough." I'm putting it a little more cornily than he put it, but here is a man who in my opinion is incapable of hurting another human being if it is within his power not to do so. That's not the image of a man who's walking around saying how ugly life is and putting people in ash cans. I've never seen a greater love scene in modern literature than those two old people in the ash cans. I've always said, it's easy to write a love scene on the back seat of a Cadillac with the leopard-skin seats. But if you really make me believe in love, two old people whose legs are cut off, who live in sawdust in an ash can, that shows great compassion and great understanding.

Edward says he wouldn't have written the same kinds of plays or wouldn't have been able to write at all had it not been for Sam Beckett. The two write quite differently, yet one was stimulated by the other. The young American read Beckett, understood Beckett, and found me through Beckett. So I'm very grateful. When I was doing *Krapp's Last Tape* in New York, I met Edward Albee. He liked what I was doing with it and asked me to do his next play.

I'd heard all my life that Chekhov was pessimistic and dull, and nothing happened in Chekhov. I think that's all nonsense. I mean, again, a man who understood the change that was necessary in that society, who appreciated the good things in the order that was passing, and the bad things in the order that was coming, but which had to come. I don't believe that any artist can be without compassion, even for the things that he's against. I don't believe that any dramatist can write a play without having a sense of life, a sense of vitality, a sense of intensity. I don't find the theater worthwhile if it simply reproduces life. That's the nature of drama, fundamentally—to intensify life, heighten life, distill life, bring it down to its ultimate.

How did you meet Beckett?

I found myself in Paris once, with some vague recollection of a play that had been mentioned to me in Zurich, called *Waiting for Godot*. I hadn't heard of the play, didn't know anything about the author. I spent about a week in Paris trying to find this play, because nobody knew where it was. Finally I found it. It was in the Théâtre de Babylon in the Left Bank, tiny, beat-up, like an off-Broadway Village garret theater. My French is about enough to get me into American Express. I saw this play and . . . I can't really describe it any other way: I was haunted by it. I didn't quite get it all. I remember when I first saw Lucky and Pozzo, I thought it was the British Empire and Ireland. Now where in the devil did I get that idea? There was something almost mystical about it.

I went back the next night. I got a copy of the play in French, I read it, so I had a little more sense of it. I went back the next night and I began to get right into its mood and atmosphere. Then I spent another week trying to find the author. He was very elusive, he didn't want to be found. I left him notes, I tried to call him up — he didn't have a telephone. I wrote him letters, I did everything. Finally, I said, "to heck with it." I couldn't find him. I'd heard that the play had been sold in English. And it was sold, to be done in London with Alec Guinness and Ralph Richardson, which struck me as a good idea. I gave up. I figured I'd lost out on that one.

As it turned out, Ralph Richardson got cold feet. He didn't want to do the play. Guinness wouldn't do it because Richardson didn't want to do it. It was finally done in a little theater off West End in London. I'd read the reviews, it sounded fascinating to me. One day, I was in Chicago — I had just given a talk in Madison, Wisconsin, my old alma mater, and I was passing through Chicago on my way back to New York. I get a phone call from a New York producer. He says, "Alan Schneider?" "Yeah." "I want you to direct a play called *Waiting for Godot*. You want to do it? We got Bert Lahr and Tommy Ewell." I said, "Yeah!" It turned out that there'd been another director, Garson Kanin, who got cold feet, didn't want to do the play. They thought of me because Thornton Wilder had heard that I read this play, or had seen the play, or I talked to him about it. Anyhow, I was hired. And the producer, in one of his rare acts of wisdom, sent me to Europe to meet Beckett.

I had been trying two years to meet Beckett. Beckett resisted, but finally he agreed, and I quote, "Give the New York director a half an hour." I crossed the ocean for this half hour with Sam Beckett. I was with Thornton Wilder, and we talked about Beckett all the time. He admired Beckett immensely, thought he was one of the greatest writers of drama in the twentieth century. I got to Paris. I went out and bought a bottle of champagne. I don't know anything about champagne, but I thought it would be suitable to get him a brand called "The Tears of Christ." So I bought him *Lacrimae Christe* champagne. I couldn't call him—he has no phone—and so I sent him what they call a pneumatique, it's this fast mail thing. You send it like in a department store where the money goes in the tube. You send a letter and you get an answer. And I got an answer back: OK, he'd be at my hotel at six o'clock, and he only had half an hour.

I get downstairs and there's this gaunt quarter-miler, in a sheepskin coat, glasses, hair sort of straggly and like the feathers of a hawk. We sit down in the hotel lobby. I've got a notebook full of questions, but he doesn't answer questions, so I just want to meet Beckett. So I take out the bottle of champagne. He looked at me and he says, "Well now, where are we gonna drink it?" And I said, "I don't know." He said, "Well, let's come over to my house. I've got a few minutes." So I went to his house, which wasn't too far from the hotel. It was a walk-up, rather a plain artist's studio, a lot of paintings on the wall—by friends of his, not famous artists—a few books, very simple, spare. And we drank the whole bottle of champagne. Then we began to drink his bottles. It was about four hours later— I'd been asking him questions in the meantime. First I'd ask him stupid questions like, "Who is Godot?" or "What is Godot?" and he'd say, "If I knew, I would have put it in the script." I don't mean to give the impression that we just got drunk, but we sort of hit it off. I asked him a lot of silly questions, and we went out to dinner. We went out to a restaurant where he'd had many, many meals with Joyce in the Left Bank. Then he said, "Look, I'm terribly sorry, I have an appointment. But if you're still staying tonight, I'll meet you at eleven o'clock. You haven't finished asking everything. Would you like me to meet you at eleven o'clock?" And I said, "Yeah." We met at another café, Fouquet's, which was a favorite hangout of James Joyce. So here I am, in seventh heaven. I meet Sam Beckett at eleven o'clock on the Champs Élysee and we talk some more. About everything. Art, life, the theater. We occasionally mention *Godot*. As we were leaving—'cause I was going to London to see this production. The producer had wanted me to see it. Sam said [speaking with a brogue], "Would it be any help to you a'tall if I went to London with you?" I said, "Would it be any help?" I said, "Wow." He said, "I can't go tonight, but can you stay till Wednesday and we'll go on Wednesday?" I stayed to Wednesday, he went with me, we went every night to see the show in London. He'd tell me [brogue] "They're doing it all wrong."

I spent about a week in London with him. We went to the show, we talked to the actors, I spent a lot of time with him. I got to know *him* more than the play. When I left, finally, to go back to America, I remember Sam telling me, "Do it this way, do it this way. This is necessary, that's necessary." Then, at the end of all those series of instructions, "Do it any way you like, do it any way you like." That's the kind of man he is. His directions are really part of the text. If he puts a pause in there, it's part of the rhythm. If you try to louse that up or change it around, I think it hurts or distorts the play. Edward's not as rigid. Some other authors I've worked with, even less rigid. But Sam, it's hard to differentiate between the text, the dialogue, and the directions, because he's writing poems. They're dramatic poetry. And the relationship between elements is pointed out as much sometimes by the directions as by the words. You want to know about Miami, Florida? About our American opening?

We went to Florida because the producer was nervous about opening it anywhere, and he got a guarantee down there that the theater wanted Bert Lahr, they wanted Tommy [Ewell], and they didn't know anything about the play. Miami. They were opening a new theater down there, sort of a winter stock outfit, Coconut Grove Playhouse. They gave the producer a fantastic amount of money. We begged him not to go down there. They hadn't *opened* yet, but the kind of play they wanted to do would be *John Loves Mary*. That's the kind of play they've done since. Our press agent was nervous, and they went through the standard operating procedure. They billed this play as "Bert Lahr, star of *Harvey*, and Tom Ewell, star of the *Seven Year Itch*, in the laugh sensation of two continents." They'd spent ninety thousand dollars fixing up the house with blue satin drapes and carpeting four inches thick in the lobby, and it had a big goldfish pool shaped like some kind of kid-

ney. They had a restaurant there where the steaks started at about
$5.75. But no dressing rooms. So Bert and Tommy dressed in an
alley. It was just madness. We rehearsed, and the show wasn't bad.
But we were all absolutely terrified. The show's supposed to open
at eight-thirty. At about ten minutes after ten, they put champagne
in the goldfish pond out there, and the people were drinking out of
it, dunking into it and drinking out of it. At about ten minutes after
ten they finally straggled in out of the lobby, and the restaurant, and
the ladies powder room, down the aisle to this beautifully decorated
theater, and we got the curtain up.

The first five minutes of the play . . . it was a fascinating so-
ciological experience. The first minutes of this play everybody
laughed at everything. Tommy Ewell came on, took his hat off, big
roar. Bert Lahr came on, sat down, took his shoe off, yok. Smash,
boom, bang, everything. About five minutes later, everybody suddenly quieted down because it wasn't funny. They didn't know
what was going on. The lines are funny, but they're not funny the
way they thought they were going to be funny, and there was dead
silence. Then there began to be coughing, then there began to be
groans and grunts and shouts of disapproval, especially when the
language got a little difficult.

One or two guys got up and left, and then five guys got up, and
then twenty-two guys got up, and I would say by the end of the first
act, half the audience had gone. They were quite vocal in their disapproval: they staggered up the aisles and went out. There was great
dismay on stage. I went back and tried to reassure Tommy and Bert,
who were by this time *white*, not with makeup. By the end of the
show, I would say another thirty-five, forty percent of the audience
left. There were ten, fifteen percent of the audience left by the end of
the show. The ushers were all high school kids with tears in their
eyes, not understanding why the audience was responding so badly
to this beautiful play. I mean, those kids kept me going, I swear to
you.

We went out, nobody was talking to anybody. Nobody's ever
seen ninety percent of an audience walk out. Then we got the reviews. They said everything from, "How dare you? This is horrible,
this is loathsome, this is dirty, this is a hoax, this is a fake, this is a

fraud. How could you perpetrate this on the great American public?" Walter Winchell wrote that he wouldn't soil his mouth with reporting on the play. A few other guys from New York who had come down said similar things.

Tennessee Williams loved it. He was there opening night. And there were a few other artists down there who came to me and put their arms around me. Luckily, we had some young people in the audience from the University of Miami, from the local high schools, who were ushers there and who also stayed to watch, and a few other scattered youngsters who loved the show. Bert got all kinds of threatening letters. I remember one in particular: "How can you, Bert Lahr, who charmed the youth of America with your portrayal as the Cowardly Lion in *The Wizard of Oz*, appear in this communistic, atheistic, existentialist play?" Well, Bert, you know, who's the sweetest, saddest man in the world, came over to me and he said, "What does 'existentialist' mean?"

We got one good review from a hotel newspaper written by the social director. Tommy Ewell had it reproduced and sent to all his friends in New York to make sure they didn't think he was in a debacle. Nobody came, in spite of that hotel review. We got the privilege of swimming at that hotel for two weeks. I would say about the end of the first week, we began to get a student audience. We lowered the ticket prices. The mink coats and Cadillacs didn't show up any more. The students, the kids, the night-school people came in, and we began to develop an audience, and by the end of the second week I would say we had half a house in there, and nobody walked out. It was not a regular theater-going audience, not the audience that has gone since to that theater, I'm sorry to say. But at least they warmed our hearts a little bit.

Of course, I felt a great sense of failure. The New York production was canceled, the tour was canceled—we were going to Washington and Philadelphia. Canceled. The producer was scared. Everything was canceled. I thought that's the end of the world. I wrote Beckett a letter, and I said, "Here I am and I failed you. I don't know what to do, and I'm terribly sorry." It was a long letter, blow by blow of what happened. He sent me a letter back, and he said, "Alan, failure has dogged me all of my life and I wouldn't be comfortable without it. And the only thing that worries me is that you're depressed." From then on I'd murder, rape, and steal for him.

I heard that lecture you gave at the university here. You used as your text two lines from Godot. *When the blind Pozzo is asked by Vladimir . . .*

He says, "Where do you go from here?" And Pozzo says, "On."

And that's what Samuel Beckett said to you: on.

That's what he said. Gotta go on.

His father may have said to him, "Never give up!"

That's right. He went on and he wrote *Endgame*, which I also directed. Since then, I've directed all of his plays.

My objection to audiences comes only when I feel that they're not really interested in being stirred or moved or involved, they want to just be amused. I mean, it's the kind of thing that happens so often on television. As someone once put it: the theater used to be concerned with the blood of life, and now it's concerned with the lipstick of life. I find whenever an audience wants to be reached, *Godot* reaches them like mad. It's not only young people, it can be old people. It's people that are not simply going to be titillated.

GILBERT MOSES

1966

He is the director of Free Southern theater. It is a company of African-American actors that performed in small towns of the Deep South during the civil rights movement of the '60s.
Among the plays they offered was *Waiting for Godot*.

Our audiences were mostly black farmworkers. They had worked hard all day and came to the theater in their workclothes. A lot of them came, trying to understand in some way the meaning of the Movement. Since it was free of charge, anyone could come.

We played mostly in small Mississippi towns—Ruleville,

Greenwood, Greenville. We discovered it to be the most exciting theatrical circuit in the United States. None had ever seen live theater before. They had *very* little formal schooling. So they carried no preconceived notions of what the play, *Waiting for Godot*, was about. They were unlike the Miami and New York audiences, who were baffled because they really didn't want to know what the play said.

Our audience knew a great deal about waiting. They had been waiting all their lives. They actually knew what it meant to be Lucky, the slave of Pozzo. When they saw Lucky with the rope around his neck, they understood immediately that that rope had two ends: that Lucky was not only the slave of Pozzo, but that Pozzo was the slave of Lucky. And that he was blind. In Ruleville, during the intermission, Fannie Lou Hamer stood up and said:* "We've seen these same people standing on the corner, dressed in the same clothes. All they're doing is waiting." Naturally, the audience made the connection with their own lives. They saw the two tramps as themselves. She related it to the Movement. "We don't have to wait anymore." She was telling them how significant the play was and how she was glad that we brought it to Ruleville.

Most people understood the play in religious terms. Godot was God and he wasn't coming—the only way to get out of the hole they were in, the little space, was to get out and do something for themselves.

One of the reasons we chose this play was because of the stunning imagery. For instance, when Lucky and Pozzo fall down and are on top of each other, Gogo, one of the tramps, falls down, too. They cry for help. Validimir, the other tramp, rationalizes the decision not to help them. And when he finally stoops down and extends a hand, he falls onto the pile himself. The audience got the point: a slave is someone who waits for somebody else to free him.

We wanted to find out the limits of our audience. We tried all

---

*A farmworker herself, she had become a leader of the freedom movement in Mississippi. It was she, who, along with others, appeared at the Democratic Party Convention in 1964, and sparked the great debate, challenging the legitimacy of the all-white pro-segregation delegation.

sorts of experiments. The play, certainly at first, seemed confusing to much of academia, and the so-called sophisticated audience. There was an arrogance here of what was considered culture in this country. We wanted to find out exactly what culture was; whether it could be brought to somebody or whether it could be created from the stone of their existence.

The audiences, say in New York theater, have become conditioned to theater as something commercial, rather than something related to their lives. They don't let a play like *Waiting for Godot* touch them. Our audience was open and willing to understand and learn.

They came unenslaved.

Oh, a lot of our older people fell asleep or walked out, not too different from the Miami and New York audiences. But most stayed, especially the young people. Their reactions were often vociferous. And very exciting to us.

We learned a great deal about acting from them. We had to be very clear and terribly honest. The audience knew right away whether it was real or not. They could not be fooled. They came here to learn and they didn't take any stuff from us. Each action had to be simple. Each move clear. When Gogo takes off his shoe—a simple thing—and complains about its being too tight, the laughter of recognition burst forth.

JOE LATTIMORE

1991

I interviewed him for my book, *Race: How Blacks and Whites Think and Feel about the American Obsession.*

Being black in America is like being forced to wear ill-fitting shoes. Some people adjust to it. It's always uncomfortable on your foot, but you've got to wear it because it's the only shoe you've got. You don't necessarily like it. Some people can bear the uncomfort more than others. Some people can block it from their mind, others can't. When you see some acting docile and some acting militant, they have one thing in common: the shoe is uncomfortable. It always has been and always will be.

———————

The kids were fascinated by the play. After the play in Ruleville, one of the kids went on stage and put on Pozzo's hat and put a rope around the neck of another kid. They played the game. The image of the two tramps, two vaudeville clowns, was exciting to them. They got the slave–master relationship immediately.

A lot of people stayed over after the play ended. We had discussions after every performance. A lot of it was confused and I began to think that we should abandon the idea. Then I realized they had been working it over in their minds. There was a lot of emotion. One man got up and as he talked and talked and talked, we realized that he sounded just like Lucky. Remember Lucky has that fifteen-minute speech during which his words fall over themselves; he's wound up like a phonograph record. It's as though he's rattling off the history of the world. This man's thoughts were wild, yet in a crazy way connected. He just couldn't get the words out fast enough. That's the man we were trying to reach.

When Lucky stops, Pozzo takes his hat off. In Holmes County, Mississippi, a man said of the scene: "You brought this play to put the thinking cap on us."

Holmes County was that all-black rural area that had a lot of troubles in the 1960s. Cars were bombed. People put up all-night guards to protect themselves, because the whites were coming any moment. Weird things were happening.

A photographer came there two weeks after our performance. There was a little girl in a local store, sitting on the table. He asked her whom she was waiting for. She said, "I'm waiting for Godot." [Laughs]

I think *Waiting for Godot* is one of the greatest plays in the twentieth century. It marks the beginning of a new playwriting era. No one can do what was before and leave it at that. This play has established a new plateau.

RICK CLUCHEY

1999

In 1955, he was a prisoner at San Quentin; sentenced to life without parole. After "eleven years, nine months and fourteen days in prison, and ten years of civil-death parole: twenty-two years in a prison designed to keep you," Governor Jerry Brown gave him a full pardon.

While in prison, Cluchey organized a theater workshop, putting on experimental plays and conventional dramas. *Waiting for Godot* was its first project. After his release, he founded a theater company, with several of his fellow San Quentin alumni as members. Most of the group's repertoire consisted of Samuel Beckett's plays. *Endgame* was the smash hit at the Edinburgh Festival of 1974. So, too, in Paris. While there, he met Beckett, who had heard about his work. For a time, he was an associate of the playwright.

We talked in the radio studio in February of 1999. He was in Chicago to perform in what Beckett called the definitive production of *Krapp's Last Tape*. He described a moment of epiphany.

On a windswept mid-November evening in 1957, a troupe of actors from nearby San Francisco arrived at San Quentin Prison. They brought with them a dead tree, a large stone, and a bullwhip, plus assorted costumes for five players. In the audience sat over 1,400 convicted men, serving long sentences for violent crimes including rape, murder, and robbery. I was one of those men and at the age of twenty-three had already served three years of my term of imprisonment. I was sentenced to life without possibility of parole for kidnapping, robbery, and violence. All around me in the huge mess hall *cum* theater, the air was charged with excitement; most of us had never seen a play before and had never been inside a theater, not even to rob it!

As the lights grew dim, the warden appeared from behind the curtain and immediately a hush fell upon the hall. He explained that this play marked the only time a professional performance of theater had been given inside the prison since the turn of the century, when Sarah Bernhardt stopped to entertain San Quentin convicts; he also expressed the hope that we'd respect this fact by our good behavior! Next he introduced the director of the play, Herbert Blau, and Blau explained to us the name of the playwright, the play, and the nature of watching some plays which are difficult to understand; he related the play to a jazz solo. Therefore we should listen to the play like music and find whatever we wanted in the interpretation! He left the stage and the curtain opened on a vacant, silent landscape, unbroken except for the endless void of darkness which engulfed it. I was reminded of a great cage. I sat transfixed as the play unfolded, the words coming forth with knife-like reason. Waiting! The play was about waiting! Waiting for somebody called Godot.

All around me the convicts were laughing! The laughter of recognition? Of course! We knew about waiting. We knew what it meant to wait for something; waiting had become an essential part of existence behind the grim walls of San Quentin. Waiting for a letter, for food, for the guards to open the cells, for a smile, for a handshake, for sleep. *Waiting.* Waiting for contact with another human being, for understanding, for love, for help, for relief from the total oppression of being trapped inside the black hole of this prison. And all about us in this sea of forgotten faces, we saw the same recognition. The situation of the characters on stage might well have been written for any member of the audience. And true enough, it was like a musical score filled with life, poetry, and tonal variations on theme which captured the imagination. We felt the mystery of this work a long, long time after the curtain fell.

The convicts all stood at once when the play ended; the applause was loud and sustained, while the San Francisco Actors' Workshop cast took their curtain calls. Everything came into focus. I had been waiting for Godot for all my prison life and didn't realize it.

E. G. MARSHALL

In the first New York production of *Waiting for Godot* he played Vladimir (Didi) opposite Bert Lahr as Estragon (Gogo).

It created a furor on opening night. Those who hated it thought they were being cheated and robbed. Others were moved to tears. At the time, we thought we'd have a short run. The producer had an ad. "Wanted: 18,000 intellectuals." Which is a heck of a way to advertise anything. He thought if he could get that many people to come, it would pay its production costs. We ran longer than expected. People were coming back to see it again and reassess their thoughts. Something of a Beckett cult came into being.

When Gogo asks me, "What are we waiting for?" I had to say, "We're waiting for Godot" twenty-eight times in twenty-eight different ways. With the last one, I whispered into his ear, "waswaswaswas." The audience knew what I was saying and burst into laughter.

Bert Lahr had a natural person's reaction to the play. He didn't intellectualize it. To him he was playing the part of a clown. I was the intellectual clown, he was the natural clown. He had no makeup, I had a modified clown makeup on. We didn't wear the Pierrot-Pierrette costumes, but tramp clown costumes. We said these are the thoughts of Pascal as enacted by clowns.

As we look back on *Godot*, it was a watershed, a milestone in theater. Beckett changed the nature of dramaturgy. All the writers who have come along since then owe him a debt.

ACT THREE

1—Solo Flight

RUTH DRAPER

1958

She was the first actor I ever saw offering a one-person evening of theater. On stage, by herself, she created a whole family of characters. It was she who influenced the great many who followed.

At the time of this conversation, she was on one of her last tours across the country. It was a balmy afternoon at the Fortnightly Club, a sanctuary for "genteel ladies," as the sun played upon her handsome, patrician features. She was in her sixties.

It was a wistful moment in her life. She had been lamenting the hard time her nephew, Paul Draper, the remarkable tap dancer, had been having during the witch-hunt days of Joe McCarthy.

Are these portraits you paint based upon actual human beings you've encountered?

I suppose it's an unconscious observation. But I never imitate anybody. I never put anybody that I see into a sketch. They're all fabricated characters. They're all invented people. Naturally, I suppose, they're based on observation. And I can't say that they're based on conscious observation. Only two or three sketches are based on actual facts, stories that I've heard or in two cases, I think, people that I have seen. That's a sketch in County Kerry based on an incident that impressed me very much, although I didn't in any sense imitate the woman. She's typical of a great many Irish peasants. And the sketch called "Three Generations in the Court of Domestic Relations" was based on an incident that I saw in court. I changed the story, but it was a picture of three women—a grandmother, mother, and a daughter. I made up the story and invented the types, but it was suggested to me by a real incident.

You do something there that is a bit of a mystery to everyone. Your sudden transformation. You're first the old immigrant grandmother, then you're the hard-working mother and suddenly you become this vibrant young girl of seventeen or eighteen. What's the trick?

I just become the person that I'm depicting. Instead of leaving the stage I do it all before the audience. That's why the transformation seems to be so quick, so immediate. Instead of leaving the stage to adjust the shawl, I just drop the shawl from my head to my shoulders, and then for the young girl I fling it off. I think it's the speed of the transformation that impresses them.

I think it's more than the speed of the transformation, the flinging off of the shawl. It seems to us who watch you that you become this other person. You become this young girl.

That is the essence of acting. That is what an actor or actress must do. Become that other person.

None of your portraits is etched in acid. Whether it be the titled lady who gives a lawn party, or the Irish peasant woman, or the three generations, or the continental actress, the frailties and foibles of humans are there, and that's it.

I think that everybody is rather ridiculous, and everybody is rather pitiful. And I try to show both sides, the humorous qualities in people, the ridiculous qualities, and the serious, human qualities. I don't know, my people are just made up of all parts, the way everybody is, I think.

It's very curious. Sometimes my mind hears a very good remark that I make on the spot, you know. If the audience is very exciting, and very lively, and very intelligent, and very responsive, I'm better. And sometimes I'll say something, and then I will hear myself. "My, that was good. I must remember that." And I never think of it again. Never do remember it. Sometimes I'm startled by a good line that I've made for the first time, and then I never remember.

It's the manner in which you use your voice that knocks me out. The inflections. In "The Italian Lesson" as this elegant woman is on the telephone, we immediately know whom she's talking to: her husband, her friend, or—bingo!—her lover.

Don't people often reveal themselves on the telephone? A certain inflection of the voice may tell of their attitude or relation to the one on the other end. I believe that's true of all of us.

AUTHOR'S NOTE. *I'm something of a chameleon on the phone. My wife immediately knows who's at the other end. I take on his or her characteristics. When Nelson Algren called, my voice took on a nasal, slow, dry-funny air. When Mahalia Jackson called, I sounded world-weary and murmured in the manner of James Baldwin, "Lord have mercy."*

Years ago, I wrote a radio script about Jimmy Durante. I read it back to him on the phone. As he reacted in his inimitably high-voltage gravelism, I was responding in like manner: "Yeah, yeah an' den Umbriago says dis —." When I hung up, my wife, who had just entered the house and heard the last fragments of the conversation, asked, "Did he like the script?"

When you told me you were interested in folk music, I thought of a series of folk songs I made up. They are really imitation folk songs. At the time, I had never visited these countries, heard the people that I imitate. I just made up the language and made up the melodies. As I find great difficulty in hearing the words of any song, as well as they're sung, I didn't think it made very much difference whether anybody understood what I was saying or not.

They amuse me very much. They always amuse musicians and singers, my satire on singing folk songs. I find that lullabies in almost every country have the same quality. They sing to the baby and then they speak of the father perhaps off on the hill minding the sheep while the baby is safe in the arms of the mother. And there's always a repetitious quality in the lilt of the song. So I made a little lullaby; I call it a Slovak Lullaby, not knowing in the least what the Slovak language sounds like, but imagining that it might be a certain mixture of Slavic sounds and Latin sounds. So I call this a Slovak Lullaby. [She sings.]

I have a Swedish polka which is very gay. A young girl dancing with her boyfriend in the village square. I had never heard Swedish, but I had heard Swedish people speak English, and I had got the lilt of their voices. And on the signs of delicatessen shops, I had noticed a great many O's with little marks over them, and SV's and SK's and curious Oos and Oh sounds that were marked so that I imagined what the language was like because I'd heard them speak English. Subsequently, as I went to Sweden, I think it does sound something like it. [She sings.]

It sounds right out of Stockholm.

Then I did an Arabian Beggar's Chant and I'd never been to Arabia, but I'd imagined that Arab music, which was the basis of Spanish music with a curious rhythm. I knew that they made use of quarter notes and eighth notes and effects of sound that would perhaps be dissonant to our ears sometimes, because they jump from one key to another. I thought it might sound like this, and when I went to Morocco later on, I found that it did. [She sings.]

Yet, as we listen, it sounds authentic, as though from a minaret even though we know you're kidding.

It's a very interesting demonstration, my work is, I think, of the need of an audience. The audience must work as well as I do. Their imagination must be fired, and then they supply all that's not there. A very interesting thing was said to me once by a man who knew a great deal about the theater and acting. He said, "You must get it over to the audience." He was wrong. What you must do is to get the audience up onto the stage and into the scene with you. The audience must contribute exactly what the performer contributes in proportion, I mean. They give their whole imagination, their concentration, their thought, their creative ability, and consequently something happens. It's a mixture.

Now the tendency in the movie audience and the television audience is just to sit still and receive. They give nothing. But in the theater the audience must give a great deal. In the ancient theater, in the Oriental theater, in the Greek theater, and in the seventeenth-century theater in Shakespeare's time, the audience supplied what was not there. When Shakespeare speaks of "how sweet the moon-light sleeps on yonder bank," there's no moonlight and no stage effects of moonlight. And they did it in daylight, so it is obvious that the audience had to supply the most tremendous amount of working imagination.

The trend in theater today and in cinema today is to deaden peoples' imagination. I'm very much interested to find that young people, the young, present generation who've never seen live acting, are terribly interested in what I do. They've never seen anything else but the screen. At last they are sharing, at last are finding in themselves the capacity to create. That's what's fun. That's what people enjoy, I think, in my work: feeling, unconsciously feeling that they are clever, that they have made the thing. They give me the credit for it, but it's really something in them. I mean they're all potential artists, all really, at heart, children. It's what children do with the greatest facility. I always think that what I do is something that, as a child, I never lost, which is the child's capacity to throw themselves completely into what they pretend to be. Children pretend that they're fairies, or pirates, or Indians, and they think you think so too when they perform for you. There's no self-consciousness. They think that you think they look like a pirate. That sounds ridiculous, but there's something very profound in that thought: if you're completely given over to what you're trying to portray, you will convince the other people too. And that's what I do.

EMLYN WILLIAMS

1960

The Welsh actor and playwright. *Night Must Fall* and *The Corn Is Green* were two of his most acclaimed plays. His adaptation of Ibsen's *The Master Builder* was performed by Laurence Olivier at the British National theater. His performances as an actor in films and in the theater invariably evoked respectful salutes. His one-man shows as Charles Dickens and, later, as Dylan Thomas occupied most of his last years as a performer.

This conversation took place during one of his Chicago performances in *A Boy Grows Up*, a compote of Thomas's autobiographical writings.

It started very gradually. There was a memorial tribute to Dylan shortly after his death. Edith Evans and Richard Burton read some poems. I was to read a couple of his stories. We had ten days to prepare. I thought I really must sit down and get them by heart. It was ten days of absolute slavery. I sat up with a towel around my head until I mastered all those words. It was worth it, because I got the idea that I'd do the same with him as I had with Dickens.

I picked on all of my favorite pieces, but of course I had no possible way of putting them together. I didn't know what the link should be. Then I realized that all the stories, all the bits and sketches that I loved had to do with his childhood from the age of four to the age of seventeen. I'm telling the story from the moment the curtain goes up to the moment it finishes.

My great fear was that a wonderful story, perfect for the last act because of its strength, would do, but it dealt with his very early childhood at the age of five and I wanted something at the age of seventeen. I struggled and juggled. Luckily, there was one when he got to London at the age of seventeen. It fit. At last, I had my links.

What a tour de force that one was. The man hopping up and down on that mattress, casually greeting you, because there was no other room, it being filled to the ceiling with furniture; Dylan with his finger stuck in a bottle; the crying woman; the girl with glasses in the bathroom. You were all those. How did you carry that off?

Strangely enough, it was not as exhausting as playing a long part in a play. I was not responsible for other people on the stage and worried about their timing and mine. I was in absolute charge. So you rehearse by yourself, arduously, concentrate, and you've got it.

I had to write the bridges between the stories to make it absolutely continuous, so that you would see or hear no change of gears.

Just to make it as if the whole thing had been written expressly for one man for the stage.

It was oral biography.

That's wonderful that you should think that, because that's what I hoped it would be, really weaving bits. I'd fiddled with them like a jigsaw puzzle.

There was a chair and there was a screen with the signature Dylan Thomas. And you walked in with a couple of loose-leaf books.

Yes. School notebooks.

You sat on the chair, or got off the chair, or bounced, or jumped, or cocked your eye. With each gesture, with each suggestion you became a different person. Did this call upon your own memories too of people like that?

Yes. A lot of it, of course, is in the actual cutting of the stories; that you must always make it clear who is speaking. It's a lot of it in the manipulation of the words with which, of course, I had great training in doing Dickens.

In The Outing, *there are Dylan Thomas's memories of his uncle; his huge uncle with the big waistcoat. How many old men did you do on that bus? His old cronies.*

Seven or eight. I suppose it's helped by having my memories of my own childhood, because my own father was an innkeeper until I was about twelve, and so I saw a great many of those men, standing up and lying down. A lot of beer drinking. I was just sitting watching, I imagine, just the same as Dylan used to.

Did you know Dylan Thomas?

No. I never met him, oddly enough. I feel in a way it was quite a good thing that I didn't. It left me free to work entirely on what he's written, not on my memory of him as a person.

I met his mother after he died. It was a very touching relationship we had.

Did his mother know you were doing him?

Oh, yes, because I wrote and I think I asked her if she minded my using certain things of his which involved her. There's a short story, you know the one, the mad one about London, when he goes to London, which talks about his mother.

Oh, yes, when he's on the train.

Yes. And I thought she might be rather hurt, and I thought I must ask her. And then from there on she sort of adopted me. It was about a year after he died that I started.

What about yourself? We know of you, too, as the playwright of two powerful works. One very moving, The Corn Is Green, *and the other, the gripping, macabre,* Night Must Fall. The Corn Is Green. *Was this autobiographical?*

Somewhat, yes. Well, more than somewhat really because it was written about my own school mistress who prepared me for Oxford, and helped me to get a scholarship there. It started me off into the theater and really started me off generally, period.

Was yours a mining village?

There are mines near, but it's in North Wales. I was never a miner myself. I almost believe I was now because people say to me, "When did you cease to be a miner?" My father was a miner for a short time. He was mostly an innkeeper. I've never been inside a mine.

Now, it is this one-man theater that has you on the hip. The actor alone on the stage.

It's a return to medieval minstrelsy, almost, isn't it? People were going around just sitting down and telling stories, really, and acting them, and being able to go around from one castle to another. I'm able to go around from one college auditorium to another, from one night to the next, and I must say it's a life I enjoy.

1964

It is a return Chicago engagement for Emlyn Williams as Charles Dickens. It is also related to the publication of his memoir, *George*. It is also his seventy-fifth birthday.

In the beginning, I dreaded writing my autobiography. I thought, I can't just sit down for two years and put I, I, I, all, everything being about me, which an actor rather shirks from really, because an actor always likes to hide behind something that he's doing, like I hide behind Charles Dickens at the moment. But once I started it, I got so involved that it was like writing about somebody else. If you're a writer and an actor, your personality changes once you're doing one and not the other.

When I first started doing Dickens and was rehearsing it, I had great difficulties adjusting myself. But as soon as I really got that beard on and was really doing my dress rehearsals, I was perfectly happy, because I was really then behind this facade of being somebody else, which was Dickens. I realized the tremendous drama and variety in Dickens. You realize that now he would have been writing plays and films. He would have been mad about films, about movies. A lot of his stuff reads like a wonderful scenario, wonderful shooting script. He was mad on the theater. If he hadn't had a cold when he was about seventeen, he would have gone to an audition at Drury Lane or somewhere. He wanted to go into the theater, wild about it. He didn't go, and became a reporter in the House of Commons. He was always acting. He was always in theatricals, always putting on plays for charity. He had a great itch really to be an actor. When he did these things, which he called readings, it wasn't a reading at all, it was a tremendous performance.

He had a great thing of social criticism, sometimes savage and sometimes political. Of course I've concentrated on the funny side of it, because he had this marvelous humor.

He saw society as a circus. Dickens was out of a poverty-stricken childhood. I think he had, not a complex exactly, but he was very class-conscious and wanted to take it out on the snobs at that time.

Naturally, when I was working on the program, my only concern was to make it entertaining and varied, to change pace all the time. But it happens to involve things which are about society, doesn't it?

Mr. and Mrs. Veneering, who are on the make—

In *Our Mutual Friend*, the Podsnaps are a step above them, and they want to get there. The Myrtles are way up. The real tycoons, you'd call them now. There's a tycoon in *Little Dorritt* who causes, as it were, a sort of Wall Street crash in London. He's this powerful man who gives these tremendous parties. Later, everything goes. He's swindled thousands of people by using their money in the wrong way, and he commits suicide in a Turkish bath. I'd love to have used it in my readings, but I felt it might have been a touch too macabre. Dickens, of course, had a great sense of the macabre, obvious in his ghost stories.

It's funny how all these elements are in Dylan Thomas, too, in a wholly different way. Of course, two different men, two different artists, different times.

There's a lot in common, because his humor is extraordinary, it's sort of surrealist too—Dylan Thomas. He had a sense of pathos, too—some of those stories of Dylan Thomas. His mother did tell me that Dickens was one of his favorite authors. Quite out of the blue. I was asking her about what he was like as a boy. And she said that Dickens was one of his idols. You'd think there'd be nothing in common because of the difference of epoch, but there is, really.

I read a couple of things about those triumphant tours Dickens did. It got rather discouraging because they said he was so astonishing a performer. Apparently, when he came on in the funny bits, the audience laughed so much they fell off their seats, and then in the pathetic bits they cried. Women swooned at the sight of him because in those days there was no radio, no television. He was this mythical figure. It was like Churchill going around now, or somebody. And I got discouraged; I thought, I can't compete with that. So I just had to imagine what he would have been like if I had been him.

Coming back as Dickens after five years doing Dylan Thomas and other things, it's absolutely fresh to me, particularly with the new things I'm doing. Every night is like a first night. You're re-creating, really. You must see it as your audience does. In a double way. A double consciousness, yes.

Dickens would have vied with some of the Welsh preachers I heard at chapel. When I did Dickens in Wales, they said it was like having one of the great preachers. Oh, the drama is tremendous in some of the preachers. The congregation—I was going to say the audience—waits for the great climaxes to come and, suddenly, they take off like an airplane. It's oratory, really, isn't it? Welsh preachers are orators. Of course, all this affected what I do in theater.

HAL HOLBROOK

1959 and 1961

> Ladies and gentlemen, I wish to present you a man whose great learn-ing and veneration for truth are exceeded only by his high moral char-acter and majestic presence. I refer in these very general terms, to myself. [Audience laughter] . . . I was born modest, but it wore off.

> Thus the young actor, on the stage of the Goodman theater in Chicago, introduces *Mark Twain Tonight*. It is a re-creation of the celebrated author's lecture tour across the country in 1905, when he was seventy.
>
> The familiar white suit, the flowing mustache, and the cigar are all there; and so, uncannily, is the presence of Mark Twain.

During my last year at Denison,* my wife and I did sketches from the lives of famous people. One of them was Mark Twain. I knew little about him, so I had to find out who he was and what he thought. I remembered reading Tom and Huck vaguely when I was fourteen. They made no impression upon me. When I read Huck, say at twenty-two, he made a little more impression. Now, my God. I think the older you get, the more you appreciate the deep lights and shadows.

---

*A liberal arts college in Ohio.

When I began to read as much of Twain as I could possibly get my hands on, I became fascinated with the character of the man himself. I had never met anyone that seemed to be telling the truth so often, alive or dead. [Laughs]

I remember so many instances where I had just been reading the paper and got terribly steamed up about something that I considered a terrible injustice or a horrible stupidity — the best way to get an ulcer is to read the paper. Or maybe I had just committed some asinine act and come out a jackass and knew it. I'd feel so embarrassed and angry. I found the only thing that would calm me down was to read Mark Twain.

A paragraph would just leap out of the page. It was as though he had just written a direct comment on what was bothering me. It was just wonderful because he turned it into humor somehow; humor that is not surface, but from deep compassion or indignation. Then I could relax and go to sleep. It was either that or pills.

His influence on my life has been profound. But I have a huge problem playing this man. Remember, I began doing this when I was twenty-two. I was a young actor struggling to create my own self and image, plunging completely into this character. Now, as I feel Mark Twain on stage, other things inside *me* keep coming out.

I spend three and a half hours every night at the dressing table making myself up as Mark Twain. As I carefully add bit, by bit, by bit, I become, bit by bit, that man. It's quite an experience sitting before that mirror transforming yourself into someone else.

The suit came first. I looked at his photographs and there was always the white suit. The cigar was, of course, the identifiable symbol. An actor in a one-man show needs an activity. The cigar is more than a prop. It is a holding onto something. Lots of times when people get up to speak and are nervous, you give them a matchbox, let 'em hold it in their hand, it's holding onto mother, you know. [Laughs] In this case, Mark Twain loved cigars. I read somewhere that he bought them by the barrel. So holding on to a cigar, rolling it in my hand, clomping it in my mouth now and then, feels as natural for me as it must have felt for him.

You're delivering things in a funny style — as though you are unaware that they are funny. There's a feeling of bland innocence, as if you didn't know the astounding irreverence you just uttered. [Laughs]

What may have helped through the years, especially in my early years, is that he never lost the spirit of youth; the youth who does not accept the answers of his elders; who must find the answer for himself. That spirit lasted for seventy-two and a half years for Mark Twain.

You're not just Mark Twain, you're Mark Twain at seventy becoming Huck, the eleven-year-old illiterate kid. The scene on the raft, for instance, where Huck battles with his conscience. How do you carry it off?

I'm not quite sure myself. It's a tough challenge. I have to really concentrate on this piece because I have to be thinking I'm Mark Twain all the time, but I must never let that thinking get in the way, so the boy can come through.

We had trouble with the record album because of the word in that scene: "nigger." This was written in 1885. I just don't see how people could come away from that scene without a wonderful feeling of humanity and the realization that Twain ennobled the Negro. The use of the word "nigger" is important: the way Pap, Huck's drunken father, uses it, the way an ignorant person uses it: "A fella, a free nigger from Ohio, that could vote. What's this country comin' to if I'm gonna let him vote?"

Remember Huck in disguise at the farmhouse door? There was a steamboat explosion. The lady of the house says, "Oh, my, was anybody hurt?" He says, "No, ma'am, just a nigger." And she says, "Oh, well, that's good, because sometimes people do get hurt." Twain turns around and uses that word as a bullwhip, as savage satire, and it stings hard.

It happened just the other night at the theater. You, Hal Holbrook—or was it Mark Twain?—got heckled from the audience. It was a stunning moment.

Oh, boy, was it! I was going into Twain on religion, right after the Huck Finn piece. He was pointing out that it was partially because of the support of the church, as well as the press, that slavery was condoned. It was preached from the pulpit, that it was a sin to help a slave escape. I had just described Huck doing that very thing when he lied to the slavers about Jim being on the raft. Slavery was a holy thing, justified in the Bible. Huckleberry figured that by helping Jim escape, why, he was going to have to go to hell, but this courageous little boy decided he'd just go to hell and do it anyway.

Mark Twain goes on to point out that in the old days the church indulged in witch-hunting because the Bible justified it. He brings in the business of the church, the terrible persecutions carried out for nine centuries. He says, "Night and day; tortured, hanged, burned whole armies of witches. And then it was discovered there was no such thing as witches."

At this point, this woman in the audience shouts, "What church are you talking about?" [Takes a deep breath.] Suddenly, I'm not Mark Twain, but a young man and a very angry one. She was voicing the very narrow-mindedness which I was trying to expel. She was also breaking the spell. She was challenging me. Of course, though she didn't realize it, it was Mark Twain she was challenging.

At that moment, my mind was whizzing around like a rocket because I didn't know what I was going to do next. I just looked at her and waited and waited. The silence was . . . the audience went [he gasps] . . . Suddenly I realized that I had all the heavy artillery coming up in the last five minutes of this number. I was furious, but I knew I had to control myself and try to be as mature in this situation as Mark Twain would have been. Mark would have leveled this woman with the material I had coming up. It was funny but filled with acid. If I did it furiously, as I felt that moment, it would have been too much. I was Mark Twain and simply said his words, which were devastating. The woman had provided all the emotional savagery.

The material I choose has to speak for 1961. He has written so much, so rich, so contemporary, I have to sift through it like a gold prospector. The stuff on Cuba and the Philippines I cannot refer to directly now. I can't mention Castro and Kennedy. But when I quote Twain on something astoundingly similar, the audience makes an immediate connection.

The subject of the silent lie is good for all time. I pulled from ten to twenty Twain pieces and created *On the Decay in the Art of Lying*. It was all Twain, based upon a number of sources. It went especially well in Europe last year. [In character] When I talk about the decay in the art of lying, I'm talking about the silent lie, the unspoken one. It requires no art, you simply keep still and conceal the truth . . . When whole nations conspire to propagate gigantic mute lies, in the interests of tyrannies and shams, why should we care anything about the trifling ones told by individuals? Why make them undesirable? Why not be honest and honorable and lie every chance we get? Why should we help the nation lie the whole day long and then object to telling one little, individual, private lie in our own interests; just for the refreshment of it, I mean, and to take the rancid taste out of our mouth. No, there's no art to this silent lying. It is timid and shabby.

I notice that you laugh easily, from the belly. Mark Twain would have delighted in you as his audience.

I'm always terribly depressed when you do a show and someone says *sshh!* when a guy's trying to laugh and enjoy himself. Gee whiz, laughing is actually a physical release of tension, a catharsis.

"Laughin' to keep from cryin'" is a blues lyric.

I remember going to see *A Raisin in the Sun*. To me, there was a rich, earthy humor in it. I was roaring with laughter. The people behind me kept giving me that look: "Listen, this is a problem play. What are you doing?"

In front of me there were about five Negro people seated. They were laughing very hard. I had gotten a little embarrassed by the people looking at me, so I tried to hold my laugh in, even though I was really having a wonderful time and I loved the play. When the play was over and the house lights came on, one of those Negro ladies turned square around to me and said in a loud voice, "You got some laugh. You oughta rent that laugh out. You'd make a million dollars." [Laughs] Boy, I felt wonderful.

2—Out of the Shadows

I am at the Regal theater on Chicago's South Side. It is the counterpart of the Apollo in New York's Harlem. The audience, as well as the performers, are black; though there is usually a smattering of whites.

She ambles onto the stage in a sort of housedress, sneakers, as Count Basie's band has finished its set. The crowd laughs as little kids laugh when they're about to eat something that tastes *so* good. She begins her soliloquy:

"Week before last I was standing on the White House lawn. Me and Dulles was talkin'. Mamie, she came out and admired my bangs. You understand what I mean. We sent Dulles across the street to get some Pepsi Colas over at the delicatessen. Dulles said, 'Moms, we called you down here because we wanted to know what age should you hip a child.' I said, 'What age would *you* hip one, Dulles?' 'Pshaw, when they get school age.' I said, 'Oh, boy, no wonder the country goin' to pot.' I say, 'As soon as a child is born, that's the time to hip it.' Whether that baby can answer you back or not, it's digging everything you're putting down, from them first words. You get it wrong, instead of telling that baby the truth, you put your big hand up in front of that child's face, no wonder they got all kinds of diseases. It gets a little older, you want to go out and have a nice time, all you gotta do is say, 'Listen, old man, I done straightened you out, you go ahead and get some shut-eye. I'm gonna cut out, I'm gonna dig you later, you're on your own.'"

I was raised with God-fearing parents and I always prayed to God. I got on my knees when I was in Buffalo, and prayed to God to open a way. And something said to me, "Go on the stage." None of my people from generations back had never been on the stage, you know. I was around fifteen years old. Young girls do run away from home sometimes.

My hometown was Brevard, North Carolina. It ain't on the map. You go to Asheville, then you take a buggy and go to Brevard, I suppose. It was a great resort, as you know, up in those mountains, the healthiest place in the world. Rich people that had, you know, estates, joining Vanderbilts up there. I wish you could see the spot where I was born, and my beautiful home. It looked like a mansion. We had plenty of servants and everything.

My father was a businessman. He had the only white barbershop, undertaker shop, grocery store, dry goods store.

You said a white barbershop.

Yes, only white people came in our barbershop.

Your grandfather was a white man?

Yes. Lawyer Duckworth from North Carolina. Wonderful man. Never denied his children; never denied my mother's children.

My grandmother was born during slavery, my great-grandmother was a grandmother in slavery. My great-grandmother was a wonderful woman. She was mostly all Cherokee Indian. She lived to be 117. Her words was like gold nuggets. I used to stay with my grandmother a lot, and after granny got so old, then she came to live with my grandmother. So she would tell me stories of slavery. Wonderful. And she would always emphasize—she couldn't say Loretta, which is my name, she'd say Retta—she'd say, "Retta, you're freeborn."

The mother of a Negro family didn't want to do some of the things she did, it's because she was forced to do it. Then, too, it was that great deep religious feeling in that faith in God to take them through. Granny used to tell me they weren't allowed to have Bibles. And they used to have to go down in the woods, the same as you would hide whiskey or something, and they'd hide them. And they'd go down at night by the moonlight and have a meeting. And they'd have to sing very low, you know. And the ones that could read, why they would read the Bible and sing those songs. And I remember Granny used to sing a song: "Before I'd be a slave,

I'd be buried in my grave and go home to my Lord and be free." Oh, she was one of the greatest people. She was the greatest. My great-grandmother. They prayed, they trusted. They knew some day it would happen. And all of the things that are happening, Granny would tell me, she told me years ago, you know.

You told me you were a wet nurse at fourteen.

Yes, it was for a family in Asheville that I was a wet nurse for. They're called the Dickersons. They lived out in the Gold Park section. This man had come to Asheville for his health. They has this baby, and no formula. A sickly child. The mother didn't have the milk for it. What was she? Around thirty-seven, I think, when she got married. Out of all of the women in, that they tested, I'm the one that stood the test and nursed that baby. And I'd grown the fondest for that child; I loved that baby like my own baby. She was a part of me. I willingly gave her part of my life. I sacrificed my own baby sometime. I would say to Lucretia, to my own baby, "Darling," I'd say, "Lord, you're a big strong baby, little Lois is weak and sick." I'd say, "Now, don't cry," I'd say, "I'm savin' some milk for little Lois." And I loved that baby. I used to tell her, I'd say, "Some day I'm going to make you proud of me," I'd tell little Lois.

I've never run into Lois. And I've tried very, very hard. Whether she's living or whether she's not, I would like to know what happened to that baby. To my baby. The mother, the Negro mother is the rock in her family, because the Negro mother in one sense has had more opportunity than the Negro father. He was denied manhood.

The show people named me Moms. Yes, both, of both races. Because, even though I was young, they would always bring their problems to me to settle. And then so many, sometimes, they get away from home and wouldn't be able to get back, and I'd send them home. Or I'd always put on a pot or something like that when I know that those ones that didn't have very much money, I'd see that they were fed. So they named me Moms, I didn't give myself that name.

There was a circuit called the TOBA, Theater Owner's Booking Association, which was the greatest thing and should be today, because it taught young people how to be entertainers. Both as in character as well as ability.

There is no such training ground today. These children will make a record or something and you'll throw them out there on the stage, and that stage is a work of art. It's not to be played with. They go out there, they don't know even how to walk on it. In those days, this TOBA time, you'd go down by the way of Washington, and in two years time you come out by the way of St. Louis, because in those days you worked sometimes two and three weeks in one place. And then they had a wonderful circuit, and then they had these little tap shows. The TOBA circuit. It was also known as Tough on Black Actors. That's what they used to say. But I don't know, it didn't stop me. From the minute I went on the stage . . . I did *The Rich Aunt from Utah*, a comedy. It was a very funny comedian on the show which later became my husband. An old man. But one of the finest men in the world.

We were playing Macon, Georgia, and a colored man by the name of Old Man Douglas, he had a theater, and above that theater he had this hotel. I had taken very ill in Macon. In Macon, any man that was caught in a woman's room had to marry her or go to jail. So I was sick, and Leroy, the comic on the show, came in to see how I was feeling. Somebody got to fighting at the hotel and the cops come in and of course they went in everybody's room. And I remember the cop said, "What are you doing?" And Leroy says, "She's sick. I just came to see her." And the cop says, "Well, you'll either marry her or go to jail." So they just called in a preacher and married us. No license, no birth certificate, nothing. [Laughs] And we're married. And Leroy was just like, more like a father to me. He was one of the finest men that ever was.

I learned so much from him about timing. Timing don't come overnight, son. That's one of the secrets about the great Duke Ellington. You can't learn in a music university to time a note. The Duke has that. Timing is everything in show business. You'd see on this TOBA time, the older people. Like in Chicago, Butter Beans Susie.

When I went into show business, I was making $12.50 a week, and had a baby. And when I got raised to $15, I thought I was rich.

Oh, boy. We go from one show to another, in different places and run into people. Like one show going out and another one coming in, Butter Beans Susie came to me after the show and says, "Girl, who are you and where are you from? You're sensational. You're the whole show." Susie said, "Between you and I, how much is the man paying you?" And I said, "Fifteen dollars." I was really proud. She says, "Oh, ain't that a shame." She says, "I'll tell you what you do, say put in your notice and quit in the next town," which was Port Arthur. And I did. And they wrote Mr. Boudreau and Bennett in New Orleans and told them, because they were headliners: Butter Beans Susie, Bessie Smith—those people were headliners.

I worked on a bill with Bessie Smith many a day. And so they booked me from New Orleans to Chicago, to the place used to be called Monogram Theater. They booked me there without a layoff at $90 a week. I'd been all over that circuit and I listened to those people, and watched them carry themselves as ladies and gentlemen. If you didn't on the TOBA time, your punishment, you had to go over it again. I don't care how great an artist you was. If you had no character, if you didn't know how to carry yourself, you had to go over that circuit again. And you'd rather be dead. [Laughs] It was rough.

One of the wittiest comedians I've ever worked with was Dusty Fletcher. He was the one that really wrote *Open the Door Richard*. That's why they had that big lawsuit. That belonged to him. There's not many comedians that can ad-lib, as you call it. He was a great ad-libber. And I like to work with somebody that can ad-lib. One time I know a very big man, now that has a television show. He says, "Moms, we'd like to have you on the show, but we never know what you're gonna say." I said, "Well . . ." [a laugh] I wasn't particular on being on it, because I don't like for no one to underrate my intelligence. After all, I love Moms too. And I know what to say and *when* to say it and where to say it. You don't entertain the audience the same way. You got to know how to switch your material, and professional instinct teaches me when to switch my material. It was just something that came along, that wonderful gift that God gave me.

You had to do everything in show business, and learn everybody's part, so if somebody takes sick, you step right in and do their part. Sing, dance, talk, everything. That was what was great about the TOBA: it taught you how to do everything and do it well. If you *could* sing . . . Of course if you couldn't sing that was a different thing, then they perfected you in whatever category that you were best in. And so I started doing comedy.

To tell the truth, you don't have to look for material, darling. The way the world's going now, it's funny. It is, it's comedy. And especially the truth. The things that I record, very few of them are jokes. Like about that baby. I *do* think that's time to wizen up a child. What I got and how I feel, and goodness knows I started young enough raising children, has a lot to do with those first words, how you raise that child. Tell that child the truth. Why lie? Because those lies will register. Then when that child tells you a lie, you wanna whip it, and that's wrong. Tell the truth. It's much easier.

[We listen to a recording of her live performance at the Apollo theater.]

"Let me tell you what happened to Moms week before last. You know where I was? *Way* down in deepest Georgia. Right here at election time. There stood a whole row of [whistles] white folks with me at the end of the line. [Laughter] We all had come to cast our votes, but don't you know that they got mad at me when I said I was sent there by the NAACP. Every time I get up to the front of the line, they push me back in the rear. And from the evil, mean look that they had on their face, I said, 'What am I doing here?' I said [chanting song], 'Please, boys. I don't wanna vote.' I said, 'Please, please don't make me vote.' [Laughter] I had a dream last night, I asked for my equal rights. Somebody said, 'Moms, you're next.' And there I stood with a rope around my neck. [Laughter] Please, Congressman Adam Clayton Powell, they ain't gonna let me vote. [Laughter] The arms reach out for me, they must want desperately. [Laughter] But if I can just break free, they've seen the last of me. In Georgia, no peace will I find, till I catch a plane north and blow Georgia out of my mind. Great God can you hear me. *Oh, yeah.* [Laughter, applause]"

Has there been a change in humor or is it the same?

Well, son, one fault, they do a lot of stealing, which Moms don't. This comedian's stealing from that comedian, this one's stealing from the other one's jokes. I believe in the Golden Rule. Thou shall not steal. In no form. Because if you steal my material, you might as well steal my money, because that's my living.

You don't have to do that because your stuff is uniquely yours.

[We listen to a recording.]

"Got me a job out here with some people, and they told me before I went to work, they said, 'Moms, don't work for that woman.' Said, 'She don't pay nobody.' I said, 'Well, I got to work. I'm gonna try it one time.' [Laughter] Sure enough, when I started working for her three weeks, she didn't give me a dime. [Laughter] I said, 'I know what I'm gonna do. I'm gonna go upstairs and get in her bed and I'm gonna lay right there till she pays me.' [Laughter] I went upstairs and got in her bed and she thought I was sick and sent for the doctor. Doctor come and he said, 'What's the matter girl?' I said, 'Nothing, only she owe me, she won't pay me, and I'm gonna lay right here till she pays.' The doctor said, 'Get over further.' Oh, she wouldn't pay nobody. [Laughter]"

LORRAINE HANSBERRY

1959

It is an apartment on Chicago's South Side, known as the Black Belt. Hers is one of the leading, more affluent families in the city's African American community. She has returned to Chicago for a visit shortly after the Broadway opening of her first play, *A Raisin in the Sun*. It had won the Drama Critics Circle Award.

I'm sure you've been told a number of times, "This is not really a Negro play. It could be about anybody."

[Sighs] Invariably. I know what they're trying to say: it is not the traditional "Negro play." It isn't a protest play. It isn't something that hits you over the head. What they're trying to say is something very good; that they believe the characters transcend category. Unfortunately, they couldn't be more wrong.

I believe one of the most sound ideas in dramatic writing is that in order to create the universal, you must pay great attention to the specific. Not only is this a play about a Negro family, specifically and definitely, culturally. It's not even a New York family or a Southern Negro family. It is specifically South Side Chicago. That kind of care, that kind of attention to detail, to the extent that people believe them, accept them. They can become anybody. But it is definitely a Negro play before it is anything else.

You call Walter Lee Younger, the son, the protagonist of the play, an affirmative hero.

He refuses to give up. There are moments when he doubts himself, retreats, does things I don't agree with. But in the end he goes beyond that point when he says not only was he cheated, but the solution is to cheat everybody else because this is the way life is. What he means is: this is the way life around *him* is. I suppose he represents my own feeling that sooner or later we're going to have to make principled decisions that will seem contrary to what we think we want.

I think it's conceivable to create a character who decides that his whole life was wrong and that he ought to go out and do something else altogether different: a complete reversal of things that *we* think are acceptable. This to me is a kind of affirmation. It isn't just rebellion, because rebellion rarely knows what it wants to do after it's through rebelling.

Nothing is really solved here as we move into a new neighborhood.

Walter Lee Younger and his family may have plenty of trouble. He probably will if he's moving anywhere in Chicago. [Laughs]

There's someone else equally powerful: the mother. In many cultures, it's the mother, the woman, who is the strength. Ma Joad in Grapes of Wrath.

Analogies often apply but there are fundamental differences. There are those of us who think it has something to do with the slave society, where she was allowed, not ascendancy, but at least control of her family; where the male was relegated to absolutely nothing. It's a mistake to confuse it with the Freudian concept of matriarchal dominance and Philip Wylie's momism. Not that there aren't negative things about it, that tyrannies don't emerge. But basically, it's a great thing. These women have become the backbone of our people in a very necessary way.

The Irish reflect this. There's a relationship between Mother Younger and Juno* that is very strong and obvious. There probably was a necessity that among oppressed people, the mother would assume a certain kind of role. The most oppressed group of any oppressed group will be its women. They are twice militant, because they're twice oppressed. So they react accordingly and there's an assumption of leadership historically.

I love Sean O'Casey. He is the playwright of the twentieth century using the most obvious instrument of Shakespeare: the human personality in its totality. I've always thought this was profoundly significant for Negro writers, not to copy, but as a model, a point of departure.

O'Casey never fools you about the Irish. You've got the Irish drunkard, the Irish braggart, the Irish liar who's always fighting the revolution and when the English show up, runs and hides under the bed, while the young girl goes out to fight the Tommies.

Genuine heroism must naturally emerge when you tell the truth about people. This, to me, is the height of artistic perception. When you believe in a people completely, they're so recognizable, because everybody has their drunkards and their braggarts and their cowards. Then you also believe them in their moments of heroic assertion, too. You don't doubt them, you don't feel this is soap opera.

Walter Lee Younger's revealed frailties made his heroic moment somewhat more believable.

That was my hope. In theater, what I don't believe in is naturalism. I think it should die a quick death. I do believe in realism. If you

---

Juno and the Paycock by Sean O'Casey.

repeat what is, show a murder and say, "This is the whole of life," you lie. Realism demands the imposition of a point of view. O'Casey's point of view has always been the wonder of the nobility of people. He uses poetic dialogue which moves it out of the realm of what I'm ever able to write into the sphere of great art. As a matter of fact, there are parallels between Negro urban speech and Irish urban speech.

People keep asking me if the play is autobiographical. No. I come from an extremely comfortable background. But I also explain that we live in a ghetto, which automatically means intimacy with all classes and all kinds of experiences. This is one of the things that the American experience has meant to Negroes. We are one people.

Though your play is not autobiographical, does the younger sister bear a resemblance to you?

Oh, yes. My brother would tell you that. [Laughs] It's an expression of conceit, really. I enjoyed making fun of this girl, who is myself eight years ago. Even though I kidded her, I have a confidence about what she represents. She's precocious, she's over-outspoken, she's everything that tends to be comic. People sigh with her. They have one at home like that. She's very much alive. She doesn't have a word in the play that I don't agree with. I would say it differently today.

My favorite character is the African suitor. I think he's a true intellectual. He is so confident in his perception of the world that he has no need for any façade. I was aware that the Broadway stage had never seen an African who didn't have his shoes hanging around his neck and a bone through his nose. The only Africans I've known have been students and he was a composite. He's something of a hangover of something that began in the '20s and '30s, when Negro intellectuals became aware of the African past, particularly in poetry and the creative arts. The girl asks him in the play. "You're always talking about freedom and independence in Africa, but what about that time when that happens and you'll have crooks and petty thieves, who'll come into power and they'll do the same things, only now they'll be black?"

He knows that, he tells her. But he simply believes in the order that things must take. Before you can start talking about independence, get it. [Laughs]

You've expressed annoyance with plays about Negroes by those outside the experience of being black. How about Carmen Jones for a starter?

It's the whole concept of the exotic, you know. In Europe, they think the gypsy's just about the most exotic thing there is. It's because he's isolated from the mainstream of European life. *Obviously*, the natural parallel in American life is the Negro. So whenever they get ready to do something like a Bizet opera, involving the gypsies of Spain, they neatly translate it into a Negro piece. I'm bored with the clichés. People may not realize how dull, and often nauseating these stereotyped notions are. *Porgy and Bess.* I'm talking about Du Bose Heyward's book, not the opera. In that beautiful music the roots of our native opera may some day be found. The book offends me, not only because it's a degrading way of looking at people. It's *bad art* because it doesn't tell the truth. There's no excuse for a stereotype. I'm not talking politically. I'm talking as an artist. Art is almost the only place where you can tell the truth.

Watch out for a young guy who's been one of the exiles and is now coming home. Jimmy Baldwin. Ever hear of him? I think he's just finished a novel. From what I've read of his essays, he's one of the most talented American writers walking around. If he can wed his particular gifts — which are way beyond most of us — we have the stuff of a great American writer. He's one, I think.

In our hometown, not too far from where we're sitting, Richard Wright was setting hearts on fire.

He's one who didn't come back. And I've not been at all impressed with his output since he left. Being away from one's roots is a killer. People say, "Don't get lost in a cause because this is what destroys art." I've been obliged to remind people that for two hundred years, the only writers in English literature we've had to boast about have been the Irish, who come from an oppressed culture. Shaw, O'Casey. From Jonathan Swift to James Joyce. I don't think it's an accident. Even though they're not protest writers in the sense we think, they were exiles. O'Casey's Dublin plays, though written in Devonshire, England, still ring and have that good Irish flavor. He never lost his roots, and I'm afraid Richard Wright has lost his.

Wright belonged to another tradition in American writing that came to flower with a novel like *Grapes of Wrath*. My husband would say Dreiser. [Laughs] I'd like to see that kind of panoramic power reemerge in the American novel. And it might come from a Negro writer. The glory of Langston Hughes was the blues quality in his poetry. When a Negro dramatist can approach a little of that feeling, he might get close to what O'Casey does in putting the Irish folk song into a play.

I sense at this particular time a new mood in the country. We've gone through ten years of misery under McCarthy and all that nonsense. To the great credit of the American people, they got rid of it and they're making new sounds. I'm glad I was here to make one.

JAMES BALDWIN

1961

He was in Chicago promoting his book of essays, *Nobody Knows My Name: More Notes of a Native Son.*

People talk to me about the strides that have been made. And all these dreary movies Hollywood keeps turning out about be kind to Negroes today and isn't this a good sign? Of course, they've never seen these movies with a Negro audience watching them.

The Defiant Ones was a celebrated movie about two convicts who escape from a Southern chain gang. One is black, Sidney Poitier. The other is white, Tony Curtis. They hop on a freight train, presumably heading toward freedom.

At the end of the movie, Sidney, who does his best in a rather dreary role, does something I just couldn't *believe* would have been done. He jumps off that train to rescue Tony Curtis. I saw this movie twice, deliberately. I saw it downtown in front of a white liberal audience. [Sighs] I suppose they were liberal. There was a great sigh of relief and clapping, and I felt this was a very noble gesture on the part of a very noble black man. And I suppose in a way it was.

Then I saw it uptown before a Negro audience. When Sid jumped off the train, there was a tremendous roar, a fury from the audience—with which I must say I agreed. They told Sidney to get back on that train, you fool. In any case, why would he go back to that chain gang when they're obviously going to be separated again? A silly Jim Crow chain gang. What's the movie supposed to prove? What the movie is designed to prove really, to white people, is that Negroes are going to forgive them for their crimes and that somehow they're going to escape scot-free. Not that I'm being vengeful at all when I say this, because I would hate to see the nightmare begin all over again with the shoe on the other foot. I'm simply talking about a human fact and the human fact is this: one cannot escape anything that one's done. One's got to pay for it. Either you pay for it willingly or you pay for it unwillingly.

AUGUST   WILSON

1998

His plays are, in effect, poetic chronicles of African-American life, from early in the century to the present. Each work explores a tumultuous decade.

We are listening to an old, scratchy recording of Ma Rainey singing "Hear Me Talkin' to You."

Ma Rainey's Black Bottom was my first play.* It dealt with the exploitation of early black performers. The setting of the play was a recording studio. I intended to get off some of the philosophical ideas of the characters, all based on the blues. It is, in fact, a celebra-

---

*Ma Rainey was a celebrated blues singer in the '20s. She was the teacher of Bessie Smith. Her frequent accompanist was Georgia Tom, who, after he was saved, became Thomas A. Dorsey, the most prolific composer of gospel songs. His most celebrated work, "Precious Lord, Take My Hand," written for Mahalia Jackson, became Martin Luther King's favorite.

tion of the blues, as well as of the person, Ma Rainey, who was called the mother of the blues. It was about being black in America, especially in the '20s. It dealt with the recording industry, which was relatively new.

I hadn't heard Ma for a long time and just hearing this scratchy record took me back to the play when we first did it in New York seventeen years ago. That particular song is in the play. I chose it because of the line: "You hear me talkin' to you, I don't bite my tongue." That was Ma being uncompromising in her truth. In essence, she didn't bite her tongue. She talked all during the play of her—and her band—being exploited by the record company.

I came into the blues by way of Ma Rainey, Bessie Smith, Ida Cox, Victoria Spivey, all of those women. It wasn't until many years later that I heard male singers. For fifteen years, I was listening to these women. It seemed like the most natural thing to do. It's also the story of the black woman's role.

How it all began? I was born and raised in Pittsburgh and lived there for the first thirty-three years of my life. It was called the Hill district. It's still there, but it is not the community it was, back in '65 for instance. It was a thriving, bustling community of 55,000 people. Today it's about 7,500. My sister still lives there. I go back, I visit, I walk the streets.

From the Hill, segregated as it was, came some of our great jazz pianists: Earl Hines, Billy Strayhorn, Pine Top Smith, Erroll Garner. And Mary Lou Williams.

It was a thriving culture that I wanted to chronicle. I came to playwriting in 1968 during the Black Power movement. We were looking for ways to alter our relationship to the society in which we live as black people. As an artist, I considered it my duty to participate, so I became involved with the theater. My friend and I started the Black Horizon theater, with the idea of using it to politicize, raise the consciousness of the people and their growing awareness of themselves as a community. I was fired in a kiln of black nationalism in the '60s. That's largely responsible for who I am today.

That was my beginning, but I wasn't a playwright then. I went home and tried to write a play, but I couldn't handle dialogue. I started a play with one guy saying, "Hey, what's happening?" The other guy said, "Nothing." I sat there for the next half hour trying to figure out, What else would they say? I couldn't. It was many years later that I came to writing plays. I started out my career as a poet. I still write poetry.

It's not accidental that the language of your plays has a poetic quality. Somehow, when I see your plays, I think of the black preacher whose prose becomes poetry and song. Martin Luther King's last sermon, the one in Memphis, before he died—remember? "I have seen the promised land . . ." That word "seen" sings. It builds and builds. . . .

Absolutely. It's that oratorical style of the black preacher. But the biggest influence on me is the blues. All the characters and their attitudes come out of the blues. It has always been in the forefront of defining black American character.

A million definitions of the blues. "The blues is nothing but a good man feelin' bad." I've heard the black man or woman laugh when recounting or singing a tale of humiliation—

The laughter is what enables you to keep going. Ma Rainey in the play says, "You don't sing because you feel bad. You sing because that's a way of understanding life, and then you go out and you're ready to meet whatever is out there."

The artist Romare Beardon has also been a big influence. It was the first time I had encountered art that showed black life that was rich and full and varied, but without the sentimentality. It just presented life on its own terms and you had to take it on those same terms. I looked at his painting and I said, "I want to write a play like this."

Romare Beardon said, "I tried to explore, in the terms of the life I know best, those things which are common to all cultures." I thought: what more could you ask for? I took that as my credo: I want to explore through the life that I know best, the commonality of all cultures.

My play of the late '20s, the early '30s, *The Piano Lesson*, came from a Romare Beardon painting. It was an homage to Mary Lou Williams. There was a woman and a young girl playing the piano. I began to explore what that might be. I interpreted it as a question: Can you acquire a sense of self-worth by denying your past?

I wanted to pose that question. So I invented this circumstance about the piano. You had this heirloom, or the legacy of black America. The question: What do you do with your legacy? How best do you put it to use? That's what the play explored.

There's a brother and a sister. He needs some money to buy a piece of land from the plantation owner, who exploited the family.

Yes, yes. The sister had this family heirloom. A slaveowner had it originally. He had traded off members of the family for this piano. It was stolen out of his house and eventually ended up in Pittsburgh in 1936. Carved on the piano is the history of the family.

But it's not just any piece of land the brother wants to buy. It is, in fact, the same piece of land they used to farm as slaves. So, if the brother can purchase that land, he will have come full circle. That's why it's so important to him. His argument is that he doesn't need the heirloom to know who he is. He carries all that inside him. If he can use that money to get some land, it will be the basis of independence, to provide for his future.

The sister wants to hold on to the piano because it does represent the family. The father, in fact, died over the piano. She wants to hold on to it, but she doesn't embrace it. She hasn't told her daughter the history of the piano.

She has a taboo. She cannot play the piano since her mother died. It's her legacy, but she's not using it. Her brother tells her, "If you were doing something with it, I would relinquish my claim to it. But you're not doing anything, so I want to take it and make a future."

You're making a strong case for the brother, yet there is something else on the sister's side. The carvings on that piano, the art work, done by a black artisan.

Their grandfather did it. It's a piece you would put in a museum, it's that finely rendered. It's art. The sister says, "We can't give this up—it is our history." But she hasn't told her daughter. The brother argues that the girl should know this. If nothing else, she needs to know the history of the piano.

This reminds me — my daughter was going to Morgan State University. She told me she joined the Black Action Society and they were talking about Timbuktu in Africa. I said, "Listen, start with your grandmother, and then think of your way back to Africa. OK?" You have to know your own personal history first and how it relates to the distant past. That's more important than Timbuktu and all the great African kingdoms.

How *The Piano Lesson* is resolved? The supernatural enters the story. There's a ghost in the house; the ghost of the slave family which owned the piano. The brother engages in some exorcism ritual. It's only when the sister breaks her self-imposed taboo, goes over to the piano and calls on her ancestors, the people whose carvings are on the piano, that some peace comes over the house, and the issue is resolved. Then, having found the perfect use of the piano, the brother relinquishes his claim. We're back to the Romare Beardon painting again, aren't we? The woman and the girl at the piano.

This play, being set in the '30s, is about the Great Depression, too.

We used to say black America is still in a depression in the '60s and '70s. The conditions haven't improved that much, you know.

CLIFFORD BURKE

1969

> An African American pensioner. Most of his days are spent as a volunteer with a community organization in the black ghetto on the West Side of Chicago. From *Hard Times.*

The Negro was born in depression. It didn't mean too much to him, the Great American Depression, as you call it. There was no such thing. The best he could be is a janitor or a porter or a shoeshine boy. It only became official when it hit the white man. If you can tell me the difference between the depression today and the Depression of 1932 for a black man, I'd like to know it. Now, it's worse, because of the prices. Know the rents they're payin' out here? I hate to tell ya.

My third play was *Fences*. It was set in the '50s. It dealt with an ex-Negro League baseball ballplayer. Unable to play in the major leagues, he was somewhat embittered. He will not allow his son to accept a football scholarship because "the white man ain't gonna let you get nowhere with them sports." Each one takes his own truth and forces it on the succeeding generation. He never realizes that times have changed. He's fifty-three years old at the time.

My favorite play is *Joe Turner's Come and Gone*, set in 1911. It's set in a Pittsburgh boarding house. He's going around with his eleven-year-old daughter, searching for his wife. They were separated seven years ago by a guy named Joe Turner.

According to W. C. Handy, who wrote the blues, Joe Turner pressed Negroes into peonage. It represents to me black America's bondage for 300 and some years. You suffer a spiritual dislocation, trying to figure out what happened to you. In this play, the character comes to understand who he is, and makes a connection with his African past. It gives him an identity and makes him aware of his image, as he puts it, and enables him to move forward.

W. C. Handy wrote "Joe Turner Blues" with the man as an exploiter. Big Bill Broonzy sang of an altogether different man. He sang of Joe Turner as a black man, who was also white. He was a good samaritan, saving a black town. He said he heard it during his young boyhood in Mississippi.

[We listen to Big Bill's *"Joe Turner Blues."*]

Isn't Joe Turner something of a generic name? There's the real Joe Turner we know, the blues singer from Kansas City.

That's funny. When this was playing in Philadelphia, a guy showed up, not knowing what the play was about. He brought about twenty Joe Turner records. He thought it was about the Kansas City singer.

Actually, that play came out of a Beardon painting. There was a figure seated in the center of the painting. He was at the table with a hat and a coat on, in a posture of absolute defeat. I began to wonder who he was. He became Harold Loomis, the character in *Joe Turner's Come and Gone*. We duplicated the set right off of the painting.

Very often it can be a certain line in a blues that sets me off. "Two trains running, neither one going my way. . . ." I took off from that and wrote *Two Trains Running*. It's set in a diner in 1969.

There's a man named Hambone, who had painted the local butcher's fence nine years earlier. The butcher had promised that if he did a good job, he'd give him a ham. Otherwise, he'd give him a chicken. He did a good job, but the butcher said he didn't. So for nine years, he's showing up every morning at the butcher shop saying, "I want my ham."

For me, that was black America saying, "I want my ham." I want what, in essence, is due me. Hambone had an unwillingness to take anything. He would not take the chicken. He wanted the ham.

Gradually, all the other characters in the play discover that they are, in essence, him. There is something in their past, in which they have compromised. So he leads them to this uncompromising vision that you should get what you deserve, and not be willing to accept anything less than that.

Forty acres and a mule. That was the promise during Reconstruction, wasn't it? A promise betrayed.

There's a young man in the play, who is so moved by Hambone's principles that he goes into action. He breaks the window of the butcher shop and takes the ham. Unfortunately, Hambone had died. So he took the ham, put it in Hambone's casket and the ham was buried with the man. The whole play drives to that point.

Seven Guitars, the year is 1948. The main character is a blues singer, who's traveled through Chicago and made a record. His mother dies, he goes home to Pittsburgh. They release the record, and it becomes a hit. The only thing is, he spent ninety days in jail and when he gets out, the guitar's in the pawn shop. He's trying to get his guitar out of pawn and get his band together. Before he can do that, he gets murdered. The play I'm working on now, set in the

'80s, deals with this theme of insane violence among these kids out there, killing one another for the very slightest reasons. You're dealing with people whose sense of self-worth is so fragile that the slightest thing can be perceived as an insult and become a cause to kill someone. One of the things I'm exploring in this play is a look at the black family. Everyone talks about the breakup of the black family. In the '30s and '40s, the welfare policy was that you couldn't have a man in the house in order to be eligible. I thought: Why not? Why not encourage the man to be in the house, instead of encouraging separation. So I began to explore—to look at the black family. I'm going all the way back to 1619 and I think it's a miracle*—the fact that the black family has survived and is as strong as it is today in 1998 America. It's a societal policy that has encouraged separation and led to single-parent households. I'm trying in this play to figure what it's all about.

The whole odyssey of black America has been a search for jobs. To put your hands to it. You can't feel like a person until you put your hands to use. I don't care if it's a job dishwashing. I've seen people who've worked in McDonald's. They are *somebody* because they have that job. Who are these people?

They are the artisans who created those carvings on that piano the sister wanted to keep in The Piano Lesson. *Those are the same people.*

[We listen to a recording of Mary Lou Williams playing a blues.]

She's part of my history. Pittsburgh. Listening to her brings it all home to me.

---

*The year 1619 was when the first slave ship landed in Charleston, South Carolina.

ARNOLD SCHWARZENEGGER

The movie actor. I interviewed him for my book, *American Dreams: Lost and Found.*

Call me Arnold.

I was born in a little Austrian town, outside Graz. It was a 300-year-old house. When I was ten years old, I had the dream of being the best in the world in something. When I was fifteen, I had a dream that I wanted to be the best bodybuilder in the world and the most muscular man.

It was not only a dream I dreamed at night. It was also a day-dream. It was so much in my mind that I felt it had to become a reality. It took me five years of hard work. Five years later, I turned this dream into reality and became Mr. Universe, the best-built man in the world.

"Winning" is a very important word. There is one that achieves what he wanted to achieve and there are hundreds of thousands that failed. It singles you out—the winner.

I came out second three times, but that is not what I call losing. The bottom line for me was: Arnold has to be the winner. I have to win more often the Mr. Universe title than anybody else. I won it five times consecutively. I hold the record as Mr. Olympia, the top professional bodybuilding championship. I won it six times. That's why I retired. There was nobody even close to me. Everybody gave up competing against me. That's what I call a winner.

When I was a small boy, my dream was not to be big physically, but big in a way that everybody listens to me when I talk, that I'm a very important person, that people recognize me and see me as something special. I had a big need for being singled out.

Also my dream was to end up in America. When I was ten years old, I dreamed of being an American. At the time I didn't know much about America, just that it was a wonderful country. I felt it was where I belonged. I didn't like being in a little country like Austria. I did everything possible to get out. I did so in 1968, when I was twenty-one years old.

If I would believe in life after death, I would say my before-life I was living in America. That's why I feel so good here. It is the country where you can turn your dream into reality. Other countries don't have those things. When I came over here to America, I felt I was in heaven. In America, we don't have an obstacle. Nobody's holding you back.

Number one in America pretty much takes care of the rest of the world. You kind of run through the rest of the world like nothing. I'm trying to make people in America aware that they should appreciate what they have here. You have the best tax advantages here and the best prices here and the best products here.

One of the things I always had was a business mind. When I was in high school, a majority of my classes were business classes. Economics and accounting and mathematics. When I came over here to this country, I really didn't speak English almost at all. I learned English and then starting taking business courses, because that's what America is best known for—business. Turning one dollar into a million dollars in a short period of time. Also when you make money, how do you keep it?

That's one of the most important things when you have money in your hand, how can you keep it? Or make more out of it? Real estate is one of the best ways of doing that. I own apartment buildings, office buildings, and raw land. That's my love, real estate.

I have emotions. But what you do, you keep them cold or you store them away for a time. You must control your emotions, you must have command over yourself. Three, four months before a competition, I could not be interfered by other people's problems. This is sometimes called selfish. It's the only way you can be if you want to achieve something. Any emotional things inside me, I try to keep cold so it doesn't interfere with my training.

Many times things really touched me. I felt them and I felt sensitive about them. But I had to talk myself out of it. I had to suppress those feelings in order to go on. Sport is one of those activities where you really have to concentrate. You must pay attention a hundred percent to the particular thing you're doing. There must be nothing else on your mind. Emotions must not interfere. Otherwise, you're thinking about your girlfriend. You're in love, your positive energies get channeled into another direction rather than going into your weight room or making money.

You have to choose at a very early date what you want: a normal life or to achieve things you want to achieve. I never wanted to win a popularity contest in doing things the way people want me to do it. I went the road I thought was best for me. A few people thought I was cold, selfish. Later they found out that's not the case. After I achieve my goal, I can be Mr. Nice Guy. You know what I mean?

California is to me a dreamland. It is the absolute combination of everything I was always looking for. It has all the money in the world there, show business there, wonderful weather there, beautiful country, ocean is there. Snow skiing in the winter, you can go in the desert the same day. You have beautiful-looking people there. They all have a tan.

I believe strongly in the philosophy of staying hungry. If you have a dream and it becomes a reality, don't stay satisfied with it too long. Make up a new dream and hunt after that one and turn it into reality. When you have that dream achieved, make up a new dream.

I am a strong believer in Western philosophy, the philosophy of success, of progress, of getting rich. The Eastern philosophy is passive, which I believe in maybe three percent of the time, and the ninety-seven percent is Western, conquering and going on. It's a beautiful philosophy, and America should keep it up.

UTA HAGEN

1994

She is an actress and has won two Tony Awards, one for her performance in *Who's Afraid of Virginia Woolf?* and the other for her work in *The Country Girl*. She was equally celebrated as St. Joan, as Desdemona to Paul Robeson's Othello, and as Blanche Du Bois in *A Streetcar Named Desire*. In her younger days, after an appearance in "a terrible play" in Brooklyn, she was described by Alexander Woolcott, drama critic of the *New Yorker*, as "the Duse of Brooklyn." She has appeared in a few television plays and "once in a while in a movie."

In Greenwich Village, the HB Playwrights Foundation, of which she is the artistic director, is alive with all sorts of activity:* several acting classes are in session; someone is painting a set; another is busy at a desk, answering the constantly-ringing telephone; several are studying scripts; and a play is in rehearsal. These peripatetic, though obviously intent, persons are all quite young.

Hagen, vibrant, "full of beans," has the enthusiasm of her young acolytes. Her appearance and demeanor belie her calendar age, seventy-five.

Since 1965, "we've done over one hundred productions. Our little theater seats eighty-one. We squeeze in a hundred. It's free. People from the community, colleagues, friends are the audience. We haven't had an empty seat in twenty-five years. The neighborhood is crazy about it."

When people tell me, "Isn't it a shame you're not working," I laugh my head off. I work from ten to twelve hours a day. We have sixty teachers, two thousand students, and are probably the least expensive theater school in the world. We used to charge three dollars a class.

In the '50s, because of inflation, we raised the fee to five dollars. After my husband died, because we were running a deficit, I raised it to seven dollars.

It's a big gimmick in America to teach to make money. People get rich off the backs of young, aspiring artists, who bankrupt themselves, borrow, and work all night long in restaurants in order to take a class. In essence, we subsidize them, but it's well worth it.

My husband always called HB our big kibbutz. Once a year, we have spring cleaning, in which everybody participates. Me, the staff, the students, and people from the neighborhood all pitch in. The

---

*Named after her late husband, Herbert Berghof.

few staff people get salaries, modest; everybody else volunteers. We even get help with the printing.

We do have grants and contributions to the foundation, but the school supports itself. We own three buildings, that's why we can manage. When we got our second building, the four-story brownstone, it was falling apart. The crazy little old lady who owned it was right out of Tennessee Williams. She had seventy-five cats and the stench was unbelievable. The board of health got her out, and we bought it for $40,000. It's probably worth half a million now. But we worked like dogs. I take home about $200, $300 a week.

Why am I doing this? For one thing, the state of the theater in the United States has never been worse. The level of work is at best mediocre. Every little off-Broadway house is looking to sell something. When they try out a play, they're already thinking, "Where will it be moved to?" It's not, "What does it mean to this community?" You've got to have a creative idea first. You can't say, "How will it sell?" before you even arrive at the idea. You can't use the community so you can move somewhere else—it is the death of art in the theater.

I am still fighting for the same idea they had in the village square, the idea I started with when I came into the theater as a very young child.

My father was a professor of art history in Göttingen, where I was born. It's known for its university. We came to the University of Wisconsin in 1936. My mother was a singer. My aunt was a prominent mezzo in Germany. My father had been everything: an actor when he was seventeen, a musician, a composer, a prize pupil of Humperdinck. His one opera was such a disaster in Berlin that he decided to become an art historian. My whole background was literature and music and painting and theater.

My first job as an actress, when I turned eighteen, was playing Ophelia to Eva Le Gallienne's Hamlet. It got amazingly respectful reviews. She played a very strong role in my young life. Her dream was of a repertory theater at reasonable prices. It was part of the great American tradition. Going back to Booth, the artists always had their own companies, were always in control of their own destinies. They were not run by real-estate operators.

That's my bitch to young artists: don't be slaves to realtors, producers who treat you like a piece of caca. In order to take control of your own lives, you've got to merit it, you've got to work your behinds off and pursue your goal relentlessly.

The Lunts immediately come to mind. Alfred Lunt and Lynn Fontanne. As a very young actress, I was in their production of *The Seagull*. They were *fan*tastic. After a show closed, they would give us all notes. On the closing night! [Laughs] It was never perfect, but that was their goal. When they died, the obituaries read as though they had never done anything except drawing-room comedy. They did everything from Shakespeare and Shaw to Dürrenmatt. They were *wonder*ful.

People say to me, "Nobody knows who you are anymore." I really don't care. One of the reasons I'm still full of beans is because I'm passionate about my beliefs. I'm happier in the pursuit of these goals than people who are pursuing their own belly buttons, their own success, without having a cause. They're chasing their tails.

They say, "I want to be a household name." I say, "What is that? Lysol? Toilet paper? Bounty? These are household names." Listen to me, I'm shouting. My heart is pounding. [Laughs heartily] I did a play called *Charlotta*. She was Goethe's mistress, the most important woman in his life. It bombed on Broadway. I said to Herbert, "I feel like I have a stillborn baby." He said, "Let's do it again." I toured it all over the country. Between 1982 and '83, I played it for months and months and months. I turned the play around, so it got better and better. When I returned to New York, I did it in Joe Papp's theater.* It was very exciting, jammed, standing ovations. Joe came backstage and said, "I think it's just tragic that you're not working." I was amazed. I said, "What do you think I was just doing on your stage?" He said, "Yeah, but that's for nothing." I nearly fell through the floor. If it's for nothing, it isn't work? Does your worth depend on how much money you get? He tried to laugh it off. Even Joe Papp, one of our best people.

It is as though money is the only thing that gives you a merit

---

*The Public Theater.

badge. How much money? How many awards? Awards are to me the funniest thing in American society. Everybody knows they are totally manufactured gimmicks [pounds table] to get more money. The Broadway season starts in the spring, so they'll cash in on the Tony Awards. They can't start in the fall because they might be forgotten by the spring. They can advertise the awards because it means more business. The same with the Oscars. Every Oscar represents millions of dollars at the box office. The dumb actors stand up there and weep, "Oh, look what I got." What did you get? Nothing. [Emotionally] I defy the whole status quo. I think it's full of shit. This is dangerous territory for me, I know. I won a couple of Tonys. Each time, I thought it was meaningless. I remember years ago, when Charlton Heston won the Oscar over Laurence Olivier. Doesn't that tell everything?

I got doctorates from three different colleges. After the third, I knew everything was a trade-off. At one college, they said, "You're going to give us your papers, aren't you?" Another asked, "Will you be on our board of directors, so when we audition people for the drama department . . ." When Nancy Hanks was head of the National Endowment for the Arts, she received nineteen honorary doctorates. She was in charge of giving out money. "If she gets an award, she may give us a grant." It is rotten.

How did I get this way? Most important were parents. They gave me values that sustained me. They never preached. I listened to them, I watched them. I had stimulating fights with them. By the time I was seventeen, I had left home, knowing exactly what I wanted and heading for it. Sink or swim, I was going to do what I wanted to do.

As a youngster, I had enormous contempt for the movies. I don't anymore. I was nineteen and married to José Ferrer. We were invited to Hollywood. Both of us did screen tests for RKO and they flipped. I thought it was dreadful. I turned down all kinds of scripts. One of them was as Esmeralda in *The Hunchback of Notre Dame*, with Charles Laughton. I told Pandro Berman, the producer, that the dialogue was terrible. "I'm used to Chekhov and Ibsen." [Laughs] I was so snotty. I was just awful. People said I was a fool.

"Look at the career you could have had, like Maureen O'Hara's."
[Laughs] I would have been suicidal.

We left Hollywood. I was never tempted again until after *Streetcar*. Suddenly, I was a hot item again. By that time, I was on every political blacklist in the country. I always say the blacklist saved me from corruption. But I don't want to be blacklisted again. [Chuckles] Oh, it was horrible.

McCarthy started with me in Pittsburgh. I spoke at a rally for Henry Wallace and I made headlines:* COMMISSAR HAGEN, RUN HER OUT OF TOWN. They printed my phone number and my hotel room in the newspapers. Wonderfully enough, we broke every house record. Somebody sent Claudia Cassidy† all this press stuff and, bless her heart, she was furious that they were trying to influence her.

My best friends during the McCarthy period were Republicans. They were more honest. Irene Selznick, the producer of *Streetcar*, said, "I would kill myself if I thought I was preventing you from doing what you believe in, but don't forget you're the star of this show and responsible for sixty-two other jobs, so take it easy." George Abbott said, "I got all these letters telling me not to hire you. You're a great actress, so what do I care?"

My most fruitful years were during the early McCarthy days — *Country Girl, Saint Joan*, and *Streetcar*. Broadway was uninfluenced by the hysteria, but they couldn't send me on the road.

They were wonderful years. I was out talking, raising money for Greek war orphans, antifascist Spanish refugees. I was on the platform with Eisenhower and Mrs. Roosevelt, and suddenly I'm called a villain. I don't really know why I got in trouble. I have never been a conscious politician in any way. I just know that some of the people I met during those years were just about the most extraordinary group I've ever known.

The FBI had two men, on taxpayers' salary, tailing me for two years. They said, "Who got you involved?" Fortunately, I have no memory for names. So I never had to tell a lie. I said, "There's been

---

*The Progressive Party candidate for president in 1948.
†Chicago's most influential drama and music critic of the time.

a woman in my house for three weeks whom I'm helping to start something for the YMCA. If you pulled my tongue out of my head, I couldn't tell you her name."

I was subpoenaed twice by the House Un-American Activities Committee. A subpoena in your hand is terrifying. My lawyers were saints. Paul Porter, the partner of Abe Fortas and Thurman Arnold, represented me for nothing. They had 150 others they called their "conscience" cases.

The night before my first hearing in Washington, the chairman of the committee phoned to say that the hearing was called off because the guy who was going to testify against me turned out to be a perjurer. I asked, "Does that mean I can forget about it?" Paul Porter said, "Oh, no."

About three years later, I was called again. I remember I was so nervous. I remember that when I took my hands off the big table, there were pools of sweat on it. I lifted my felt skirt to wipe the sweat off. My heart was pounding.

"Did you appear in Chicago in 1948 on a Saturday in October, at noon, with Gerhardt Eisler?"

"No."

"We have a tape of you at that meeting."

Whooo, my heart was going wild. I said, "It couldn't have been. On Saturday, I would have played a matinee. I do two shows. It's impossible." I don't remember ever meeting Gerhardt Eisler.

Paul Porter said, "We'd like a copy of that tape." It was never mentioned again, because there was no such tape. Paul said, "I forgot to tell you. They have a number of such tactics they use to intimidate you. They'll bring up anything that they think will throw you and you'll be so rattled that you don't know what you're doing." They almost succeeded. It was the only time in my life I've ever been frightened, and I'll always hate them for that.

Have you ever had any second thoughts?

Never! Never, never, never, never. I never could follow dogma, I really couldn't. I remember when I was twelve, at a Girl Scout camp. They said, "You don't put your foot over this boundary line." I went [taps on table in deliberate fashion, indicating footsteps "crossing the line"]. If somebody says there's something you can't do or you must do, I immediately rebel. It has to be *my* choice. I love hot and heavy argument—I learned that from my parents—but the minute it's one way or else, forget it. That's why I could never have been a good Communist.

I'm told that the young today are more conforming. It's tragic. Youth has always been a period of rebelling. If they conform when they are young, what will they be when they're older? Fascists? The kids I know are aspiring artists and may be somewhat different.

I treat my younger students, my older ones, and my middle-aged ones as colleagues. A teacher is in big trouble when she stops listening to young people. When they begin, they have *wildly* idealistic goals. What is heartbreaking is to see them pitched into the theater as it exists and see them turn sour and mean and bitter and opportunistic by the time they're thirty. At nineteen, twenty, they're [takes a deep breath] like this. My job is to teach them not to lose that feeling. Call it passing the torch, if you want to.

FLASH FORWARD. *In 1997, she played the role of Melanie Klein, the child psychiatrist, colleague of Freud. The play:* Mrs. Klein. *Several leading drama critics acclaimed her performance as the most memorable since Laurette Taylor's in* The Glass Menagerie.

4—Winners and Losers

WILLIAM SAROYAN

1977

Your name, Saroyan, has become almost an adjective. Saroyanesque. A synonym for a longing, a wistfulness, free association. A zest for life. In your Pulitzer Prize–winning play, The Time of Your Life, *a young hoofer played by Gene Kelly is soliloquizing as he tap dances in a San Francisco saloon, during the Great Depression. Gene Kelly: "Thursday, the 12th. Maybe the headline's about me, I'll take a quick look. No. The headline is not about me. It's about Hitler. Seven thousand miles away?! I'm here. Who the hell is Hitler? Who's behind the eight ball? I turn around. Everybody's behind the eight ball."*

Style is unaccountable. The writer may not know too much about it. I don't know too much about it. One thing I do know: Dickens often found that the next day, after working all night, he frequently couldn't imagine what he had written. He'd be eager to get to it, and now and then was so deeply moved, either to tears or to laughter. If you work, as in the days when I drank limitless coffee and smoked one cigarette after another, if you work with that prolonged intensity over many hours, you forget what it was that you wrote. The next day, when you're going to go and check it, you get surprised. And sometimes it is so good that you take the view, well I didn't write it, but thank God somebody wrote it.

The human being unaccountable, he is all surprise. There is no end to the variations within one person, let alone in the multitudes. So what are we up against? We're up against no excuse ever to be bored. Nobody has a right ever to be bored. Why are we all bored?

There's a young kid, who plays the role of Wesley in The Time of Your Life. *He says, "This play is not about losers, it's about winners."*

You must understand a language which is beyond the words. This is implying that the only winner is the loser who knows that he's a loser. Who the hell else could possibly win unless he was self-deceived? We're all losers. But if we get to a recognition of the unavoidableness, the inevitability of being losers, then we've already made a win. It isn't much, but we've made that much of a win.

BILL VEECK

1978

He's nursing a beer at the table in the Bard's Room, a casual restaurant-saloon under the stands of Comisky Park, serving freeloaders, journalists, friends, and the occasional wayfaring stranger. He is the president of the Chicago White Sox. He had been the general manager of the St. Louis Browns when they were the worst team in major league baseball and the Cleveland Indians when they were the world champions. He is sixty-four.

For the most part, we're losers. We're losers in a country where winning means you're great, you're beautiful, you're moral. If you don't make a lot of money, you're a loser. The bigness, the machines, the establishment imbue us with the idea that unless you make a lot of money, you're nothing. Happiness has nothing to do with it. I'm challenging that and I'm having a lot of fun doing it.

We have a lousy team out in the field right now, but they're singing in the stands. We have just about the worst ball club and the oldest park in the country. We have an exploding scoreboard in Comisky Park. At first, they declared it illegal, immoral, fattening, terrible, too bush. [Laughs]

Funny how you pick things up. It came from reading Saroyan's play, *The Time of Your Life*. All took place in a saloon. There's a pinball machine and the fella, he goes up to the bartender and he wants more nickels. He plays and plays, no luck; and just before the final curtain, he hits a winner. The bells rang and the flags went up and it played "Dixie" and all sorts of extravagant things. That's what happens on our exploding scoreboard. Saroyan was sayin' something. You keep tryin' and tryin' and you finally do hit a winner. You hope, you dream, the guy's gonna hit a homer. Suddenly, he hits it. The rockets go off, the bombs burst in air. [Laughs] The loser has his day.

Mark Twain, he was our prime, great loser. Nothing he did in the material world came to any good. He lost money at everything: the printing machine, the typewriter. Every investment he ever made. In the end he did find the human race contemptible, and the reason for it is rather difficult to really pin down. He had for so long, especially in the years in which he wrote *Huckleberry Finn*, recognized the essential criminality that the human being was capable of. At the same time loved the human race, and found that illiterate kid, Huck Finn—so unlikely to be a good example of a human being—should be such a magnificent guy, especially in the matter of trying to deliver Jim from the tyranny of enslavement, and how if he did this deliverance he'd go to hell. He says, "All right, then I'll go to hell."

That little glow, the star that's in Huck Finn, appears in many of your characters whether it be in Nick's Tavern in The Time of Your Life, *or whether it be the Armenian poet in* My Heart's in the Highlands, *or the tramps in* The Cave Dwellers. *All of them are Huck Finns. They're waifs—they're waifs of the world. But they survive.*

I really hadn't given it that thought, but I think that this is accurate. There is that quality, and we can trace it back to the fact that I am the last of four children born to immigrants. The other three were born in the old country. We were outsiders. But also we're all outsiders. You're an outsider from something or somebody.

When I talk to my son, I know that we're not talking the same language. He's a poet and a writer and an eccentric, and a very fine man, and a man that I love deeply and admire very much. Now I ask his sister, who is a couple of years younger than him, I say, "Tell me about Aram now." And she can tell. And I says, "Why am I getting it wrong?" She tries to help me. The daughter can communicate, but the son can't.

In 1935, I went to Armenia for the first time. During my absence three editors and writers from the Armenian press, who write in the Armenian language, called on my mother. "We have come to pay our respects to the mother of William Saroyan. Mrs. Saroyan, you must be very proud of your son." And my mother said, "He's crazy. Please sit down and I'll bring you some tea." [Laughter] When you say the zest for life, it's a helplessness. You don't have much choice in the accident of identity. That's why it's so important for all of us to find it in our hearts to be patient and to try to understand and to love people that are exactly the opposite of ourselves. It's easy to like people that are like you, but how about this fellow over here? I'm very swift, and this fellow is very slow, very slow, very slow. It's my job to dig him, to try to understand what goes on there. I've met some new writers through my son, and I can see that they've got a lot of stuff, but it's not in my language, it's alien. So I have to discipline myself to go along with it.

If they seek you out for some sort of counsel, give it with some sense of responsibility. The only counsel I'm willing to give kids is that I have found that it's better to work than not to work. I mean, if you are going to write, work at it. Make a muscle of yourself, of your spirit. Let it have muscle. Don't be totally at the mercy of inspiration. They ask me: "Where do you get your ideas?" If you sit and work the ideas will come.

At your best you're much better than who you are because who you are is every day, but art is not every day. Art is the essence of the whole human race. A fragment of that essence which is inexhaustible, that'll go on and on and on. We'll never despair of the usefulness and importance of language, of the putting of words together to communicate whatever it might be. That will go on. Whether spoken, as it was for centuries in my country—and I'm sure in all people's, we have the bards who sing and talk—or whether it's written. Now McLuhan says with the competition of all these mediums, electronics, and so forth, we're not gonna need them. We're gonna sit around like this and talk. Well, that's all right, that's also writing. But we also need that very integrating force of the printed page, the quietude of a man going to one side. There's nobody bothering him and he is communing. This is close to prayer. We needn't be embarrassed about such terms because it's true. I find that reading, all kinds of reading is basic to my participation in the human experience I wouldn't give up reading for anything. That's one of the reasons I write, so I'll have good stuff to read. [Laughs]

My father was very good in writing English as a small boy. He went to a Presbyterian school, and that's how he became a preacher. He was a great extemporaneous talker. If some preacher got sick, he could take the man's place and say: "What's the theme and how much time do I have?" And they'd say, "Give us the return of the Prodigal Son, and take an hour." And he'd do it. Walter Huston used to tell me, "I don't know about these theories that they have about schools of acting. All I do is I come in, 'What's the play and what time is curtain?' "

What he was saying is "Everything that they are learning by their instructions, I know by experience." I don't even know anything about grammar, except that I know about *my* writing.

I never knew the first thing about what a play is, and that's why I wrote *My Heart's in the Highlands* as a first play. It breaks all the rules. First of all, it's a long one-act play. It's not even a play. Second, it has none of the things which the conventional play is supposed to have. And I marvel at the fact that it was produced at all. But that was the idea. I felt in order to break through, I had to release a lot of creative energy.

In The Time of Your Life *there's a little newsboy who wants to be a singer. He sells a lot of papers to the rich drunk who's the benefactor there, Joe. When you were a newsboy in San Francisco, you have a memory of a guy who gave you a silver dollar.*

One of the profound experiences of my life. The White Fawn Saloon was a long bar on Mariposa Street. I had a right as a newsboy to see if anybody wanted to buy a paper. I didn't care whether they bought it or not because the place fascinated me. Over the bar were these huge old oil paintings. There would be a racehorse and some prizefighters, and some oil paintings of Lillian Russell*-type ladies.

---

*The glamor girl of the 1890s — celebrated for her figure and beauty.

They were beautiful. And all of these guys were there drinking, and I'd pass down the line and say, "Paper, mister?" One day, a fella says, "Yes," and he hands me a silver dollar, and so I ask the bartender to please give me change, and the man says, "No, I want you to have that." And I was stunned, because he wasn't drunk. But I never could forget that. This was not a rich man, this was a man who for some reason wanted a kid to have a buck, and ever after this I said to myself, "I'm gonna do the same thing." For years, I used to do it.

That guy who gave me the silver dollar so long ago may have been the inspiration for Joe, the drunk benefactor in *The Time of Your Life*. He talks a doubletalk. He says, "Bet McCarthy." "What the hell should I bet McCarthy? The horse is no good." He's just listened to a man who's name is McCarthy. And he says, "Go and bet him."

He's a hunch horse player, you're a hunch writer.

Yeah. I seize upon and try to make likely to happen all of the good accidents of timing. And if you get these good accidents of timing, suddenly you've got Nijinsky.

JOSÉ QUINTERO

1973

He is the director most responsible for the revival of interest in the plays of Eugene O'Neill. America's greatest playwright had been neglected for at least a decade until Quintero's off-Broadway production of *The Iceman Cometh*, in 1950. It had originally received mixed reviews.

Jason Robards is the actor closely associated with him — beginning from their triumph in *The Iceman Cometh* — putting forth O'Neill's last series of plays, his autobiographical saga of the Tyrone (O'Neill) family. The cycle was to begin with the Irish potato famine and continue up to today. Three of these plays, *Long Day's Journey into Night*, *A Touch of the Poet*, and *Moon for the Misbegotten* were produced. O'Neill died before the cycle was completed.

> Quintero is in Chicago as *Moon for the Misbegotten* is play-
> ing here. Robards is Jamie, O'Neill's ill-starred older brother.
> He had played the same role in *Long Day's Journey into Night*.

O'Neill writing of his own life makes you dig into your own. Using
his own family, he was creating a universal family. It matched mine
and it certainly matched Jason's. It matched every person's who
came to see this play.

I remember saying to Jason, "How does it feel to be successful?"
By this time, he had done *The Iceman* and had become recognized.
We were awaiting the opening of *Long Day's Journey*. He said to
me, "How's it feel to you?" We both understood. Neither one of us
had been educated for success. We were never the good boys in the
house. We were failures in school. Success was a frightening thing.
Like we had fooled people. O'Neill understood the very texture of
guilt in success.

I was flabbergasted when I received a call from his widow, Carlotta. It was just after I did *The Iceman*. She said, "How would you
like to direct and produce *Long Day's Journey into Night*?" Every
producer on Broadway was going after this play. And I had to say,
"Excuse me." And I got sick to my stomach. I really, actually got
sick to my stomach. I said, "Yes" and had to excuse myself.

Why would she give it to me? She said it had to do with my
wrists. Apparently Mr. O'Neill had very narrow wrists and mine
were narrow. She said, "That's how I know that you understand
him."

I think O'Neill had something to do with my early upbringing.
I'm from Panama, yet he helped shape me and my environment. He
may have written about the Irish but it wasn't foreign to me. The
way laundresses hang sheets out to dry . . . I had a sense that he
had caught me performing certain acts.

Interest in him had been dormant, except for the Swedes.

He was very grateful. One of the last people to visit Mrs. O'Neill in
the hospital was a Swede, Ingrid Bergman. O'Neill had met her
years ago while he was working on his cycle. She did *Anna Christie*
in San Francisco. She was finished with pictures. Carlotta picked

her up after the theater and she spent hours talking with O'Neill. He wanted her to play in the cycle. That's the reason, she came back to America after an absence of twenty-two years. To keep the promise she made to O'Neill.

He called the cycle plays of the self-dispossessed. He had it all figured out, layer on layer, building through this family, a sort of history of our society. *More Stately Mansions* was to follow *A Touch of the Poet*. And drafts of four other plays. He studied the genealogy, everything.

And then one night, knowing his strength was failing, knowing he could never complete the task, he and Carlotta sat in front of their fireplace in Marblehead and burned the six plays, page by page. He knew his end was at hand. It was probably the saddest moment in the history of American theater.

Maybe that's why, of all the members of the Tyrone family, I feel closest to Jamie. O'Neill had the outlet of writing. Jamie had no outlet at all. It was all within him, all the torture, all the terror. The waste. . . .

Waste? What about the miserly father, James Tyrone? He might have been a really great actor, yet he settled for playing this one role in Count of Monte Cristo *because it made him a bundle of money.*

During a rehearsal one time, I was talking to Bradford Dillman, who played O'Neill. "All right, call him a miser. He was a miser to you and your brother and your mother. Remember, he was a potato-famine Irishman, who knew what poverty was. It was imprinted into him. He himself was the one that he cheated the most. He had been a brilliant young actor. Edwin Booth said, "That young man plays Brutus better than I ever could." The old man cheated himself of touching the heavens because a money-making play came along. Success.

Success meaning what?

What is it? I don't know if it happens in other parts of the world, but in America it's an overnight thing. All of a sudden. The night *Long Day's Journey* opened—the newspapers had come out—I got very drunk. I was very unhappy. A director feels at the opening that he is no longer needed, no longer part of it. When I got home, there were six offers. For plays, for pictures. For anything. It is just too, too fast.

O'Neill fought this whole idea of "success." He paid for it by isolation. He stubbornly refused to cut the plays just so it would fit the commuters. He had great fights with the Theatre Guild. They wanted it tailor-made, up at eight, curtain before eleven. It had nothing to do with the play. As you say, he wouldn't cut his vision to fit the time.

Some say he often over-wrote and his plays may have needed cutting. I'm reminded of an old barroom fighter, who would swing wildly, but then comes that roundhouse punch — wham! And you are knocked out cold.

It's that part of you trying to get at the very kernel of where the power is, where it really hurts, where the energy really starts. And then it goes, pow!

JOSÉ QUINTERO AND JASON ROBARDS

1976

They are in Chicago, during the run of O'Neill's long one-act play, *Hughie*. It is, for the most part, a one-man play: Robards as Erie Smith, a small time gambler in a seedy hotel.

Quintero: I don't think he ever wrote about something he himself had not experienced. The language of O'Neill is not the kind that a writer, sitting in a room all of his life, invents.

It's an American poetry. They always talked of O'Neill's heavy language because few can speak it like Jason and Colleen Dewhurst. It's rich.

Robards: Once you start in it, you can't pull back. He takes you there whether you feel like it or not, you know. Sometimes you do eight performances a week. You say, "I can't make it. I don't have the energy." And all of a sudden, you'll find by the time you're half-way into it, you've been transported out of any feelings of your own and he takes you from there.

Quintero: How can you deal with tea cups and embroidery when you're concentrating on the big passions that rule our lives? Love and hate are braided like a woman's hair. I know of no family that can escape that. I don't care how rich they are or how poor or how middle class they are.

Robards: He says you can't make it alone. You die. In *Iceman*, the guys in Harry Hope's saloon, these poor, godforsaken rummies, need each other and their pipe dreams too. Along comes Hickey, that's me, and he brings death by destroying their pipe dreams.

He doesn't know it but he has the biggest pipe dream of all. He knows that he killed his wife, but he thinks he did it out of love. When he finds out later, through his own guts, that he did it out of hate—he mixed hate and love—he goes crazy. Then you know the true insanity. He realizes what he's done, he's killed these guys too, because he was selling them the wrong salvation.

Quintero: People think O'Neill is dark, heavy, and gloomy. He's really positive. Think of these guys in the saloon. Regardless how shabby their dream, man can't live without a dream.

What about Erie Smith in Hughie? *What's his dream?*

Robards: He gets his name from Erie, P.A. A hick burg he calls it. He's on the fringe of the rackets and barely gets by. He said he used to run errands for Arnold Rothstein, the famous gambler, who fixed the World Series of 1919. He can pay for his room, cigarettes, a couple of drinks, a little food. That's about it.

But with the hotel night clerk, Hughie, he was able to pump himself up and make himself Arnold Rothstein. He was big time in Hughie's eyes. But now Hughie is dead. Erie has lost his modus operandi for life. His luck is gone. He can't win even on a two-bit crap game. And he can't get by on his loneliness. He has no one now. He has no Hughie. He can't even build his dream and go to bed and sleep.

Quintero: The clerk in any hotel is an important figure in terms of identity for the occupants. Even in first-rate hotels, he sits behind the pulpit, greets you. You are somebody. It matches your idea of yourself. Imagine a night clerk in a third-rate hotel where the identity of these people is cracked, broken like a piece of cheap porcelain. That night clerk acquires a dreadful importance.

Now here's where O'Neill is positive and he believes in man again. Erie struggles to blow life into the dead Hughie. He's had a tough fight because Hughie alive was burnt out. So Erie invents him and brings him out.

Robards: He's totally creative. Erie Smith is fantastic in the richness of his fantasy. Hughie doesn't appear in the play. We find out about him from Erie's gab with the new clerk. A fresh, wise punk in Erie's eyes. He tries to con him with the same lies he told Hughie. The conquest of Ziegfeld Follies babes and all that.

Anything to avoid going upstairs to that lonely room.

Robards: We always figured if he did go upstairs this time, he'd go out the window. Hughie's death drove Erie off on a four-day bat. He's come back for the funeral. He figures it's his only hope.

What awaits him in that room is death. He has made an outside debt. He's borrowed money to give Hughie a funeral wreath of flowers. He has to pay up or they'll kill him. If he doesn't get life back, which may help him get his luck back, he's finished.

This is a play about salvation.

Quintero: That's why it's so positive. But it's a struggle every time we do one of his plays. I mean, the old man is still fighting for recognition.

The old man? You're referring to O'Neill himself when you say that.

Quintero: Yes, I am.

That's a hell of a note, isn't it? O'Neill still has to battle for recognition, to be remembered.

Quintero: What's fascinating about *Hughie*—do you know the last words O'Neill ever spoke? "I knew it. I knew it. Born in a hotel room, and goddamn it, died in a hotel room." And he fell back on his pillows and never spoke again. I have a fantasy about him. When he returned to Carlotta and they went to what everyone would think was a fancy hotel, he was trembling all over. And what look did that clerk give him, I wonder. He saw a palsied old man. He knew that if he went upstairs, the next time he'd ride that elevator down, he'd be in a coffin. And it turned out to be true.

A hotel is also a place for transients.

Robards: Tumbleweeds.

Quintero: You have a line in which you say, "I'm not transient."

Robards: "I've been camping here off and on for the last fifteen years."

Quintero: What he's really saying to this new clerk, "You should recognize me even if you are new."

Erie referred to him as a young punk. That could have been me. Back in the early '30s, I worked for a few months as a night clerk in a men's hotel on Chicago's skid row. Who the hell is Erie Smith?

Robards: Erie calls him "a fresh young punk. You couldn't tell him nothin'." And he couldn't con him.

What a horrible moment that must have been for Erie Smith, after Hughie's death. Here's someone to whom he's just a has-been, a never-was. What happens to Erie's position in that hotel of which he was the star guest in Hughie's eyes.

Robards: Remember, he bought a fancy floral wreath for Hughie's funeral. He borrowed the money, "from dead wrong g's." If he doesn't pay back, he's a dead man. He says, "What the hell, I always took a chance. When I lose, I pay. I'm no welsher. And it sure was worth it to give Hughie the big-time send-off." He'd never welsh on him.

Quintero: There's a dignity in him. He had that floral wreath done in the shape of a horseshoe, so Hughie went to his death as a big-timer. Erie might accept the dying, but to die like somebody is entirely different than to die like nobody.

Thanks to the beau geste of Erie Smith, a loser, Hughie goes to his grave a laughing winner.

Robards: Remember Erie gets this new clerk to come out from behind the desk and shoot craps with him.

Quintero: That the dice is loaded makes no difference. But that somebody believes in his luck, that's what it's about.

Robards: He's got life again. He's got his luck back. We know that he'll go on. By Tuesday, he'll have gotten in a crummy crap game and paid the guys back and he'll be OK. He'll have this guy every night. A continuation.

Quintero: Can you imagine that clerk playing dice with one of the biggest guys on the main stem? An intimate friend of Arnold Rothstein.

But Erie Smith is given a dignity Arnold Rothstein never had. We've been told that the big-time, glamorous gambler was killed because he welshed on a bet. Erie would never welsh. Though full of self-deceit, full of pipe dreams, O'Neill shows us a passion for life.

Quintero: He chooses Erie, a small-time gambler and liar, the kind of guy we don't associate with, and forces us to identify with him. He strips us of all pretense.

Let's say I can't get a job, ten years pass, as with O'Neill, and nobody recognizes me. I corner somebody and begin to tell him about the successes I've had, exaggerating, of course. I would be Erie. All of us are Eries.

Robards: O'Neill got all his stuff together in those last years. Through the years, he went through so many stages. He experimented with masks: *The Great God Brown*, With electricity: *Dynamo*. Inner thoughts spoken: *Strange Interlude* and *Mourning Becomes Electra*. And all of a sudden, he had five plays that just poured out of him.

Quintero: Imagine him in that hotel room, upstairs, with his hands trembling. He couldn't hold a pencil, he couldn't write. They disobeyed him. Not one of his plays had been produced in ten years. He was Erie. Most of all, he understood himself.

Robards: In a strange way, we still feel connected to him. The role you play gets out of your hands. It ceases to be lines, cue, and business. It ceases to be the play, really. It's as though somebody's putting a hand on your back and pushing you forward. It's beyond mechanics.

Quintero: He's the one friend we can always count on. He never fails us. Do you ever think of him as dead? I don't.

E. G. MARSHALL

1981

The actor is best known for his frequent appearances in tele-vision dramas and occasional films.

In the original production of *The Iceman Cometh*, he took over the role of Hickey.

When I heard that Eugene O'Neill was coming back and the The-atre Guild was going to do this play, I said: "Get in this production, even if you carry a spear, because this is going to be an event of historic importance."

In a rather large room, I read for O'Neill and a group of Guild people. He shook my hand and right away I felt: *I like this man.* I felt very warm toward him right away.

He wanted me to play Hickey. They said I was much too young for it. In the casting, they were shuffling people all around. It was either Dudley Digges or James Barton to play Harry Hope, who ran the saloon. They decided it was Barton to do Hickey. After we opened, O'Neill was very unhappy. Finally, he insisted.

O'Neill came in and worked with me on it. Boy, did we! We played it in several cities and eventually wound up in Chicago.

I'll tell you something funny. Just to show how he could be wrong about actors. He thought I was the best actor in America. [Laughs] People were saying: Why doesn't he write you a play? I said, "Mr. O'Neill doesn't write plays for actors. He writes plays for posterity."

In the history of world theater, has there ever been a speech as long as Hickey's confession to the guys in Harry Hope's saloon?

I can't recall any of that length. Not in Shakespeare, not the Greeks. When word got out that there was a forty-five minute speech — or forty-seven—you could see them looking at their watches and timing it. Waiting to see if he was going to make it. Yup, he made it.

Hickey wants these beaten-down guys to face reality. Get rid of your pipe dreams. There's the one flash moment, when he realizes he hated his wife all of these years, after saying how much he loved her. As these words escape from his mouth, he realizes that he's had a pipe dream, the wildest of all.

O'Neill told me so many stories about the flophouses he frequented, where his older brother finally wound up. He loved to tell these stories. Funny ones, too. The one about the old rummy who died and the guys were gonna give him a good funeral. Of course, they braced themselves with booze beforehand. One of the pallbearers fell in the grave that was dug. He couldn't stop laughing as he was telling this story. I guess you have to do that in talking about some event that's so grotesque.

I heard him tell a young woman reporter, "No, I don't have a success goal. I have a happiness goal. And happiness, that's the biggest pipe dream of them all." He was not an optimist. He didn't think optimists were rational people.

Of course, he would never compromise. Like his father did. I think that's what moved him most of all. His father, who could have been a great classical actor, was seduced by a guaranteed $50,000 a year, eternally doing *The Count of Monte Cristo*. He could have been greater than Booth, but decided to go for commerce. He said: "No, don't live your life for a false reason. Be true to what your dream is."

EDWARD ALBEE

1968

He is in Chicago during the tour of *A Delicate Balance*. Several of his other plays had been here: *Who's Afraid of Virginia Woolf, Zoo Story, American Dream*, and *The Death of Bessie Smith*.

We are in the radio station on the thirtieth floor of the building. We are staring outside the window. It offers us a foggy, panoramic view of the city's West and South sides. It is not a natural fog that pervades; it is man-made smoke, obstinately hanging over these precincts.

It is a few days after the assassination of Martin Luther King, Jr. Younger members of the city's African American community, overcome by grief and inexorable rage, have set fires at random, here, there, to some of the blocks. The smoke is a searing reminder.

So many people—those we call respectable—find it much easier to sleep their way through life, or avoid responsibility. If you live in a country like the United States, which is a revolutionary society, and keep forgetting that fact, finally, your freedom of choice vanishes. Of course, my plays have political content. I believe that symbols shouldn't be c-y-m-b-a-l-s—I don't think they should clang and make a great deal of noise. There's one play of mine, *Who's Afraid of Virginia Woolf*, which had a rather large political content. Not too many people saw it. They were listening to the noise of the arguments, and they weren't listening to the metaphors.

The choice of names, George and Martha, wasn't accidental. If anybody wanted to see them as representing the principles of the American Revolution with the illusory offspring of it, that was just dandy with me. Not too many people did bother to find that.

Here, the illusory offspring of the mother and father of our country are fighting over what? Fantasy? Also living fantasy, too.

Exactly, yes. The need of crutches, false illusions, the whole business which always ties in with politics. I'm not talking about war and politics, but almost the nature of a revolutionary society. When I was in the Soviet Union about five years ago, in their history courses they don't teach about the American Revolution. They start history with the French Revolution. I talked to lots of college students and school kids in the Soviet Union. They'd never heard of what we might call the second American Revolution, the one that started in 1932. The New Deal. There's a lack of self-awareness, in this country.

I think of your one act play: American Dream. *It's interesting that the grandmother there, who is to be put away, is, in a way, the observer.*

She's not too far away from the alcoholic sister-in-law, in A Delicate Balance.

People who are out of the arena, people who are too young to fold it up yet, who are too old to care about folding up, the pariahs of society: they have a great deal to teach us. I remember when I was a kid, I got along much better with my grandmothers than I did with my parents. I suppose every kid does. We were both a little bit out of the mainstream. We didn't have the crushing, nullifying responsibilities that force so many people to make compromises.

We come to Zoo Story *then. The kid who's met the advertising guy on the park bench, kid who's in trouble, seems disturbed,*

He seems disturbed, but he's not the disturbed man at all really. He's willing to go to the extent of sacrificing himself in order to teach. And it's really the complacent, establishment figure on the bench who's disturbed. The worse things get around us, the more problems we get into, the more people try to remove themselves from them. We have a great deal of violence in this country now. It isn't something that created itself out of whole cloth, nor is it a communist conspiracy as our reactionary friends would have us believe. But the reaction of so many people to necessary violence, such as the one out there last week, is a kind of fascist reaction. It's further withdrawal from responsibility. And when it comes down to the point, finally, that if we don't live up to the principles on which the country was founded, the revolutionary principles of a continually growing revolutionary society, then we deserve to have happen to us what intelligent people are telling us is going to happen.

We're a very violent society by nature, but we have such a puritanical, repressive streak in us at the same time that we're almost schizophrenic as a country. Yes, it is so, in a larger sense, other than merely ward politics—that is, the level at which politics seems to express itself in this country—and people don't bother to concern themselves at a local level terribly much, do they? They let the bosses run all that. I was startled last night. I was listening to a program: college kids were talking about the draft and about their feelings about government. One kid said something which I was shocked to hear. I'm afraid it is too constant a statement in this country. He said, "I am personally offended that my government is not making sufficient, proper decisions that I've got to, at my age, involve myself in the foreign policy of my country, and make decisions about whether or not I will agree or not agree to be drafted based upon whether or not I approve of the foreign policy of the country." Now that's an extraordinary remark to make! It's too bad. He wants the decisions to be made. He wants to be proud to serve in the armed forces and doesn't want to have to question the validity of what the government asks him to do. It's as if the government were an entity that exists without the people.

I sometimes get the feeling that the only way people are going to hear anything is if they're screamed at, if they feel personally threatened. Then they usually make a wrong judgment.

I've been going around to universities talking for a number of years now. And compared to what it used to be a few years before that, kids are indeed—with the exception of this one kid—a good deal more aware and more involved. I'm less disturbed by the occasional odd direction that the involvement takes than a lot of people are. I'd rather have the involvement and have it misdirected occasionally than have no involvement at all.

Usually, one or two people always walk out of every play of mine, either through good taste or because they're offended, one of the two. But I'd be more disturbed the nights that nobody walks out of the play of mine if I didn't realize the incredible apathy that people bring to the theater with them—which connects with political responsibility, too. If people would go into the theater realizing that it's an arena of engagement, rather than escape, and if people would go to the theater to be upset and disturbed rather than merely being pacified and having their values reaffirmed, then on Broadway each year you'd have more than one or two half-way decent plays surviving. People have got to realize that art isn't easy, and the audience must bring to the art at least part of the responsibility that the perpetrator brought to it.

I'm not a didactic playwright. I usually find out what the target is after I finish the play. Obviously I let the subconscious do a great deal of work for me, and I don't start trying to write a thesis play. But

I don't think I've written a play yet that doesn't have a thesis behind it. If a play doesn't have resonance and overtones that are larger, or extend further, than the individuals in the play itself, then one hasn't written a worthwhile play.

It's the function of creative people to disturb the peace. Some people ask me, "Why don't you write plays that I know exactly what the specific answer to the questions you're raising is by the end of the play?" And I always have to answer these people by saying that I find I can ask an awful lot more interesting questions if I don't have to supply the answers to them. If I limited the content of my plays to what I could give specific answers to, I think I'd write very dull plays. And also, there are some people who say, "Why don't you write happy plays?"

Your plays have violent laughs.

Laughter should be awfully close to violence and tears.

Whether it be the laughter that is brought to the audience by Claire, the alcoholic sister in A Delicate Balance; *whether it be Martha and George in their fights; whether it be Jerry telling the story. It turns out to be a horrifying story of himself and the dog.*

The one thing that joins all these outsiders in my plays together is that they do care enough. They care enough to attack and to try to impart a sense of awareness in life to other people. So they're disturbers too. Of peace. That peace of people who wish to sleep through life. Those people who were happy with our government between 1952 and 1960, for example.

Sometimes you can get the right effect for the wrong reason. John Chapman, one of our more erudite critics, who works for the *New York Daily News*, added six months to the life of *Who's Afraid of Virginia Woolf*, in New York, by saying it was a play for dirty-minded women. And the next day at the box office, the lines of dirty-minded women stretched around the block. The worst thing is indifference. Indifference and apathy.

———

1995

He is the only playwright who has won three-and-a-half Pulitzer Prizes. He has officially won three: for *Seascape*, for *A Delicate Balance*, and for his current play, *Three Tall Women*. The Pulitzer Prize judges had chosen *Who's Afraid of Virginia Woolf* as the winner, but were overruled by the corporate executives who had the final say. They said no.

So it's three and a half, which is nice.

We met for the first time in 1968, a dramatic year, especially for Chicago. You were here for A Delicate Balance. *In this current play,* Three Tall Women, *there are three figures. There's a young boy, but the three major figures are the old woman, A, who is ninety-two years old: vital, cantankerous, self-centered, but above all brimming with life and power. Another is a middle-aged, fifty-two, caretaker, governess, B, taking abuse from her. The third is a young woman who comes from the lawyer's office to look over her accounts, C.*

Three Tall Women deals with a subject that most of us have to face at one time or another, getting old, getting helpless, becoming senile; the encroachment of death; the falling away of all of the people that we've known; the collapse of the values we've accepted in our lives. It also deals with being able to see the future and think about the past. Of course, without being able to change it.

In the first act, we learn an awful lot about the old woman, who talks constantly; sometimes drifting in and out of senile dementia; and other times very much on target. And we learn a good deal about her life. And at the end of the first act, she suffers a debilitating stroke. At the beginning of act two, same set—she's in bed when she has the stroke—there she is still, hooked up now to life support systems. The two women from act one are there, but they look rather different; they're dressed quite differently. It soon becomes evident that they are the old woman at various stages of her life: at twenty-six and at fifty-two. Through some miracle of playwright's trickery, they are able to be together.

Then the old woman herself—it turns out to be a dummy on the bed. She comes in, still at ninety, and the three of them have a conversation about the inability to change the future, the mistakes we make, and how we turn from one thing into another. Every single thing we do in our life seems to be going in a straight line. All of a sudden the path diverges and we have to make a choice. So you make a choice and go to the left, say, if you're a democrat. You go to the right if you're a republican. You go twenty feet more, and all of a sudden there are three choices, and you've gotta make one of them. Every single choice you make determines what's going to happen to you for the rest of your life. It has to. The trick, I guess, is to make the most adventuresome choices. The old woman's three selves come to some kind of, if not conciliation, at least compromise with each other by the end of the play.

The audience reactions are interesting. Absolutely stunned, and I'm sure they talk about it long after the curtain comes down. Your purpose is to impel conversation and reflections, debates and heat.

But sometimes silence at first. I remember when my first play, *Zoo Story*, had its world premiere in West Berlin, in German, in 1959. I spent most of my time during the performance of the play watching the audience. We came to the end of the play, *Zoo Story*, and one person performs a kind of crucifixion on himself and gets himself killed.

When the curtain came down, there was absolute silence from the Berlin audience for what struck me as being ten minutes. What was the silence? Ten seconds maybe, of shock and recognition, and then the applause started. I love to write a play that does drive people into a kind of silence.

I suppose what creates some of the audience silence in Three Tall Women *is that it deals with the ultimate, mortality. You don't applaud mortality.*

No, you don't. It's something we try to think very, very little about in this society of ours.

But there's something else that attracts people to your plays: the vitality. Whether it be Martha and George and their vitriolic arguments, the power *of them and the effect on the young couple. Whether it's* Delicate Balance *and this guy's recognition that something went cockeyed. It's furious stuff.*

I was an orphan and I was adopted into that family. The Keith–Albee vaudeville management circuit.

I remember going to the vaudeville shows at the Palace. The phrase Orpheum–Keith–Albee *circuit is familiar.*

They owned the greatest number of vaudeville theaters and they were the ones who would give a vaudeville performer fifty weeks work a year.

There's a matriarch of the family, your adoptive mother. Was she the model for the role of A?

I have to give you a double answer there. Yes. Most of the events that occur in the play that happen to A are things that happened to her. But I invented the character a little bit. Because I wasn't trying to write a revenge play. I was trying to get an accurate portrait of what happens to somebody, so I had to distance myself and, and forget how I had felt about the stuff that happened between us, because we didn't get along well at all, all of our lives together. I had to distance myself from that so that I could write a fairly objective piece about her.

This play is, strangely enough, dealing as it does with mortality, also exhilarating. It seems kind of cockeyed, doesn't it?

You find it exhilarating that it deals with mortality?

Yeah.

Well, that's the last big adventure, isn't it? As far as we know. And people certainly should participate in it, it seems to me. The way they should participate in their entire lives. Dylan Thomas said, "Don't go gentle into it," right? Well, he was right.

The worst thing would be, it seems to me, to come to the end of it, of your life, and discover that you've wasted it; that you haven't participated in it fully, that you haven't been willing to make mistakes, that you haven't been willing to take chances, and that you've coasted through it. What could be worse than that? That's one of the themes of *A Delicate Balance*, that after a point of not making decisions, you become so rigid and so set in your ways, that when a desperately important, humanist decision comes up, like taking in your best friends in the world, you can't do it.

While we may not be responsible for everything that does happen to us, we certainly are responsible for everything that doesn't.

A, this old woman, is full of all sorts of appalling bigotries. Yet, she has this zest for staying alive, in spite of all of the encroachments. And maybe she had to close down her parameters in order to concentrate on surviving. That's possible. That's one of the things I was examining in the play, and that's one of the reasons that even though I knew the woman the character was based on so well, I wanted to remove myself sufficiently to be objective about her. Some people who knew her have told me the character I have created, though she's a horror, is nicer than the real woman was.

When I write a play I have some sense of what the play is about and how it's going to go. But I was writing along early in act two of *this* play, and one of the characters said, "We have a son." And it wasn't until she had said that line that I realized the next line that I was going to write was a stage direction: the boy enters. I didn't know that I was going to do that. Obviously, I'd made up my mind unconsciously, but consciously I didn't know I was going to put him on stage. That's one of the things that's fun about writing. Surprising yourself that way. Or revealing to yourself what you have planned and not been able to articulate it yet.

You had a problem here, and that's the actual woman, and yourself, the adopted son.

We didn't get along at all. And I left home when I was eighteen. And didn't talk to her, didn't see her for the next thirty-some years. It was a question of her saying: "You become the kind of son we wanted when we adopted you or get out." And I figured, well, hey, it's me, you know. I can't be what I'm not. I can't be what other people need me to be. I've got to be what I want to be. So I shrugged and left.

But you as a playwright are also God, therefore you have to be benign toward this antagonistic force.

Being God, I suppose I could've distorted her. That's why I kept trying to be so objective: keep your own reactions, Edward, out of this; keep, keep your own vengeful feelings, your own hurt out of it. Give us the woman as she was and let's see her objectively. Now that was what I had to do in writing this particular play. I had to limit my participation to making sure that it was accurate and fair.

She's aware of her shrinking self. It is natural, as you get older, a certain age—octogenarian and beyond—there is a shrinkage. Of course there is. A physical shrinkage along with the other kinds. She is less tall. She once towered over her husband. She was close to six feet. There's a reference in the play that she took her husband away from a vaudeville woman performer that he was going with at the time.

Charlotte Greenwood!

It was Charlotte Greenwood, yeah. In the play she refers to the husband dating a vaudeville performer: the eight foot one who did the splits. That's the one that my adopted father was dating.

I'll be damned! I remember Charlotte Greenwood. She played in a couple of movies, too. But she was a famous star known for her height and the splits.

I knew you'd know who that was.

And she can't stand losers who miss the boat.

She always stayed on top.

Is she right as far as that young twenty-six-year-old girl, the lawyer, is concerned, that she's gonna be like her?

There's no chance for her to change. Since she *is* the younger version of the older woman. She's not another person. That's awful to know what's going to happen to us, that we can't change.

That may explain the audience's momentary silence.

Sure it does.

It was another kind of silence I heard when I saw Zoo Story.

The guy who's in the park, is a settled young middle-aged executive, who has made too many life decisions that he's not going to reconsider. The other guy, Jerry, is an outsider. Some people think that he's crazy—I don't. I think he's too sane, maybe, and unwilling to make all of the compromises that most people do to accommodate themselves to our society. The argument of the play is the outsider, Jerry, trying to batter Peter, the other character, into an awareness of how to live completely and fully. And Peter resisting. No, I've got it made, I've got it all right. Don't rock my boat. Jerry keeps trying to teach all the time, and realizes that Peter is not going to accept it. There's one point in the play which ties into its religious theme, where Peter does the three denials: denies three times that he knows what's being said to him by Jerry. Jerry is left with no alternative but to teach by self-sacrifice. So he arranges a fight and throws a knife at Peter, who takes it, and Jerry says "So be it," runs on the knife, and dies. Peter, of course, can never recover from this experience, and probably, without wanting to, has learned a little bit more about how to live fully from Jerry. That's what upset a lot of people. That's why the silence.

That theme: the meaninglessness of the guy's life—the other guy's trying to teach him there's something else—also applies to the protagonist of A Delicate Balance.

Tobias didn't make any decision. He regrets it, and there's a fury inside him that explodes.

So we come to Martha and George in Virginia Woolf *and the battle royal.*

What George is trying to do in *Who's Afraid of Virginia Woolf*, by exorcising the nonexistent child, which they started to use as a weapon against each other, is to save their marriage. To destroy the falsity of it. To bring it right down to, to level ground and say, "Let's see if we can build something true and honest on this thing." They do love each other very much, and the play is about trying to save the marriage. Whether they succeed or not, I don't know. See, I don't know whether they've got the guts, the intelligence, and the courage to be able to survive without the falsity, without the false illusion. I don't know. Maybe they can. I'm not sure.

We're talking about false illusions again. The jewelry that the old woman, A, is talking about turns out to be fake. There's an illusion of richness, there's an illusion of the beauty of the diamonds and the rubies. They're fake.

Maybe I've only written one play, since I seem to write about the same stuff. All writers have a couple of themes and that's it. As Blanche says in *Streetcar*, "I tell what ought to be true."

5—The Clowns

Paris. I'm clambering up five flights of stairs toward his small flat along Rue de Boucherie. I breathe laboriously and pause at each landing, desperately looking heavenward. It is a case of life recapitulating art, the herculean task of steep stair-climbing being one of his more celebrated routines. His character is Bip. Bip is Everyman. His hallmark, aside from the mime's white uniform, is a slightly battered top hat with a single rose adding a touch of panache. It is my second encounter with Marceau; we had met in Chicago, during his first American tour a year ago.

The mime expresses the deepest feelings and aspirations of the human being: our first frustrations, our hopes, joys, sorrows, and dreams. The mime art cannot lie. When you rely on words, it's possible sometimes to say things you don't even feel or think. I don't say the word is not a fine and great art. Every art has its greatness and its limits. But in the art of mime, it is so pure: if you lie, you see it immediately, because it's a gesture, it is the moment of truth. You cannot lie with gestures. You're not understood if you lie, and if you're not understood, there is nothing. The mime has to be clear, simple, and people have to identify him with themselves when they see him. I think it has to attain a great degree in the form, like music. You have to attain a degree of poetry, to which everybody can identify himself in the highest level. That doesn't mean intellectual, because everything which is falsely intellectual is too abstract, and we have no contact with it.

You show what is invisible, you make it visible; and what is visible, you make it invisible. That's poetry. For instance, you struggle with the elements every day, a fight with elements. Struggling against the wind; going upstairs and downstairs; pulling in a tug of war; being at the fair; being in a small café; being in a public garden;

representing youth, old age, and death. These are the things without which you cannot live. You have to portray a character which is recognizable. You can identify with him because he belongs to the society. Bip is at a social party; Bip is skating; Bip is traveling on the sea; Bip is a frustrated street musician. Bip wants to die because his fiancée has left him, his love. Or Bip is a lion tamer.

What made Chaplin so great, he found in his early films the Little Tramp. The little man. I think he's a great, great mime. He expressed everything in the movies. But the technique I express is in the theater, which is quite a different art. In the movies, people want illusions through reality. In the theater, they find reality through illusions. They are completely different techniques. In the theater, when the hero dies, everybody knows he doesn't die really. In the movie, he dies really for the public. In the theater they know it is illusion, but they get the poetry, and they are moved, as they are moved in a concerto of Bach or Mozart. They are moved by the form, by the poetry, and also by the meaning: through the illusion they get the reality.

Bip and the traveling rose is a continuation of Harlequin, of Pierrot, the white clown, you know, Punch. There is a continuity in the history. This character has never ceased to be mixed in the society. In the theater world he represented a type of man. The man who has no right to speak, the man who is oppressed, the man who is in a world which has no place for him and his struggles. But also Bip is a combination: he is not only frustrated; he loves, he creates, he struggles, and he has a sense of humor, making people laugh even if the situation is sad. I think we have this in Chekhov, we have it in Molière, we have it Shakespeare. You laugh very often. And suddenly, you cry.

This character, Bip, he can play a prince, he can be a hero, but people know that he is dreaming. He has a hope of doing, achieving real things, like Don Quixote, he is a person who has always perspectives. When there is no more perspective, there is no more hope, there is no more life. Mitterand* said recently, "To explain

---

*François Mitterand was the president of France at the time.

the mystery of their life, people have invented theater." And its most pure form is pantomime. In the Bible it is said, first there was action and then there were words. We know the limits and the possibilities of our art and we have to make people forget that our art is difficult. We have to make people forget that we are working on a stage. We have to live in a high degree of art and motion, and make people come closer to us. But there has to be a distance always between the public and us. The public has to come to the theater because they want to see dreams, they want to see illusion, they want to see magic. If they're not spellbound by magic, there is no necessity for them to go to the theater. They are fine at home. We sleep to have magic. That's why there are dreams. And if you go to the theater, we have to offer you that: dreams.

To create illusion, you have to begin with nothing. You have to begin by re-creating completely reality and motion. To re-create, at every moment, the fragments of daily life. But not to re-create it like a photograph. Let us say like a painter.

I think that mime has to combine the grace of a dancer, and the psychology of an actor. We have to express through gestures psychological, tragical, comical situations. Let us say like the old silent films, Buster Keaton, Harry Langdon, Harold Lloyd, Chaplin, of course, Stan Laurel and Hardy. But of course with different ways, because we are theater.

Sometimes, there is a different reaction in different pieces. In Japan I did "The Staircase," climbing up all those flights. Nobody laughed. When I did it in New York and Chicago and San Francisco, everybody laughed. I found out why. In Japan, houses are small, stairs have no use. The American public laughed because they identified. Let us say you live in the thirtieth floor and you have to go upstairs. That's funny. And that's why they laughed. When I appeared at the second floor, I look higher, and I say, "My God," and it goes on again. But they laughed because they think of the funny idea of every day's life. People can only laugh if they recognize themselves in satire or tragedy.

There is something of Pirandello in what I do: that we are not one man, but we are many. We have not one face, but many. We change. We are a mixture of contradictions, of conflicts. In *The*

Mask Maker, there is the idea that we have not only one face, but several. We change. It is inevitable. I am very happy to grow a little older. I was just thirty-seven this month. People say the more you grow in age, the more you lose possibilities. I would say it's the contrary. That is the great drama for human people. The more you grow in age, the more you grow in spirit and in your experiences, but the less you grow in your physical possibilities. This great divorce makes the tragedy of man. If you could combine wise people and the power of youth, the world could live in harmony. And you would not give to people who are older the complex that they are no more useful to society. It is the problem of Faust, of Goethe.

They say heroes die young because hereoes very often take very great risks, that older ones will not take. But many people develop and mature and grow and see more and more. Shaw, Picasso, Chaplin, Einstein. Many other great men in politics and in art and science. And for actors it is the same. Louis Jouvet* made his first film when he was forty-five years old. Many people in art think if they have not said everything at thirty, they are old. I think you begin to live at thirty-five. Experience is necessary.

Mime is not only skill of muscles and body, mime is spirit, heart as well. I know more now, and that's why I prefer to play as I play now than as I played five years ago. There are some pictures of when I was twenty in mime. I had no tenderness. Maybe as a child, but not when I was twenty, twenty-five. I could not play now for the public as I played before. My standards are higher.

If the young man is beautiful only at twenty, and he is worshipped because he's beautiful, if he has nothing else it is a tragedy for him. What will happen to him? What would happen to Rudolph Valentino at fifty, sixty, if he would not grow? It's tragedy. He was worshipped. I think to be worshipped is always dangerous, because we are not gods. To be respected for real value, yes. It takes time.

I can only do Bip in a social world. Bip as a tailor, Bip as a lion-tamer, Bip as a skater, Bip as a street musician, Bip as an office clerk. I can't see Bip going to the psychologist. Through every day's work,

---

*One of the most admired of French actors in theater and in movies.

I want to find out the sensibility, the spirit of life, the essence, what we need, what we love, why we live.

Especially in mime, you cannot do things without having the real experience of it first, If I go on a tightrope, I have to show people that there is a rope which does not exist. I have been a real tightrope walker. Every year we visit homes for old actors. Old actors always challenge you. I was asked to do a *real* tightrope walk. They said, "Marceau, you do a tightrope walk on the floor, do it really in the air." And I said, "My God, I have never done it." And I worked two months on a real tightrope. I will tell you something terrible. There is a real risk on the air, but people see you, they are not afraid, because you give the impression of security. On the floor when I do it, people shout, are afraid something would happen to me. I said, "That is illusion." Here is a real risk, in the air, and nobody cares. On the floor, there is no risk and people shout. Why? I said, "Because on the air I give an illusion of security. And people are sure nothing can happen to me. On the floor I give a feeling of insecurity, and this is the essence, and that's why they are afraid." Illusion is everything.

There is always an element of the fragility of things which seem solid. Nothing is so solid. It's not pessimistic at all, but it is a thing that we have to realize: at any moment of your life, you can be slapped and taken away. In the moment, you are the strongest. You see the hero, you see the bullfighter. One moment, bing. The bull gets him. Finished. Camus, when he died tragically, was full of hopes and projects, suddenly this stupid accident.* That is, as Goethe said, we have always to do things as if it will be the last time we do it. And that is something marvelous to think. If you have not achieved something people will condemn you for what you have not done. That's why you have to do it the best way possible. If you can.

That's why I chose, in my material, always the conflict of security and insecurity, and what they call, *l'élément destructeur*, the element which comes and destroys.

The name Bip comes from Pip of Dickens, when I read *Great*

---

*Albert Camus was killed in an auto accident, along with his publisher.

Expectations. Because after all, without expectations, there is no life.

JACQUES TATI

1958

He is in Chicago, promoting his film *Mon Oncle*. It is a follow-up to the movie for which he has become celebrated, *Mr. Hulot's Holiday*. He writes, directs, and acts in all his works.

At the radio studio, we had an hour or so of conversation concerning both films. He seemed quite pleased; I was happy. The station's announcer, who had pinch hit for the absent engineer, came out of the control room. He looked sickly; ashen-faced. Uh-oh. He whispered the bad news to me; he had forgotten to press the On button. The tape was blank. I looked toward my guest; I'm certain my face was ashen. He understood immediately. His eyes widened; his face brightened. "No good?" I nodded. He laughed; he was delighted. It was as though he had proved his point about technology and its control over the human. It was the unexpected metaphor for all his films.

He invited me (and the announcer, whose hand he shook) to the posh hotel where he was quartered; we resumed our conversation there.

I try to have the people in my pictures as natural as they are when you watch them from this window, regarding them in the street. This can't be done on a set and the director starts to say, "Lights! Camera! Action!" The man starts to say, "Well, I was—" The director says, "Cut! Sorry, try it again." I don't want my people to feel they are shooting a picture. I want them in a situation where they are natural. When in a rehearsal, I see a man coming exactly when I want, I have a little sign with the cameraman and the camera starts, and he doesn't know he is being caught.

Sometimes when the amateurs make a photo with their little

cameras, you find people are so natural and funny. You see funny faces coming and funny feet. When they try to get on the bus, if they knew they were on camera, they would not be as natural. I want them to say, "I know that man. I don't know where I've seen him, but, yes, I know him." I let the people observe with me. You will find people you like or dislike. They ask me, "Does your picture have a story? What is its construction?" I want the audience to use their own imagination and make their own construction. When I say the picture is not my picture, it starts to be your picture. You have a painting, a wonderful impressionist painting, what does it suggest? You stand in front of it, you look at it, a quarter of an hour, twenty minutes, and then you start to find that it's a rare river.

People say to me, "Oh, You're against television." No, not at all. I'm not against it. But when they say, "This is the best beer, you must drink it," no. "That is a funny man, he has to be funny. That is a very serious man, he has to be dramatic. That man is a monster, he has to make you afraid." No.

People say to me, "You're against modern equipment, against modern architecture." I'm not. I am against conformity. Same chair, same lamps, same table, same car, same street. Then we're going to have numbers. Numbers are good for a football team, but to live with numbers, well, I don't like so much.

Mr. Hulot* was breaking this mold when he arrived at the resort. He was awkward, ungainly, too tall, walked funny, with loping kangaroolike steps, and upset a set pattern. He was a misfit.

Yes. The businessman was spending his holiday on the telephone, still doing business. The old officer was talking about the last war. The young intellectual was trying to reorganize Europe—not easy, especially when you are on holiday. The shopkeeper is speaking of the kind of material he is going to buy next year. This is the way they spend their holiday.

Mr. Hulot arrives, the moment he opens the door, he wants to enjoy himself and the others also. He upsets things. The others are

---

*The role Tati himself played.

against him because he's not of the regime. He doesn't follow what is supposed to be the right thing to do. He wants to be independent for his two weeks' vacation. But you're not supposed to do that.

There were certain people at that resort, whom he liberated — the silent ones.

Yes, the man who always walked behind his wife, who never said a word. He was happy with Hulot, who made him smile. The little old school teacher, who seemed so unhappy. When Hulot took her for a ride, a mixed-up ride, she got excited. They thought they were misfits until Hulot came. When they said good-bye, they shook his hand and hoped to see him next year. He made them remember this holiday with a smile.

I find the same trouble with television, a pattern that is set. The people use the same dialogue. They put their hands in their face the same way. They play with the little papers they have on the table the same way.*

When I went in the shop, the girl was selling something, already started to have a television style. She says, "Oh, you have to take it because really it's the best." We speak with a uniform dialogue and a uniform attitude and it's very sad.

I went one day in the shop to buy a tie and the man acts exactly like the man on television selling a similar tie. I say, "Are you doing that on purpose to sell me the tie like I saw the man on television." He says, "Why?" I say, "Because you are as good as the man I saw on the television." He was very happy. He was complimented. He lost his own personality. I feel sad.

I make a picture, I hope, to help people a little bit, not to have a better house, not to have better clothes, not to have a better salary, but to preserve their thinking. Especially their sense of humor.

In my new picture, it's a successful family. The magazine is happy to come to write a story on Mr. and Mrs. Arpel on their new house, a new garden, a new fountain, and a new car. And even the books are new. They have a little boy, who has new clothes and goes

---

*This is a reference to the *Tonight* show on which he appeared. Jack Paar was the host.

to the best school. But Mr. Arpel is so busy a manufacturer, he doesn't have time to spend with his son. Mrs. Arpel has wonderful modern kitchen equipment.

The uncle lives in an old section, where the people are on the street, they are talking to each other and if something bad happens in one house, you know that next door will help. And they smile and they laugh. The others have such wonderful houses and wonderful clothes. But inside they are bitter.

The little boy enjoys himself every time the uncle comes to fetch him. He's happy in the old man's neighborhood. The father starts to be cross. "I pay for the whole situation. I pay the car, the house, his school." So he gets jealous. They try to teach a lesson to the uncle, who is a little bit of Mr. Hulot. They tell him he must live better, have money, have a nice house, modern.

In the end, it is the uncle, the old Hulot, who teaches the father a lesson. "This young kid wants to play sometimes, to go to my old section and whistle and put hands in a pocket, and anyway, to be free. Your house is wonderful, but it's like a prison in gold."

In the moving-picture industry today, everything is so well made. All the people are very well made. There are never mistakes. I hope I will always make mistakes. My pictures are all mine, from beginning to end. I want to tell my story in my own way. I wish to tell this to the younger generation. The individuality of people is getting lost.

1962, Paris

I am a prisoner of Hulot's character and I'm happy to be so. It is difficult for me to change my car because I don't want to be the other. It is impossible for me to come in a Rolls-Royce with a chauffeur, and somebody will open the door. What would Mr. Hulot think? I'm obliged to drive my old car. I am a lovely prisoner of a man that I like.

That is why I always defend the dialogue of the ordinary people, the worker in the little car, the shoemaker. The little details they observe. It's much more clever than the conversation you hear in a big cocktail party, where you always hear the same sound, the same words. "Oh, it was wonderful, the greatest. Marvelous." And they don't mean it. What do you call it? Packaged conversation, yes.

When I was in New York, they offered me quite big money to make a commercial for television with Mr. Hulot's character. That kind of money would help me to repaint my house, to change my car, to buy maybe a fur coat for my wife. That was one side. On the other side, were the students who I was speaking to and all the people who liked Mr. Hulot. If I accept the television commercial, I'm selling Mr. Hulot. He is telling them this beer so-and-so is the best, fly by this airline. I am not allowed to do this for the people who think Mr. Hulot is their friend. If I meet them again, I don't want them to say, "Oh, we saw you and you told us which cigarette we should have to smoke." Never.

I receive letters from students from those countries where they cannot say what they want to say. They write to me: "For us, Mr. Hulot is a free man." I do hope I will always be that. If you will look all around, in Paris, Chicago, in New York, any place, there is in everyday life much more Hulot than you can imagine.

ZERO MOSTEL

1961

He is appearing in Chicago in Eugene Ionesco's play, *Rhinoceros*. After some years on the blacklist, during the '50s, he returned to the stage in the acclaimed off-Broadway production of *Ulysses in Nighttown*. He won all the major awards for his portrayal of Leopold Bloom.

An irrepressible clown, he is forever on, even when he is off stage. During a conversation with him (even though "conversation" may not be the precise word), the other party must just hold on to his hat and enjoy an exhilarating ride.

Hasn't the clown in theater always been the one to tell the truth, to speak truth to power?

When you consider the great clowns, think of Molière. His theory of drama was based on the clown. The word for actor in French is "comedian." It is not actor. The truthful actor is a comedian, who heightens drama and enlarges life, rather than offering us a piece of realistic acting. Molière's *Impromptu at Versailles* was the first modern play for larger-than-life acting.

Much of the acting you see in theater today is what I like to call the *mishpocha* play, the family play. There is a wife, a husband and a daughter, who is in trouble, pregnant. Those are things that happen in your house—it's dull. What I like to see is something larger than that. It's like painting. Picasso is great because he heightens the truth and therefore you can't mistake it. That false realism hides it. it's just reportage.

When you see great theater or a great actor or a great painter, you're never the same. When you see W. C. Fields, some of that dignity that he has—against all the terrible things of our time—rubs off on you. When you see a great actor or a great play, it does something to you. You're never the same. Fields says, "If you cheat, you'll get ahead. Your family is rotten. Beat children. Be completely disorganized and you'll get ahead." He doesn't say, "That's what we *should* be." It's his attack on those things, on society as it is, that makes him a great clown. His reaction against false sentiment was wonderful. If a kid bites you in the finger, maybe you should bite him back. I think he simply refuses to conform, don't you think?

Ionesco prods you. He doesn't offer any solutions. He doesn't say, "Society is like this and this is my comment on it." He just says: "Think." He doesn't tell you *how* to think. He wants you to do it yourself. People come out thinking they are not rhinoceroses. They never see themselves. They always say someone else looks like a rhinoceros. The mere fact that they say, "We are not rhinoceroses," is saying, "We'll not behave like them." That's a gain.

In the play, Beringer, who seems the weakest, doesn't change, doesn't turn into the beast. He doesn't change because he's incapable of changing into the beast. I think he's the hero because in him may be the unconscious feeling for the good.

Sometimes we're attracted to a cause and we don't know why. But we feel it's good. There's just something good about Beringer.

He groans, tries to do the animal snorts. He wants his skin to change, to look lovely, like a rhinoceros, but it doesn't suit him. Then he says, "Well, I'll never surrender." There's that goodness. When you really pin 'em down, people are good.

EUGENE IONESCO

1962

Paris. 14, rue Rivoli, a fifth-floor walk-up. There's a mix-up. He tries to reach me: postpone interview, doctor's appointment. I fail to get message. His nineteen year-old daughter, Marie-France, graciously invites me in. Soon, he'll be here. My interpreter, Michelle Vian, Sartre's secretary, is *hors de combat*, with a bad cold. Boy. Ionesco and his wife arrive. They are both little, frail; he a leprechaun, baldish, wisps of hair at the sides. The missus is not at all pleased to see me. I don't blame her. She sits on the couch furiously turning the pages of *Le Figaro*. I suggest another time. He says, no, please, sit. His daughter will interpret. She is scared; her English isn't that good. There is a French–English dictionary on her lap. There are many, many long pauses, as she looks up a word. During those tortuous moments, he is looking at me; I am looking at him. He knows no English; I know no French. I lift my glass; he lifts his. We are brothers in helplessness.

Somehow or other, after a fashion we—dare I say it?— communicate.

The Theater of the Absurd has often been associated with me. The phrase is the critics' invention, not mine. Human existence may be absurd. We can't fully understand it. We enunciate it through the comic. He frees us.

Realism represents only one aspect of the world. The truth is much deeper. The abstract artist came along. Yes, there is a parallel between the revolution in art and in the theater. The theater was slower than painting and music in catching up. I am not a surrealist myself, but I have been influenced by them. This goes along with the revolution in science, philosophy, and psychology.

The idea that communication is difficult in my kind of theater is an invention of the critics. It is not really impossible for people to communicate. The difficulty comes about because we're taught to be lazy, indifferent to one another. And because we don't laugh. A play is an adventure in imagination, a challenge for the audience to think. A writer can't give up food already digested. He gives the audience raw meat. It is for them to chew, to digest. In *Rhinoceros*, you have an ideology coming in a country, and most people follow it. It is uniformity, and Beringer does not accept it. He is alone. Yet the idea is to live independently, thinking for one's self, and not the mass mind.

Einstein said, "I hate flags and military music and troops marching around." This was Beringer, too, without his saying it or even thinking about it. You have to keep your own personality. Every ideology has a slogan. You must mistrust them all, to question, to find the answer in yourself.

[He adds, gently touching his daughter's cheek] You see, we did communicate—the trouble was in the translation. We need more practice. [His daughter begins to cry softly. The missus is still turning the pages of *Le Figaro*.]

———

You see Ionesco as an optimist?

Is Ionesco a good man of hope? I think so. It's so wonderful to sit through this play. It's vaudeville. It has a big canvas. [He lapses into a thick Italian accent.] It has a broada brusha strokes.

You are also a painter. That enthralls you as much as theater?

Si. I was influenced by an Italian painter called Dominico Foppa, the great Milanese artiste. He also made the broada brusha strokes. Vaudeville. Broad brush strokes. Truth from clowns.

There's Beckett's Waiting for Godot. *Your Estragon to Burgess Meredith's Vladimir. Gogo and Didi.*

No one knows why he's called Gogo. When they ask him: "What's your name?," he says, "Adam." I'm always tickled by something I don't understand. Remember Bobby Clark,* that great clown? In the middle of singing a duet, he steps out front and says, "Did somebody see my horse go by?" Wonderful.

Many a painting, you see it, you're attracted to it, you don't know why. You look at it, you say, "There's something about it. I can't put my finger on it." You can't put your finger on it, but you sense it's unique, an invention, a creative piece of work. We see a Rembrandt portrait. What we're attracted to is not the remarkable likeness. Of the fifty extant Rembrandt self-portraits, he looks quite different in every one of them. So there's a quality other than that that attracts us. I'm crazy about that element when I see it in something. When you read Shakespeare, you read ten million versions of what one line may mean. It's wonderful, the creation of that language.

Joyce, of course, comes to mind. You called him the papa of them all.

Beckett, Ionesco, Genet, they all derive from the writings of Joyce. *Rhinoceros* could easily have come from the Circe scene in *Ulysses*, where men turned into pigs. Hallucinations make them turn into all sorts of things. Joyce originated that invented language, colorful, deep, mysterious. You need five dictionaries and nine languages to read it. It's all one and it's marvelous. [Into the microphone] I just hit Studs on the arm.

The clown. You have been—

[Into the microphone] Again I hit him!

—one of the most imaginative. As Leopold Bloom, you were a tragic-comic figure. Vaudeville, Scripture, folklore, music-hall songs, burlesque. . . .

It's all there, written down. Every piece of pantomime I did, Joyce had described, word for word. You didn't have to alter a word or a gesture.

---

*With his partner, McCullough, he was a star of musical comedies and vaudeville. His hallmarks were painted-on spectacles, a rubbery cigar, a crouchlike walk (later adopted by Groucho Marx), and an airy insouciance.

Does the same approach apply to painting, since you consider that your calling as much as theater?

Yes. What is he doing, the action painter, Jackson Pollock? What does it mean? Is it for our times? Who's to tell what is for our times? Too many painters painted for their times and nobody knew it. It was only later that we found out. I'm just fascinated by the wonderful things the human hand can do. I have to have the tolerance to sit through it and maybe find out something about it.

Jackson Pollock's drips reflect something of our time, maybe the worthlessness of much of it. The great art critic John Berger offered a marvelous picture of Pollock. "He paints as if he never had any communication in the world. He lived in a cell and there happened to be paint there, and this is how he expressed himself, since there was no language." We live in a nuthouse. A large part of our thinking is nutty and he reflects it. A reflection of our time and it's done by hand. With imagination.

I always distrust a man who says, "It's odd. I don't like it." Or, "I know what I like." Our conception of art is based upon a *little* sampling. It's never based on a huge knowledge. [A sudden hissing sound] Oh, excuse me, my cigarette just flew across the studio — Where was I?

Art.

Where am I going? What are we doing here? Waiting for Godot? Waiting for this to be over. It will never be over. Oh-h-h . . .

We live in a nuthouse, you said.

I don't say "we." There's a part of our house that is terribly nutty. When you read about atomic energy and the missile race, *that's* nutty. When they talk of its warlike use, that's nutty. The building of shelters. We're doomed if it's dropped. We're in Pollock's little shelter and hiding from something.

I see a parallel between Bosch and Breughel and Pollock. I see an almost natural development from Ensor to Pollock. They both reflected the nuthouse.

You have to know Bosch's *Garden of Earthly Delight*. His feelings of hell, of religious fanaticism. Breughel's paintings of the Flemish proverbs. Ensor's paintings of medicines, doctors, and quacks.

It occurs to me that your being a painter has colored the way you perform on stage. Your hand, the delicate crook of a finger . . .

Because I paint, my gestures come from an inner urge. I don't know why I do a certain gesture. It must be clean. Clarity is a great thing in art. Simple. I don't mean so simple that even an idiot can understand it. It must be complex, too. It must have substance. [Suddenly, a low roar.] Give me back my matches! [Into microphone] My host is a petty thief. [Softly] He gave me back my matches.

Ionesco, I'm told, was dissatisfied with most of the productions of Rhinoceros.

All playwrights are enemies of the productions of their plays. He has a preconceived notion about his work. It's your own creation, your own baby. When it's done, it's like you lost your child. You and I knew a great character, didn't we? Sol Burry. He wrote a wonderful play. *Winner of the Big Prize.* It's about the end of the era in burlesque. It was about commerce versus art. He wrote eleven versions of the play. He was offered dozens of opportunities and turned them all down. He would never write anything else. He wanted that play for himself, his baby.

FLASHBACK. *Sol Burry was an ex-burlesque comic, whose conversational tone was in the high-decibel range. His voice, even during intimate exchange, could be heard by wayfaring strangers one hundred yards distant.*

On one such occasion, he and I are lounging at the entrance of the old Royalton Hotel in New York; before this slightly seedy, charming old theatrical place had been transmogrified into a high fashion, upscale, monstrous in-place for power lunches.

He had read a pretty bad play that I had written and was letting me (and dozens of passers-by) know it. His dialect was pure New Yorkese. "Toikel, your play is manure, because it's too cosmic. Where are the dee-tails? Dickens. Chekhov. Where are the little t'ings in life? That's what art is about—the little t'ings in life."

At that moment, a taxi pulls up. George Jean Nathan, the eminent drama critic, and his companion, Julie Haydon, the actress, emerge. They have lived at the Royalton for years. Instead of entering the hotel, they stroll toward 6th Avenue. Haydon has a little dog on the leash.

Burry nudges me and, hand cupped over mouth, whispers, "That's Jawge Jean Nat'an, sage of the American theayter. Let's folla them an' eavesdrop an' you might glean a poil of wisdom about art."

We shuffle about ten feet behind the couple. There is a silence. As they approach the corner, Nathan says to Haydon, indicating the dog, "Take Max around the post." A sharp jab from Burry. "Did you heah that, Toikel? Take Max around the post. The little t'ings in life. That's a poil of wisdom. Boin that in your brain."

Ionesco insisted his was the way to do a certain scene. I disagreed. It's where I turn into a rhinoceros. All other actors, everywhere in the world, went off stage, put on green makeup and a horn and came out as a rhinoceros. I thought you could never really become a rhinoceros. Even its skin. They'd still say it's a suit. You must do it with the inner quality of the beast, the bestiality that you have in yourself.

I said to Ionesco, "I'm not leaving the stage. The transformation has to happen before their eyes." We argued. Then I showed him how it was done. "You're right," he said, "That's the only way to do it."

How did you do it?

Accidents happen. I was a perfectly lucid human when Beringer came to visit me. I smacked my foot on the floor and dust came up. I said to myself, "That's a good thing. Keep it in." So I kept whacking my foot on the floor and the dust would come off the stage—they're all dusty. That was an alarming thing to see. Sometimes you do the reverse of what is written. I was supposed to go into the bathroom and come out raving mad. I thought that was wrong. I played the rhinoceros comically. [He utters a high-pitched cry-whimper.] That was more terrifying than if I'd bellowed.

That squeaky cry as against the violent foot —

Makes it more violent. The sudden contrast is frightening. And then when I bust through the window pane, they wanted me to put a rhinoceros head on. I said no, that would destroy the illusion.

You call upon the imagination of the audience. I'm reminded of what Ruth Draper once said: "I merely call upon the imagination of the audience."

Of course. She made them *think*, And that, sir, is what theater is all about. [Bellows] Where are my matches?

1976

He is in a Chicago hotel room, during the tour of *Fiddler on the Roof*. Nearby is our mutual friend, Win Stracke, a lieder singer whose other passion is the folk song. Zero insists on Win starting things off with his favorite bad-man ballad, "Sam Hall." During our conversation, he intermittently requests an encore of the bad man's on-the-scaffold curse: "Let this be my parting knell/I will see you all in hell/and I hope you sizzle well/Damn your eyes."

You're something of a singer yourself, Signor Mostelli.

[In an Italian accent] Si, I'm a singer. What for you want to know?

You came from Parma, I believe.

From Parma, si. Where the hams come from. Smoked.

You are considered the most exciting tenor since Caruso.

Caruso, poof. [A flow of Italian double-talk, gibberish, musical references.]

You're noted for your Rhadames in Aida, *your Rodolfo in* Bohème —

Mimi I do as a tenor. Tosca as a tenor. The only one.

You mean Cavaradossi.

Non, non, Cavaradossi homosexual. Otherwise, why they shoot him. They put real bullets. He's a no good. [He sings a passage from the aria, *visi d'arte*.] Then I jump over the parapet. I broka the floor.

So you also sing high, soprano.

If you stick me, I sing high. You don't stick me, I sing low.

What is your opinion of Giuseppe De Stefano?

He's a pig. Pappaduce!

Franco Corelli?

He's a bigger pig.

Luciano Pavarotti?

He's a two pigs.

Tito Gobbi?

[Softly, with reverence] He's a bar'tone.

This is the seventy-fifth anniversary of our magazine, The Musical Courier. *Every opera singer from Martinelli to Bjorling to Domingo has taken ads. Are you interested in a page or two?*

What for? No ads, please. What for Mostelli needs ad? Everybody knows Mostelli, *grande artista.*

In your last appearance at La Scala, our correspondent thought you were alarmingly flat and off-key.

I'll take ten pages!

Now, in another life, you are an actor. During our last encounter, you touched on improvisation.

You are always imprisoned by a method as an actor. It should seem improvised. I don't believe you should analyze a part down to the point where all its juices are gone. I think it should always seem as if it's the first time you've done it. I don't like the method where you study the history of the character, the psychological gesture and sense memory. Then they ask you to play freely. It's impossible. If I go in with a bellyache, I use it. If I have a headache, obviously it would be different. Sometimes it hits one note, sometimes another. Of course, there's the idiot director. I don't have anything against them if they have something to offer. A good director steals from a good actor. A bad director tells the actor what to do in his terms.

I think most art is instinctual. There's an impulse that's different every time. No painter can paint the same way. If he paints the same way every time, he's a commercial artist. Good artists are great and bad, but never in between.

So Piatagorsky does not play the cello the same way every night. And certainly not a jazz artist.

I heard Horowitz, that memorable concert after a twelve-year absence. People wept, fell apart. His playing was astounding. I came back to his dressing room. He's sitting there with a cigarette, lying back. He said [a Russian accent]: "Zero, was not too boring?" I think a true artist doubts himself always. Although you may look confident, you doubt. I don't think I'm ever satisfied with what I do. I always say, "I could have done it better."

Horowitz is almost childlike. When I'd say, "Hello, Vladimir," he'd say, "Oh, don't touch me very much." The next day, "Sinus is bad." That's his hello. He says, "So what doing now, Zero?" I say, "I'm doing *Fiddler on the Roof.*" It was 1964. So he said, "I would like to see that."

When he came back after the performance, I was stretched out on the floor. He said, "Zero, what's the matter?" I said, "Wasn't too boring?" He had no conception what a Broadway show was like. "How many times you do this show? Once every so often?" I said, "Eight times a week." He says, "Not me. Once every twelve years." De Pachman, the great eccentric, would play a movement and then say, "I think I could play it better." And he'd play it again for the audience. Richter did that, too.

All the great artists have doubts. You can't say, "This is the best performance," or "This is the best painting." There may be forty best ones. One has nothing to do with the other. There's a Breughel, a Rembrandt, a Matisse. When I saw the *Grande Jatte*—it was the first large Seurat I'd ever seen—

At the Art Institute, Chicago.

I was young. I said it was the greatest thing I'd ever seen in my life.* It made me feel good all over. Then I saw a Matisse there and a Chagall that knocked me out. Maybe his best. [Stops short] There I go. I don't know if it was his best. It doesn't matter. I saw a Gauguin that makes you cry. What makes one a Rembrandt, one an El Greco, one a Vermeer? There are no set rules in art. It goes for writing as well as painting. How do you rate Joyce as a writer? He can't write a sweet little Guy De Maupassant story. Obviously, Joyce might have said, "I'm going to turn things inside out." He doesn't say it willfully. It just pours out of him some way. They may describe someone's painting as religious. What's that got to do with it? It's painted a certain way and it's that *way* that makes it unique.

Technique is something you must have, but once you've mastered it, throw it out the window. This is particularly true in acting. I'd like to see someone with fire, something that I may not be able to understand even. But someone with only passion isn't much good, either. You must always assume some kind of discipline behind it.

Braque was probably the brightest of the painters. Usually painters when they speak of their own work don't really say what it's about. He says, "A painting is finished when you have eradicated the original conception." I believe that. A hack ends with what he begins, when everything is in its place. It has a joke. A good ending that ties up everything neatly and works out fine. And is boring.

It's very interesting in Joyce. Stephen, in the bordello, takes the ash plant and smashes the light. He says, N-O-T-H-U-N-G. His mother appears, or a hand reaching out like a crab to crush him. Nothung is the sword in Wagner's *Ring*. But it is also—I've read it a hundred times—nothung is Not Hung. And nothing. Multi-levels.

---

*The French film director, René Clair, always made it a point, when visiting America, to stop off in Chicago to see the *Grande Jatte*. "It made my day so much better."

Your being acquainted with Wagner may have also helped in doing Ulysses. Just as your knowledge of Chagall may have helped in your portrayal of Tevye in Fiddler on the Roof.

Of course. Everything you know becomes part of everything you do. A lot of these kids don't want to go to school. "I want to be an actor." They think acting is simple. They can be a certain kind of actor, a dull one. The more you know, the more is reflected in your work.

Many of the theater critics never really dug Joyce. I never knew a critic who really recognized an artist. It takes one artist to recognize another. Apollonaire recognized a Picasso; Berlioz, a Beethoven. Mendelssohn found Bach. He had been lost.

[The tape recorder broke down — the second time — and we resumed at the radio studio.]

When did you first find out you were a mechanical wizard? I've traveled through half the town with this little, rotten Japanese set, going on and off.

Isn't an accident sometimes a catapult for a fresh idea? Something not in the books.

An accident can sometimes be wonderful. In a rehearsal period that often happens. It may work out for the benefit of the play. It depends on a work. If it's Shakespeare, I don't think we should add much. If it's Neil Simon, why not?

With Joyce, it's a listening and finding out. Listen to Leopold Bloom recalling his youth: [His face assumes an air of wonder and longing and loss.]

I was in my teens, a growing boy . . . The mingling odors of the ladies' cloak rooms . . . Instincts of the herd. The dark sex smell of the theaters and bridal's vice. And then the heat. There were sun spots that summer. End of school and tipsy cake. Halcyon days. I was precocious. Youth. I sacrificed to the forest the flowers that bloom in the spring. Lottie Clark, flaxen hair. I saw her at night, toileting through closed curtains, with poor papa's opera glasses . . . She rolled down the hill at Rialto Bridge to tempt me. With a flow of amorous spirit, she climbed the crooked tree. A saint couldn't resist. The demon possessed me. Done. Over. Besides, who saw?

I don't think anybody wrote images of that kind in the history of literature.

There is a recurring refrain running through our several hours together, seventeen years ago and now: art as a fusion of mystery and clarity. Isn't that something of a paradox?

You see a Cézanne and everybody says, "That's a mountain." Or it's an apple or it's an orange. It's not enough to know it's a mountain. What kind of mountain is it? That's the mystery.

René Clair, the French movie director, said he gave up doing it because he couldn't find young actors who were like Chaplin. Total actors. He mentioned you. Jean-Louis Barrault spoke of too many of the others being "hands in the pocket" actors.

Charlie Chaplin, at a party, tells a story. A father, a mother, a daughter, a son, a villain. He did all the roles. He did all the voices, jumping up and down in his chair.

We did something together. He was the matador and I was the bull. As he made passes at me with his imaginary cape, he flirted with a girl. Then he whacked the hell out of me, kicked me in the behind and hit me with his cape, tied the cape on me and made love. Always with his eye on the girl. For one moment, he took his eyes off me and I stabbed him. I got him with my horns. I, the bull, picked him up and carried him off. As he was dying, he was throwing kisses at the girl. As Charlie says farewell with a kiss, I say farewell to you, Cherubino!

[He sings a passage from Figaro's aria, *non piu andrai*, as we march out of the studio.]

EXUENT

EPILOGUE

1966 and 1978

During the early years of television, one of its most popular and respected programs was *Kukla, Fran, and Ollie*. It was a puppet show, coming out of Chicago. He was the creator as well as the entire cast of the Kuklapolitan Players; with the exception of Fran Allison, an actress-singer, who was the "straight man."

During these radio conversations, he, besides being himself, became several of the Kuklapolitans. Among them were Kukla, the diffident impresario; Ollie J. Dragon, with his protruding prehensile tooth; Mme. Ophelia Oglepuss, the amplebosomed grande dame, a patron of the arts; Colonel Cracky, a courtly Southern gentleman; and Beulah Witch, a raffish one.

I've often wondered why one is a puppeteer. I think he wants to run the whole show. There's a feeling of total power. You do everything. He wants to act all the characters, he wants to make all the costumes, he wants to paint the scenery, he wants to work the lights, he wants to pull the curtains, and he wants to sing. Yes, he's something of a control freak.

Kukla was the first hand puppet I ever created. I had worked with marionettes until then, string puppets. This was back in 1935, '36. I was affiliated with the W.P.A. Federal Theater and the Chicago Park District.

Thornton Wilder, who was teaching at the University of Chicago at the time, directed us in a play Gertrude Stein had written for puppets. It was called *Identity or I Am Because My Little Dog Knows Me*. I'll never forget his advice: "Don't worry about the meaning of the words, just think how beautiful they are."

We played on the backs of trucks, we played at Hull House—I remember meeting Jane Addams. We played down in Maxwell

Street* in the middle of crowds. We were pelted with tomatoes. We played in county hospitals. We did show after show, day after day, everywhere in the city. We rode the streetcar from one end of town to the other.

As a child, I loved the movies, especially the silents. I didn't see much theater when I was a little kid. We couldn't afford it. But we saw all the stage shows at the Balaban and Katz theaters. Remember those? All the best vaudeville acts. My mother was a natural musician and my father loved to sing and clown around a lot. I was about six, seven. I'd go home and build a little theater of orange crates and Christmas tree lights; with dolls and teddy bears. My imagination was touched, as I, without realizing, created a world of my own. The other kids on the block were a bit rough and this was my sanctuary.

You found a protection in this world you created—power.

Not the kind of power wielded over another person. Not in a neighborhood-bully way. Power over myself, maybe. Creatively.

Kukla means doll in Russian. Years ago, when I was at a party fooling around with my one puppet, Tamara Toumanova, the Russian ballerina, cried out, "Kukla!" He's my right-hand man, Ollie is my left hand.

They say the right hand is the doer, the left hand, the dreamer, the outsider. Kukla, the responsible one. Ollie, the carefree, the different.

Oddly enough, Ollie reflects the average man more than Kukla, even though we assigned him left-handed qualities. Kukla is really the outsider. You don't know where he came from. He has no childhood. He has no memory of parents. Ollie would be delighted to tell you of his parents.

OLLIE: Ollie J. Dragon, here. J for Jethro, it's an old New England name. My mother owns a ski lodge in Dragon Retreat, Vermont. It was once my ancestral home. [He sings.] I breathe the scent of wildflowers so rare/a sweetening breeze/I taste the precious nectar so

---

*Chicago's celebrated open market for most of this century.

pure, flowing from the maple trees/I sleep my soundest knowing full well that the dawn will herald another delightful day at Dragon Retreat/with my father and my mother. [Deeply moved] It is so sad. I'm sorry. I can't go on.

How much of you, Burr, is in the Kuklapolitans? Ollie's memory of his childhood . . . ?

It is obliquely the story of my life, of my parents, my dreams, my hopes, my doubts. As I was listening to Ollie's song, it oozed with sentimentality, sugary sweet. It was all tongue in cheek or as Ollie would say, tooth in cheek. Sometimes, we gang up on our child-hood memories. We're ashamed of being innocent. It's like being afraid of the neighborhood bully. Kukla was never ashamed of his innocence. Ollie, who believed in it, had to kid me with that song.

Remember the high moment for psychoanalysis when artists were running to their psychiatrists You were afraid to say you had a beautiful childhood and that you loved your mother and father. I loved them, but I didn't dare say it, so I let Ollie say it for me.

May I call upon one of your other colleagues? I see her now. Mme. Ophelia Oglepuss.

She is beaming.

Do you recall, Madame O, when I last saw you, you were wearing a purple opera cape?

MME. O: Yes, my darling. It was designed after Claudia Muzio's. It was purple velvet with fringe and bead work.

Did your parents name you Ophelia after Hamlet's tragic heroine?

I never talk about my past. I'm interested only in the present.

Madame Oglepuss—

You may call me Ophelia, dear boy.

—you have always been interested in culture.

Yes, yes, I have. I've always had high standards. I've tried my best with the Kuklapolitans to bring good things to television. I'm afraid that my influence has been slight, as you can tell from television today.

I've seen you opening nights at the Opera House —

My dear, I was privileged to be present, quiet as a little mouse, at the dress rehearsal of *Fanciulla del West* just the other day.

The Girl of the Golden West?

[A touch patronizingly] Yes, my dear. Si. [Sighs] Oh, I've been available for that role for several years, shall we say?

Of course. Forgive me. I had forgotten you were a singer.

Am, darling, not *was*.

But the girl in that opera is — rather young.

That's why I'm so perfect for it. My dear, haven't you ever heard my *Traviata*? [She sings a passage of *addio del passato* in the manner of Florence Foster Jenkins.*] That, of course, was Claudia's. Have you heard my *Tosca*? [A touch of *vissi d'arte* here.]

Wow, you're powerful.

That was one of the words they used — powerful.

What was the other word?

Read my reviews, darling.

I see your dear friend, Colonel Cracky coming this way.

Oh, yes. [She calls out.] Remember, Richard, we're doing lunch at the Arts Club. [She vanishes.]

Colonel Cracky, are you from the Deep South?

COL. C: As deep as you can get. Ophelia and I have been good friends for many years. We court.

---

*Florence Foster Jenkins was a "character," who, with her accompanist, Cosme McMoon, offered annual concerts of "opera arias" at New York's Town Hall. Bedecked in evening gown, feather boa and all, she packed the place.

Are you an opera aficionado, too?

Well, no, no. Actually, I'm more interested in the musical theater. I do like Victor Herbert and Rudolph Friml. Those good strong popular shows. You know, that sort of thing.

Like The Vagabond King?

Oh, my boy, yes, indeed. When I was younger, I understudied Mr. Dennis King.* That was my first role. Burgundy and all that. [He sort of sings a passage from the hit song, *Stout-Hearted Men.*] "And to heck with Burgundy!" I trust we're on the public airwaves. [Sings] "And to Hades with Burgundy." It's not as good.

MME. O: [Her voice is heard off stage] Richard!

COL. C: My mother's calling me. Excuse me.
   [A cackle is heard. Beulah Witch appears.]

BEULAH: I'm not cackling, I'm joking. I tell you, when these two get on, they never get off. Studs, baby, how in the world can you put up with that stuff? You're so tolerant and patient. How's everything, honey?

You're rather free and easy in your talk—

I'm free and easy in my life, honey. I'm liberated. I was the first witch to ride astride. The first witch to ride in black jeans. It shocked my mother. She was a side-saddle rider. Mother's used to it now and goes right along. She's very up to date. Not liberated, but up to date.

   Why am I so breezy? When you fly around a lot on that broomstick, you get a mouthful of air from time to time. That accounts for my breeziness. [Cackles] I don't like to fly around Chicago much any more. Between the John Hancock and the Sears, you can't have fun anymore. So many restrictions. The girls won't hold their convention here anymore. Skirmished with the police. Our whole sorority was busted one year for flying too low.

---

*Dennis King was renowned for his role of François Villon in *The Vagabond King*.

As a feminist, do you have thoughts about the ERA?

Do I? And about Phyllis Schlaffly,* too. But I won't tell you what they are. We're on the air, honey. Why Don't you ask Ophelia how she feels?

MME. O: Yes, dear. Why you put up with this girl is more than I'll ever know. Beulah, Beulah, Beulah, look at you. You're just tacky coming into the studio like this.

BEULAH: Honest to Pete, baby, you're the limit.

MME. O: Since you've asked, Phyllis Schlaffly's right, you know. I mean, really, I think women's lib has gone too far.

BEULAH: Oh baby, we're going to get in one big argument.

You're friends so long, you're aware of each other's idiosyncrasies.

BEULAH: That's the U S of A, kiddo. Take an opposite side, and yet be friends.

MME. O: I'm not so sure.

This argument between Madame Oglepuss and Beulah—the one we just heard—was spontaneous, sure, as of this moment, but the seeds were planted by the program you had yesterday with Gloria Steinem on the ERA. We heard you, the three of us.

The same sort of thing happened recently on the *Today* show. We followed Peter Brook, the director, who was on tape. It was the day after the *Marat/Sade* play opened in New York. There were mixed reviews and Brook was complaining about American critics and American audiences. I had something else planned and I just threw it all out the window. Beulah Witch came on and gave a review of *Marat/Sade*. She never mentioned it by name. She came on as a representative of the Kuklapolitan Woman's Drama League. She said:

BEULAH: It was just shocking. There was this, they had this bathtub. Well, I just can't tell you, I can't describe it because, well it's just

---

*One of the leading opponents of the ERA (Equal Rights Amendment).

so shocking. They had this, if I can say this word on the air, bathtub on the stage, and there was this person in the, oh, I just hate to say this word, bathtub. And, well, I can't tell you.

Fletcher Rabbit was interviewing her. He said:

FLETCHER: Well, Miss Witch, how did you like the ending?

BEULAH: Well, I couldn't stay, I had to make my train.

FLETCHER: Well, could you tell us what it was about?

BEULAH: It was shocking, that's all I can say. And I just don't think it's a proper subject to talk about on the television. And you'll excuse me.

And so she went off and Fran came on, and, of course, the crew broke up, and Fran started to laugh. And there again, completely ad-libbed—we had no idea we were going to do this—Fran put . . . I didn't know how to end it. Fran put the perfect accent on it by looking at the camera and saying, "You know, this is surprising. I don't understand what she's talking about because the play that Beulah saw last night was a children's version of *The Three Little Pigs*." And then Beulah came out and said:

BEULAH: Yes! There was this pig in the bathtub.

Burr, how do you separate your two worlds, yours and theirs?

They're really one world to me. And that could be troublesome. It's hard for me to get out of character sometimes. I remember one time, years ago, we took the 20th Century to New York often. Fran's compartment was next to mine and I could hear her getting ready for bed. I sensed that she could hear me. Suddenly, I had Beulah Witch and Madame Oglepuss get into an argument: who was going to take the upper berth and who the lower? And Beulah ribbing Madame Oglepuss about her frilly nightgown and so much cold cream. I heard Fran begin to laugh and laugh and laugh at everything I said. I couldn't stop the two of 'em. I couldn't get to bed. It has always been hard for me to come out at the end of the show on TV. I had to wait awhile until all the others had left. They are all my other selves and I can't abandon them that easily.

FLASHBACK. *In the '50s, after my TV program,* Studs' Place, *was taken off the air, I latched onto a late-night show, with perhaps a couple of dozen insomniacs as the audience. Burr phoned me one night: "Madame Oglepuss has confided to me that she'd love to appear on your program and discuss opera and other cultural matters."*

It was a memorable, bordering on surreal, hour for me. Though the man was no more than ten feet away from me, standing behind a Kuklapolitan stage, it was only Ophelia's presence I felt, not his. I was somewhat awed by the dowager; she was très *formidable!*

After the show, we adjourned to a nearby bar. I was understandably high, exhilarated. "How did you like it, Burr?" No response. I asked him again—perhaps he hadn't heard me. Again, silence. Oh, well, I'll let it pass—obviously, he didn't think much of it. A colleague whispered to me: "Ask him how Madame Oglepuss liked it." I did. Burr looked at me, his face aglow, "She loved *it!"*